Weaving Women's Lives

WEAVING WOMEN'S LIVES

Three Generations in a Navajo Family

Louise Lamphere

with Eva Price
Carole Cadman
and Valerie Darwin

University of NEW MEXICO Press   ALBUQUERQUE

Printed in the United States of America
13 12 11 10 09 08 07 1 2 3 4 5 6 7

Library of Congress Cataloging-in-Publication Data

Lamphere, Louise.
Weaving women's lives : three generations in a Navajo family / Louise Lamphere ; with Eva Price, Carole Cadman, and Valerie Darwin.
p. cm.
Includes bibliographical references and index.
ISBN 978-0-8263-4278-2 (pbk. : alk. paper)
1. Price, Eva, 1928– 2. Cadman, Carole, 1948– 3. Darwin, Valerie. 4. Navajo women weavers—Biography. 5. Navajo textile fabrics. 6. Navajo Indians—Social life and customs. I. Price, Eva, 1928– II. Cadman, Carole, 1948– III. Darwin, Valerie. IV. Title.
E99.N3.L36 S65 2007
746.1'409239726—dc22
[B]

2007026914

Design and composition: Melissa Tandysh

To Mary Sandman,

Our Beloved

Great-Grandmother,

Grandmother,

and Mother

☙

CONTENTS

LIST OF ILLUSTRATIONS

ACKNOWLEDGMENTS

More than forty years of connection have made this book possible. And there are many sources of support that have helped us along the way.

Louise Lamphere would like to thank those whose financial assistance was essential. A 1994 Snead-Wertheim Lectureship through the University of New Mexico Board of Regents provided funds to initiate this project, including our visit to the Wheelwright Museum and the initial interviews with Eva. Our thanks to the Snead and Wertheim families who established this lectureship for Anthropology and History faculty to support their research. Between 1995 and 1997, the Research Allocations Committee at the University of New Mexico awarded grants for additional interviews with Eva as well as taped conversations with Carole and Valerie. Louise also received funding from the UNM Arts and Sciences Dean's Special Research Fund. During her 1998–99 sabbatical year, the Center for Working Families at the University of California invited Louise to be a Visiting Senior Researcher, providing financial support for reworking a number of chapters of this book. Louise would like to thank Director Arlie Hochschild, Associate Director Barrie Thorne, and all the participants in the Center seminar for their encouraging comments and suggestions on chapter drafts.

Louise would like to thank Leroy Morgan and Carole Yazzie-Shaw, who transcribed Eva's Navajo narratives and then provided translations into English. Carole was especially helpful in finding smooth translations that still kept close to the meaning of the Navajo words and phrases. More recently, Beth Hadas, formerly of UNM Press, carefully read the last draft, gave helpful suggestions on how the manuscript could be more readable, corrected grammar, and guided the manuscript through the acceptance process. Melvatha Chee has corrected the Navajo throughout the manuscript. Both deserve thanks and appreciation for their careful work. Thanks also to the staff at UNM Press including our editor, Lisa Pacheco, and book designer, Melissa Tandysh. Finally, Louise would like to thank Margaret Randall, whose photographs grace the pages of this book and whose portrait of Eva, Carole, and Valerie is on the cover. Peter Evans, Louise's long-term partner, and Peter Bret Lamphere, her son, also deserve special thanks for all the years they have supported Louise as she worked on this book. Their encouragement, advice, and presence in her life have been a source of sustenance even at the busiest and most hectic times.

Eva Price would like to thank her children, Carole, Timothy, Randolph, Rudolph, and Randy, for all the love and help they have given to her over the years. She also is thankful that Louise has become part of her family over the past four decades.

Carole Cadman would like to thank her children Valerie, Erica, Jay, and Aaron for their love and support. She also wants to thank her mother, Eva, for putting her here on this earth. She also is thankful for Mary Sandman, her grandmother, who taught her the importance of the Navajo clan system and who her relatives or *k'é* were. She showed Carole how to make important Navajo foods like the 'alkąąd or cornmeal cake, made during the girl's puberty ceremony, the Kinaaldá, and *taa'niil*, Navajo cornmeal mush.

Valerie Darwin would like to thank the many inspirational women in her life: her mother Carole, her grandmother Eva, her great-grandmother Mary, and her aunt Louise for the many teachings of how to love and be genuine as a mother and a leader. These women have taught Valerie to acknowledge and practice Navajo tradition. The women in Valerie's life have also taught Valerie to live and survive as an educated and successful Navajo woman. Valerie would also like to thank her loving husband, Donovan, and her energetic children, Jacob and Dylan, for fulfilling her life in so many ways. Valerie's life as a wife, mother, and daughter has been a remarkable experience and such an honored blessing—thank you to all who have made her life meaningful.

CHAPTER ONE

Weaving Women's Lives

EACH SEMESTER I USED TO INVITE VALERIE DARWIN TO TALK to my introductory anthropology class at the University of New Mexico about her experiences when she was twelve years old and participated in the Kinaaldá, the Navajo girl's puberty ceremony. It is an important coming-of-age ritual for young women whose families still practice traditional Navajo religion. Valerie is the granddaughter of Eva Price, a woman I lived with in 1965 when I was conducting field research for my PhD dissertation on Navajo patterns of cooperation and family life. In the first few years after her 2000 graduation, she told my students about how she draws on traditional Navajo beliefs and values to sustain her current life as a young professional health educator, wife, and mother.[1] As I sat at the back of the class and observed her presentation, I saw a confident, articulate young woman, someone who expressed her ideas well in public and who invited others to ask questions and share their views. I was reminded of how much her experience at the university allowed Valerie to transform herself from a reserved high school student from the rural Navajo reservation who had found an urban environment and the large, imposing bureaucracy of the university a daunting challenge. Her body language, her gestures, and her "presence" indicated how well she could navigate new situations, cut through problems created by bureaucratic rules, and help resolve family crises—all skills she learned in college. Her upbringing and her Kinaaldá have become important sources of her present strength.

Valerie always began her talk by telling students how reluctant she was to participate in the ritual. "I was kind of skeptical; I was kind of afraid. I was kind of embarrassed at the fact that my mom and my grandma wanted to have this Kinaaldá for me. You know you're young and you think, God, nobody should know this about me." As she showed the slides and talked about the ceremony, she commented that as a college student, and later as a professional, she found that it helped to mold her own philosophy and approach to life. "All the stuff that I did, like work real hard and push myself . . . today, I think when I start to do something, I want to finish it. When I'm in a bind or when I'm in trouble I work real hard to fix it . . . to make it better. Just the philosophy that went along with the Kinaaldá ceremony kind of incorporated into the culture that I live in now. Kind of like, when you fall you pick yourself up and you fix what's broken, or you push yourself to the full extent to get what you want. You are outspoken and you express your feelings. You don't sit back and not present to people around you who you are. . . . You make yourself visible. Things like running [in the Kinaaldá]—the significance of that is like pushing yourself harder every time. Today when I look at my Kinaaldá, I'm glad that my mom and my grandma placed this opportunity upon me. . . . It's really helped to play a large part in my life."

Students were always more engaged by the lecture than they were by the book that I had assigned. Most of the students (whether Anglo American, Hispano, Asian, or African American) knew little about the Navajo, whose reservation is only 135 miles from Albuquerque and the University of New Mexico. Even the Navajo students in the class were often far-removed from the pastoral economy that shaped the lives of their grandparents and great-grandparents. Although more has been written on the Navajo than any other Native American culture, still there is no book that I feel adequately follows the transformation of Navajo experience during the twentieth century and details women's lives as well as those of their male kinfolk. For example, my own book, *To Run After Them* (1977), a study of cooperation in Eva's community, concentrates on the details of kinship and social structure and there are not enough individual voices for the book to come alive for students. To communicate the continually changing nature of Navajo culture, I felt I needed a book that spanned several generations and examined the way individuals, particularly women, utilized traditional Navajo conceptions and beliefs but also included new practices and ideas from the larger U.S. economy and society in which the Navajo have been incorporated for 150 years. I needed a book that presented the voices of women themselves, but placed them within the context of the larger American society in which both they—and women like myself—live.

My interest in writing such a book on Navajo women for college students (including Navajo youth) coincided with Eva Price's own desire for a book that would pass on her teachings about Navajo life to her children and grandchildren. I have known Eva for forty years and writing this book with her, her daughter Carole, and her granddaughter Valerie was possible because of our long and close relationship. We see this book as a collaboration, though each participant brings a different point of view, and I, as the primary author, have shaped the presentation of the narratives we tape-recorded together.

The book began initially as Eva's life history narrative focused on her and only later expanded to include two additional generations. Eva and I had talked a number of times during the nineteen eighties about making a book about her life. I had given her a copy of my first book on the Navajo and also a copy of Franc Newcomb's book on "Hosteen Klah" (more correctly spelled Hastiin Tł'aaí), a well-known singer who was Eva's ancestor. I received a Snead-Wertheim grant that enabled me to pay Carole and Eva for the hours of taping and provide funds for supplies, transportation, and groceries for several trips to Sheep Springs.

Eva has always felt it is important to teach her children and grandchildren the ways of behaving that will give them a long life along the path to *hózhǫ́* (blessings, harmony, or all that is positive and balanced in the universe). She articulated these sentiments best during an interview on July 17, 1994, conducted near Oak Springs in the Chuska Mountains close to Eva's old summer home. The two of us were sitting outdoors on a blanket. At times she spoke in English (indicated in **boldface** type) and at times in Navajo. She began by responding to my questions about what she would say to her grandchildren about her own philosophy of life, but the conversation soon turned to our relationship and to how she viewed the book we were "making." About her grandchildren, she said,

"It makes you feel good and happy. The way I talk, they understand me. They listen. They don't hitchhike on the road. They don't run away from the home, and they don't drink. They don't do nothing. That's what . . . especially my daughter Carole. I love them, with all my heart. To this day, she's with me and has helped me. . . . I talk to my grandchildren and I love them. They listen to these words, my words. You won't see them on the side of the road **hitchhiking**. And they don't drink either. They don't do bad things. As I stand, they are grateful for this. And thus far, I exist with my grandchildren. And then they have entered higher education finishing the twelfth grade and on to **college** for three years. This is my oldest grandchild. So this makes me very happy. I am grateful."

From here it seemed an easy transition to her relationship with me. "And we also think of you in the same way, Louise, with a lot of love, after so many years, since we have come to know you. You have remembered us and unlike anyone else you have helped us the way you do. Thus far, I am also grateful for this. As one of us, in good thinking and in a good place, just like this I think of you as one of my own; this is how I think about it." Since I didn't understand all of this (said in Navajo) and since Carole, who usually translated for me, was not present, Eva translated her own thoughts into English, **"We love you for so many years, when we meet together and visit you. We just love . . . as you're my daughter, like Carole, and my son Timothy, and Randa, and Rudolph, and Randy. I love them, the way I feel."** Feeling a little embarrassed by this sentiment, I acknowledged that we had indeed known each other for a long time—almost thirty years.

Eva reported talking to her paternal clan relative about the book. "I'm going to make a **book**. I told him I'm making a **book** about my grandfather Hastiin Tł'aaí, the places I herded sheep, the places I've been, and my memories. So I think about my grandkids and the way it's going to be in a generation. They are going to say, 'Hey, this is our grandma, right here.'" Eva acknowledged that she had been thinking about doing this for "so many years." She knew that others might criticize her for doing a book and talking to a white woman, however, she felt that she was looking toward the future. Most people, she pointed out, just think about where they will sleep, what they will do the next day, but have no thought about communicating their memories for their children and grandchildren.

Eva cautioned me in English before we began our taped sessions, **"I'm not going to tell you the main one. I'm just going to tell you a little bit here** [meaning the story of only one of the branches of her family]. **In our tradition, you can't tell the whole thing. You won't last long if you tell everything . . . it's the old traditional way."** As Carole, Eva's daughter, put it, "The whole secret of the old people is you can't tell everything you know." As Kluckhohn, Aberle, and other anthropologists have recognized in Navajo culture, knowledge is power and is not to be given away. It must be imparted or told as part of a reciprocal relationship; there needs to be an exchange, often of goods, in return for knowledge. Thus, Navajos make payments to a *hataałii* (singer) to perform ceremonies, an apprentice makes a series of payments to the hataałii from whom he learns a ceremony or *hatáál* (sing or chant), and the Diyin Dine'é (Holy People) come to the ceremony and cure the patient when they are given the correct offerings (*'yeel*) (Aberle 1967).

Telling all of one's own stories shortens a life. Conversely, keeping some knowledge to oneself lengthens life. Eva gave the example of her mother, who lived a long time through not imparting much of her sacred knowledge to others. "My mom," Eva said, "she didn't tell us anything about her background. We asked her about some of the things she knows, traditional things, the Blessing Way, the Squaw Dance. But she didn't tell us anything . . . nothing. She lived to be a hundred years old."

At several other points during our taped conversations, Eva cautioned me that she would not tell me all of what she knew, and she felt that others should do the same. In explaining to Rena Nelson what we were doing and in asking Rena to tell us about her relative, Hastiin Tł'aaí, Eva said, "Your name will be in the **book**, but I will not tell everything. It's like a chant and the singer who says, 'The songs are within you; you do not give people the information within you. Don't do it. Some [songs] will protect you, they say.' That is the reason why you give out only the surface information. So only tell a few things." When I inquired about Navajo sacred knowledge, Eva and Carole would often steer me away from the subject or tell me only a little. For example, when I asked for stories of the Emergence of the Holy Ones, their journey through a series of underworlds up into the present world called the Hajíínéí or Upward Reaching Way, Carole repeated her mother's admonition, "If you tell the whole thing that you know, it's not right. So she'll tell just a portion; she'll go ahead and let you in on that . . . but not all of it. Because she said, some parts are sacred and some parts aren't."

Revealing a life from the Navajo point of view is obviously an undertaking fraught with ambivalence. Clearly Eva was interested primarily in recording the secular parts of her life, avoiding discussions of religious and sacred knowledge. Paying her an honorarium (in this case $6 an hour) from the Snead-Wertheim funds was appropriate, just as paying a hataałii is necessary in return for his performing a curing ceremony. At times it was hard for Eva to answer my questions without imparting knowledge that should be kept to oneself.

After several sessions with Eva in 1994, I began to think about expanding the book to include Carole's story as well as that of her daughter Valerie, who was a University of New Mexico student at the time. Carole's memories of events that figured in Eva's life added richness to the narrative. Particularly when we began to talk about Eva's first husband (Carole's father) and to discuss Eva's life with Joe and her sickness, the interviews became more of a three-way conversation, with Carole inserting her own version of events in addition to translating her mother's words. Besides, since Valerie had become a student at the University of New Mexico where I teach, I had seen her grow and change as she adapted to college and urban life. It became clear that a book on three generations would more clearly fit my own needs and would also give a fuller picture of Eva's own family.

Meeting Eva

I first met Eva Price in 1965, when I was conducting fieldwork for my dissertation in social anthropology at Harvard University. That summer my friend and fellow anthropologist Terry Reynolds had borrowed a *hooghan* (Navajo house) from a family in Sheep Springs, a small New Mexico community on the eastern side of the Navajo Reservation.[2] In the fall, I started living with the Navajo woman we had hired as our interpreter that summer along with three of her five children. During these months I saw Eva and her husband Joe at several Chapter meetings, held on Sundays about once a month in the modern Chapter House built by the Navajo Tribe for local community meetings.[3] My previous field experience had been in the off-reservation community of Ramah, New Mexico, where I had lived during the summers of 1963 and 1964. Sheep Springs, in contrast, was on the reservation in a relatively densely populated area where important Navajo historical figures like Narbona and Manuelito had lived in the nineteenth century. It was a pastoral and agricultural community where families had seasonal homes. They would spend winters living on the flatlands and foothills where their flocks could be protected from snow and colder temperatures, and then move their sheep to the Chuska Mountains in the summer. The Chuskas, covered with ponderosa pine and Gambel oak on the lower "bench" area and with Douglas fir and aspen at the top, reminded me of the foothills and lower reaches of the Rocky Mountains outside Denver, Colorado, where I spent my childhood and teenage summers at camp.

Joe Price, a World War II veteran, spoke good English and sometimes served as an interpreter at the Chapter meetings. I remember him explaining the new Community Action Program, part of the Johnson administration's "War on Poverty," as it was enacted on the Navajo Reservation. Eva also attended Chapter meetings, and as I learned who various people in the Sheep Springs community were, I came to recognize this short, slim woman in her thirties. With her hair tied in a traditional Navajo bun, Eva dressed in calico blouses and skirts, a slightly modernized version of the heavy velveteen blouses and silk skirts that older women wore to public meetings or Navajo ceremonies. In September, I had seen her among the twenty-five or so women who were part of a ten-day Tribal Works Project at the Chapter House. Some women were carding wool for traditional Navajo rugs while others, including Eva, made clothes on five or six sewing machines. Eva was sewing a beautiful, wine-colored, velveteen blouse that would later be sold so that proceeds could go back to the Chapter. In October I learned that Joe Price had gone to Wyoming to work for the railroad, a typical wage job for many Navajo men in the nineteen fifties and sixties. The workers repaired track for the Union Pacific Railroad, labor that took them away from the reservation up to eight months of the year.

Even though I knew Joe was no longer at home, I was surprised when Eva came up to me one November day when I was putting gas into my Volkswagen outside the Sheep Springs Trading Post. I vividly remember her standing by the gas pumps and explaining that she wanted me to come and live with her and her children, now that her husband was away for several months. We spoke in English and it was clear that Eva had been to school. One of the advantages of working on the Eastern Navajo Reservation, rather than in Ramah or the western parts of the Reservation, was that it was easy to find women in their thirties who spoke English. This was crucial for me, since I had learned only a smattering of Navajo. Becoming more fluent in this difficult language was even harder in the days before the taped lessons and classes that are now offered at several universities in the Southwest. Eva had heard that I was living in the community with a family and seemed genuinely interested in having me around. I have a striking memory of her standing near her yellow and black Pontiac, driven by some relative since Eva had never learned to drive. As she delivered her request, she looked down at her shoes. Polite Navajos never look a stranger squarely in the eye. She explained that she wanted me to come and stay with her and her four boys. Not only was her husband working for the railroad, but her daughter Carole was away at the BIA boarding school at Fort Wingate twenty miles east of Gallup.

I had been planning to live with several different families over the year. Navajos reside in scattered, extended-family residence groups (clusters of hooghans, cabins, and sheep corrals) rather than in villages. So I discovered that when I lived with one family, I got to know them well but had very little contact with Navajos outside their kin network. Clearly, to get a good sense of patterns of everyday Navajo life, I needed to live a few months each with a wide range of families. I had not figured out who might be willing to take me in, so Eva's request was a welcome surprise. I quickly accepted, feeling this would open up relations with a whole new set of community members, and I made arrangements to stay with her after Thanksgiving. I had rented an apartment in Gallup, fifty miles away, where I spent two days a week. There I did my laundry, took showers, and typed up my field notes. The other days—usually weekends that were busy with Chapter meetings and traditional ceremonies—I spent with my interpreter's family. During the fall months I stayed with her in her summer cabin, helped her move to her winter home, and spent time piñon picking and going to an Enemy Way or Squaw Dance.[4] I had learned a great deal, but needed new connections and a new set of opportunities.

The Monday after Thanksgiving, I drove out from Gallup and arrived at Eva's house around 3:00 p.m. In the fall, the flat plain that stretches from the hills near Gallup toward Shiprock seems dry and barren, but it still provides winter forage for small flocks of sheep. The Chuska Mountains form a deep blue silhouette to the West, while dun-colored hills near Naschitti, and further north of Sheep Springs at Cross Hills and Yellow Hills, jut out and even emerge on the other side of Highway 666 (now Highway 491). I am always taken by the wide expanse of blue sky, often filled with billowy, white cumulus clouds, that frames this reservation landscape. Eva lives near Yellow Hills, a table-like mesa, several miles north of the Sheep Springs Trading Post along the two-lane highway, a road heavily traveled by Navajo pickups and cars as well as eighteen-wheelers traveling along the eastern edge of the Reservation. I pulled into a residence group that included two very small, one-room houses (inhabited, I later discovered, by Eva's mother, Mary Sandman, and Eva's brother Grant), a sheep corral, and a two-room log cabin chinked with cement, a modern improvement that is more permanent than mud. Eva was outside cleaning her yellow Pontiac. She had gotten up early and asked Lena Denetclaw, her neighbor, to drive Carole back to Fort Wingate after the Thanksgiving weekend.

She and Lena had just returned from the hundred-mile round trip. After cleaning the car, she took me inside the cabin and I put some of my things (a sleeping bag, pillow, and a bag with a few clothes) in the back room, which served as a bedroom. After talking a little she said she was going to cook for the "school kids" (Timmy and Randa, her two oldest sons aged twelve and eleven) who would arrive home at about 4:00 p.m. The cabin was equipped with electricity—unlike the household where I had been living, which was too far away from the electric lines—and a woodstove in the front room. Water was hauled in large metal containers from a tribally improved well several miles away.

Eva peeled and sliced some white potatoes, rinsing the slices in a metal wash pan filled with water before plopping them into a cast-iron frying pan on the woodstove. The sizzle of the hot lard sent a pungent aroma into the air as the potatoes browned. She made dough from flour, water, a little baking powder, and salt, kneading it around in another wash pan until it made a nice, round lump. After letting it rise for a few minutes she broke off a ball, pulling it into shape. Then she slapped it between her hands until it became a flat, round piece of bread. She slipped these pieces of dough into another skillet of hot lard where they fried to a golden brown while she made the next piece.

The boys arrived home, and the four of us sat down to eat at the Formica-topped table along with Rudy, her five-year-old, and Randy, the two-year-old baby. Eva had made some coffee for me in a tin coffeepot, and she drank herb tea that she had boiled in a pan on the woodstove.

After eating, Eva began to tell me more about her children, her mother, her sister, and her sister-in-law who lived across the highway. As a crucial part of opening up her life to me, she told me her mother's and father's matrilineal clans as well as Joe's, and explained to me why Shoemaker's Wife, a clan relative of her father's, lived with her as well. This conversation began a forty-year-old relationship that has included my participation in many important family events—girl's puberty ritual and other traditional ceremonies as well as high school graduations and funerals. Our relationship expanded to encompass ties with her daughter Carole and her granddaughter

Valerie, as well as Eva's sons, their wives and children, and Carole's other three children.[5]

Anthropologists have regularly established close relationships with an individual or family in the communities where they have conducted research.[6] There is a long tradition of this in the Southwest. Matilda Coxe Stevenson had close ties to We-wha, the *la'mana* or "two spirited" man/woman at Zuni in the eighteen seventies (Miller 2007). Elsie Clews Parsons was adopted into her Hopi hostess's clan in the nineteen twenties when her hair was washed at Suchomovi on First Mesa (Parsons 1921:98). Among the Navajo many of us were not adopted into a family through a ceremony but became "my relative" (*shik'éí*) more informally. As Gladys Reichard reports in *Spider Woman*, she was incorporated into Red Point's family through the device of being taught the correct kin terms of reference for family members. She then referred to Red Point as "my grandfather" (*shicheii*) and his daughters as "my older/younger sister" (*shádí/shideezhí*) and she in turn was called "my granddaughter" or "my older/younger sister" (Reichard 1934:35). In a similar manner David Aberle was incorporated into the Beck family in Piñon (Beck 2006), and Maureen Schwarz became close to Sadie Billie of Tsaile who sponsored and oversaw the Kinaaldá of her daughter Regan (Schwarz 1997:ix). My relationship with Eva Price and her family is far from unique, but, until recently, we have been reluctant to make our relationships part of our writing and analysis of Navajo culture, continuity, and change. In this book I weave episodes from my own life with the narratives of Eva, Carole, and Valerie in order to highlight our different positionalities within the same political economy and the way our cultural, class, and racial/ethnic backgrounds have shaped our experiences of similar situations (parental drinking, schooling, missionary activities) differently.

Metaphors That Link Narratives and Lives

Much has changed for Eva and her family since the nineteen sixties. The boys are middle-aged men now, with teenage and grown children, and Carole has four children, including Valerie, and five grandchildren. The family is much more enmeshed in the wage economy, and grandchildren are spread between Salt Lake City, Utah, and Albuquerque, New Mexico. I have been attentive to three issues in capturing the history of Eva's family up until the nineteen sixties when I met them, and in detailing their lives during the last forty years. First, I want to situate Eva's family and Navajo culture within U.S. society rather than present the Navajo as an isolated, separate indigenous culture. When I conducted my dissertation research, the impact of Anglo rule (the Indian wars and the Long Walk, the beginnings of the reservation system, the advent of the trading post, and the consequences of Stock Reduction) was treated as background quite separate from Navajo religion, social structure, and values. This approach suggested that the Navajo were an isolated people, which surely is not true now if it ever was. To counter this tendency, I have introduced Navajo and broader American history to contextualize the narrative for readers who are not familiar with the important events and policies, both economic and political, that have shaped contemporary Navajo lives. I have also included stories from my own life, since I am a Westerner who grew up in Denver, Colorado, who has made Albuquerque home for more than twenty years. I am part of the same regional political economy and influenced by some of the same forces that have shaped the lives of Eva, Carole, and Valerie, though race and class make our experiences very different. I see race and class as dividers that are a powerful complement to the differences in cultural meanings, language, and ways of knowing that separate populations. I am always reminded of this when Eva or her relatives come to visit my Albuquerque house, built in 1987 and blessed by Eva before my partner Peter Evans, my son Peter Bret, and I moved in. This two-story adobe house with four bedrooms and more than two thousand square feet is much grander than the two other houses I have owned in the Albuquerque area. I call it my "yuppie palace," and when Erica, Carole's younger daughter, first saw the house in the late nineteen eighties, she declared, "Boy, you must be rich!" Even though we were able to build the house because of the profit we made from selling our house in Rhode Island, it is certainly a visible reminder of the class differences that divide a family of middle-aged full professors and the average Navajo family.

Second, although I hope to make readers sensitive to race and class differences in Navajo interactions with others, I also want to emphasize the vibrancy and strength of Navajo culture. Even though Navajos have incorporated Anglo-American material culture into their lives, such as driving pickups, playing video games, watching TV, and eating Kentucky Fried Chicken, many still speak the Navajo language, utilize Navajo healing ceremonies, draw strength from traditional beliefs, and retain preferences for Navajo food. This is in addition to the growing importance of the Native American Church and various Christian denominations in the lives of many Navajos. The narratives of Eva, Carole, and Valerie vividly illustrate this process of incorporation and mixing while retaining distinctive Navajo beliefs, values, and orientations. As the discussion continues later in this chapter, I have searched for metaphors that will adequately convey the way Navajos bring elements of American culture into their lives while retaining a distinctive Navajo way of life.

My third goal in this narrative is to highlight the voices of Eva, Carole, and Valerie and organize the material from their perspective. For Eva the organizing theme is the importance of place. A metaphor that emerges from her narrative is the image of the cornstalk. The first three chapters, which tell the history of Eva's clan and the lives of her mother and father, are organized around this theme and that metaphor. We began working on this book in the summer of 1994 with a trip to the Wheelwright Museum to see the rugs and some of the ceremonial items that had been made by the well-known Navajo singer (hataałii) Hosteen Klah or Tł'aaí, who was a member of Eva's clan and a revered ancestor. The museum was originally built by Mary Wheelwright to house Tł'aaí's sandpaintings, ceremonial paraphernalia, and rugs depicting sandpaintings woven by Tł'aaí and his nieces. Eva sees herself as preserving Hastiin Tł'aaí's memory and that of his mother, 'Asdzą́ą́ Hashkéhí (Angry Woman or Mad Woman). She envisions her family's past as a cornstalk, with branches growing from a central stem—a main stalk. 'Asdzą́ą́ Hashkéhí was the main stalk and other family members branched off of her. Over the next few months, we visited places where Tł'aaí and his mother lived or herded sheep and where other members of her clan, the Dziłtł'ahnii or Mountain Recess People,

FIGURE 1.1 Corn is an important part of Eva's life as well as a metaphor for her clan relationships. Most years, until she was in her mid-seventies, she and her sons planted a cornfield in the irrigated area about one-quarter mile from her Yellow Hills home. Hoeing the corn (shown here in 2000), collecting corn pollen, and harvesting were annual summer activities.

PHOTOGRAPH BY MARGARET RANDALL.

had lived in scattered homesites in the Chuska Mountains and the flatlands to the East. She also took me to her birthplace and summer childhood home (at Dził Zéé'asgai or Mountain with a White Neck), her first winter home (at Łizhin Deez'áhí or Black Rock Standing), and the second winter home where she still lives at Łitso Dah 'Ask'idí or Yellow Hills. During these trips the centrality of place in Navajo life emerged. It was as if she wanted me to locate her life and that of her relatives in the landscape, so I have kept this structure in chapters 2–4. It also seemed that Eva's stories in which her mother figured prominently were those at Dził Zéé'asgai (Mountain with a White Neck) while the memory of her father surfaced more in relation to their winter homesites on the flatlands (Łizhin Deez'áhí and Łitso Dah 'Ask'idí, including the nearby fields).

Other writers have recognized the importance of place in the lives of the Navajo, the Apache, and Native Americans more generally. As Keith Basso reminds us, "For Indian men and women, the past lies embedded in features of the earth—in canyons and lakes, mountains and arroyos, rocks and vacant fields—which together endow their lands with multiple forms of significance that reach into their lives and shape the ways they think. Knowledge of places is therefore closely linked to knowledge of the self, to grasping one's position in the larger scheme of things, including one's own community, and to securing a confident sense of who one is as a person" (1996:34).

This focus on landscape and place contrasts sharply, in my mind, with my own bias toward linear, historical time. I have constantly felt the tug of wanting to know *when something happened* and to construct a chronology of events, making sure I know what happened first and then what came afterward.

In the end, I have arranged these narratives in a timeline, but have tried to disrupt it, first by emphasizing the importance of place, but also by coming back to the importance of relationality, the central focus on kin in Navajo culture. A timeline seemed a necessary part of my emphasis on the important relationship of Navajos to non-Navajos, particularly Anglos, and to the American economic system of which they have been a part since 1848. I wanted to stress the increasing penetration of the larger U.S. economy and American culture into the lives of Navajos.

Younger generations of Navajos have learned to focus on particular dates—birthdays, school graduations, marriages, and sometimes deaths—in narrating or thinking about their experiences during a particular year. Carole and Valerie seemed much more comfortable than Eva with the chronological approach, but even so, I felt I was being an obsessive Euro-American in trying to discover a date for every event—Carole's time in Utah with a Mormon family, the dates she held a particular job, which year Valerie had her Kinaaldá, and so on. With my fading memory, I sometimes cannot even guess where I was at a particular time period or in what year some event took place, though I still feel compelled to do so, so I have relaxed my emphasis on the exact chronology of events.

More importantly, there are two other metaphors I find useful in thinking about Eva's, Carole's, and Valerie's narratives: those of weaving and stirring. I came to see the value of these metaphors when I looked back at the significance of several gifts Eva brought me when we began working on the book. They were primarily traditional symbols of Navajo womanhood, either in terms of women's role as weavers in Navajo culture or in terms of their association with Changing Woman ('Asdzą́ą́ Nádleehé), the most important female Holy One (Diyin Diné). Only much later as I reflected on these gifts did I come to understand their significance. The first was a weaving comb (*bee 'adzooí*) that women weavers use to pound the weft threads down after they have strung them through the warp. Eva also brought me a batten, (*bee ník'í'níłtłish*) another weaving tool.[7] The third item associated with weaving was a spindle (*bee 'adizí*), a long stick with a whorl close to the end that sits on the ground. The other end is pointed to allow the spinner to shape and twist the carded wool around it. Eva and her neighbor Lena had taught me to weave in 1965–66. Eva had helped me to string a rug that I could complete once I left the Navajo Reservation. It had been years since I had done any weaving, but I often watched Eva, an accomplished Two Grey Hills rug weaver, work when I visited and she had given me four very special rugs over the years.

The fourth gift from Eva was a bundle of *'ádístsiįn*—the long sticks from the greasewood plant that are used to stir the batter for the cake ('alkąąd) that is a central part of the Navajo girl's puberty

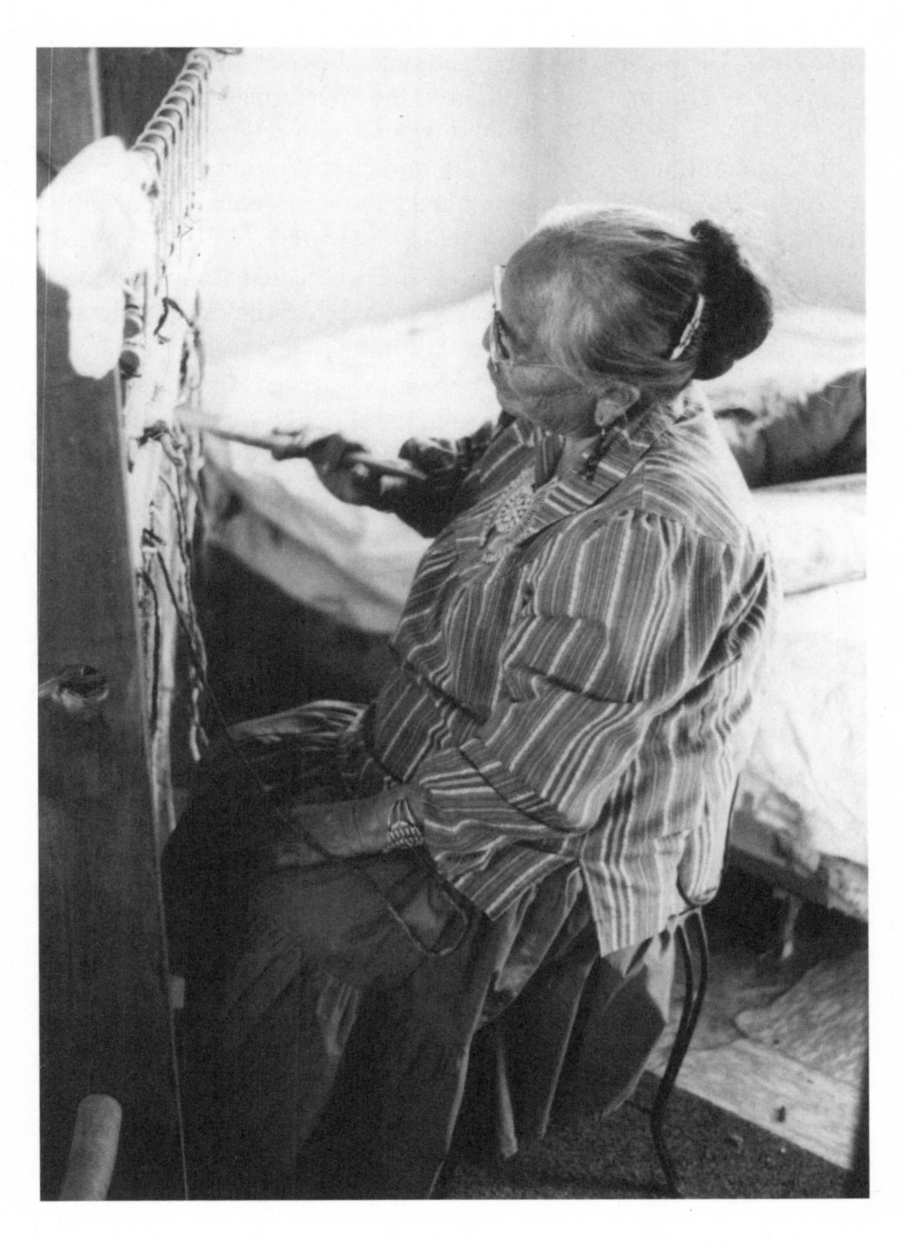

FIGURE 1.2 Eva is a skilled weaver who, throughout her adult life, has woven rugs in the Two Grey Hills style. Here she uses a weaver's comb to tap down the weft threads.

PHOTOGRAPH BY AUTHOR.

ceremony, the Kinaaldá. The ceremony (described in chapter 4) is a replica of the first puberty ceremony performed for Changing Woman ('Asdząą Nádleehé) who was found on Gobernador Knob (Ch'óol'į'í) and raised by First Man and First Woman. She later bore the Hero Twins (Monster Slayer and Born for Water) who killed the Monsters that had been wreaking havoc in the Glittering World (or Earth Surface). Changing Woman also created the first Navajo matrilineal clans. Navajo women who have had their own Kinaaldá often have a set of these sticks in their homes.

The weaving tools point to the act of weaving itself, the stringing of a weft thread in and out between the threads of a warp to create a pattern where it is possible to see distinct colors, but where the individual threads are woven into a whole that is a blend of several colors. This seems an apt metaphor for the ways in which Navajo women pull together elements of both Navajo and Anglo culture in making a new pattern for their lives. At other times, the metaphor of stirring seems more appropriate. Just as the 'ádístsiin are used to stir hot water and ground corn together to make a smooth batter, Navajo women put together elements of Navajo culture and the larger U.S. society in a way that makes it impossible to see the distinct and separate elements. In using these two metaphors I am trying to avoid the usual analysis of change in Native American culture that stresses one of two models.

The first is the assimilation model that assumes that as they progress along a continuum from "traditional" to "assimilated," Navajos and other Native Americans "lose" their culture and language and become more and more "white" or "American," not only in terms of material culture (housing, dress, food, etc.), but also in terms of cultural knowledge and identity. Individual Navajos can thus be classed as either "traditional," "semitraditional," or "assimilated" or "acculturated" (i.e., "modern"). The other model posits that Navajos and other Native Americans are "between two worlds" or have one foot in the nineteenth century and the other in the twenty-first (see Benedek 1995:7–12). Such a model leaves the impression that Navajos are "torn" between two opposites or "stuck" in a "no-win" situation. Instead, I want to suggest a much more dynamic, less dualistic view of the intersection of Navajo culture with the larger American political economy and culture. Navajos, like whites or Anglos, African Americans, Hispanos, and others in the United States have experienced the Great Depression and World War II and have been affected by social trends like the spread of public education and the increasing impact of the media. At work in these periods and through these trends are larger political and economic forces that shape the possibilities and choices available to individuals. By treating Eva's, Carole's, and Valerie's lives as part of the same wider Western political economy that my own family is part of, I want to show change not just as loss or the product of "conflicting cultures." I want to emphasize the ways each of us has been shaped by different generational experiences, the ways we use different economic and cultural resources to weave a set of life patterns. The importance of Navajo cultural conceptions, social patterns, and ceremonies does not disappear over time. Instead ideas and rituals are retained or re-utilized in differing contexts.

CHAPTER TWO

The Main Stalk

Placing the Mountain Recess People on the Landscape

We came from our grandmother, as if she was the main stalk of the corn and we were her branches.

—Eva Price, October 15, 1994

EVA'S FAMILY HISTORY BEGINS WITH 'ASDZĄ́Ą́ HASHKÉHÍ (Angry Woman or Mad Woman). She was also known as 'Asdzą́ą́ Ts'ósí or Thin Woman.[1] She is the "main stalk" and Eva's family came from her: "Just like corn, we have spread out and we are of the many that have sprouted." 'Asdzą́ą́ Hashkéhí's most famous relative was Hastiin Tł'aaí (mentioned in chapter 1), commonly known as Hosteen Klah, the well-known singer for whom the Wheelwright Museum of the American Indian, formerly the Museum of Ceremonial Art, in Santa Fe, New Mexico, was built.

'Asdzą́ą́ Hashkéhí's story, as Eva tells it, is deeply involved with one of the most tragic events of Navajo history, the Long Walk to the Bosque Redondo where the Navajo were incarcerated from 1864–68.[2] It is a story about place; about displacement and a return home, to the Chuska Mountains and Dził Ditł'oi ("Fuzzy Mountain"), the summer home of 'Asdzą́ą́ Hashkéhí. In 1864, General James H. Carleton sent Kit Carson with an army of one thousand on a campaign to defeat the Navajos and resettle them at Fort Sumner in Eastern New Mexico, at a site known as Bosque Redondo or Hwééldi in Navajo. Resettlement would free mineral-rich Navajo territory for white settlement and at the same time "civilize" the Navajos, turning them from seminomadic pastoralists into sedentary agriculturalists. Carson and his troops burned Navajo fields and orchards in Canyon de Chelly, the heartland of Navajo settlement. As winter approached, many starving Navajos began to surrender. Soldiers took them first to Fort Wingate (near present day San Rafael just south of Grants), and then marched them more than 250 miles across what is now the state of New Mexico to Fort Sumner on a barren, nearly treeless, plain. More than 8,500 Navajo people were incarcerated for four years, a period of hunger and sickness. Crops failed because of drought and pests, and the Navajo became dependent on government rations. Finally, General William Tecumseh Sherman and twenty-nine Navajo headmen (Navajo *naat'áanii* or leaders) signed the Treaty of 1868 in May of that year, which gave the Navajo a fraction of their former territory as a reservation. Soldiers then escorted the surviving Navajo families back to the new Fort Wingate, giving them livestock, tools, flour, and other rations to start their lives again in their homeland between the four sacred mountains (Brown 1971, Locke 1976, Iverson and Russell 2000, Terrell 1970).

Unlike most accounts of the Long Walk, which emphasize the role of the U.S. military and Anglo domination, Eva's account also mentions Mexicans who held her ancestor captive. Rather than centering on the journey to Bosque Redondo and the hardships there, it focuses on 'Asdzą́ą́ Hashkéhí's journey home to establish her family again in the Chuska Mountains.

"Tł'aaí's mother came back from Fort Sumner. She had been kidnapped. One of the Mexicans that had enslaved her, he had made her his wife. So she was taken, never to return home. They said it was very cold, like it is now. It was dark with fog and cold. So they say that there were two Mexicans watching her. They brought in a lot of wood and piled it up for her. And when they piled it up for her, it was very dark and fog outside.

"So they say that she would cry and would not eat. When the fog settled in, the two were gone somewhere and she looked around for them and she saw no one around. They would lock her in, always locked, but when she tried the door it opened beautifully, it is said. Then without giving it a second thought, she thought she would run away, but there was a very large dog tied up outside so that she would not be able to escape. And then she began to think that she would run away and began to walk in one direction. She walked and she walked and she walked. She had walked for a long distance when she heard a noise behind her. The dog had escaped its leash and it had come after her.

"And then she came upon a very large river. There was a tremendous amount of water flowing across. 'Now how will I ever get across?' she thought to herself and said so. So then she spoke to the water, 'Tó 'ałtah naashchíín, Tó biyáázh, stop flowing. I am returning home,' she said. They say this is what she did. When she spoke to it, it didn't take long for the water to go down. When the water became about this much, she walked across. They say that the dog followed her. She walked and walked with it. It was far away. I'm not sure how far she went, and the dog spent the night at the place where the water flows, an arroyo.

"They slept in there and the dog took care of her as she spoke to it. And then she continued to travel with it. Then sometime that day she told the dog to go home back to its relatives, and the dog went back home without hesitation.

"They say that it was cedar that helped her survive. She would break off a small piece of cedar and keep it in her mouth, which kept her mouth moist.

"It took her seven days to return home. She went up the Chuska Mountains and as she was coming back she noticed someone behind her. So then she thought that this would be the end of her life, because she thought that it was one of the Mexicans. But as he came closer, she could see that it was a Navajo. It was her uncle. Her feet were puffy and swollen. She could barely walk, but she did. So then he threw her on top of the horse like this from behind. Then he took her back to where they lived somewhere on top of that mountain range.[3] And so this is where our grandmother came from and so did we. Just like corn, we have spread out, and we are of the many that have sprouted.

"Yes, Tł'aaí was born on that range somewhere. That's what my mother used to tell me. After peace was reestablished, some of them were let go. They were taken care of by the police [soldiers]. It is said that they were let go in wagons when peace was reestablished."[4]

Hastiin Tł'aaí

After 'Asdzą́ą́ Hashkéhí, the "main stalk," Hastiin Tł'aaí, the repository of traditional knowledge and thinking (*nitsáhákees*), is the most important among Eva's relatives. She refers to him as *shidá'í* (my maternal uncle), shicheii (my maternal grandfather), and *shá hastói*

FIGURE 2.1 Portrait of Hastiin Tł'aaí.

COURTESY OF WHEELWRIGHT MUSEUM OF THE AMERICAN INDIAN.

(a term of respect for older, male kinsmen). Tł'aaí was a *nádleeh*, one who is in a constant state of change, or a "third gender."[5]

He never married and combined the characteristics of both sexes—a singer (male) and weaver (female). As a hataałii (singer), he provided a legacy of healing that Eva has carried on in her own work as a handtrembler and healer.[6] When we began work on this book, Eva and I went to the Wheelwright Museum in Santa Fe to visit Tł'aaí's grave, examine the rugs he and his nieces wove, and view the ceremonial objects from his medicine bags (*jish*) still held by the Museum in 1994.[7]

Lynette Miller of the Wheelwright Museum spent the day with us, showing us a number of the rugs that Tł'aaí wove with his nieces, Gladys Manuelito and Irene Ball.[8] We took pictures near the monument to Hastiin Tł'aaí and saw the grave where he was buried in 1937, several months before the museum was dedicated. We listened

FIGURE 2.2 Eva examining Hastiin Tł'aaí's ritual paraphernalia at the Wheelwright Museum in 1994.

PHOTOGRAPH BY AUTHOR.

to some of the tapes of Tł'aaí singing songs from the Blessing Way that had been recorded in 1930, and we examined ceremonial objects in storage at the museum, some of which were from Hastiin Tł'aaí's jish or medicine bundles.[9]

It was an emotional occasion, and Eva recorded her thoughts for me while we were sitting in the room where the drawers had been brought for us to examine.

"Greetings Louise and my daughter Carole. We have traveled far. We have come here for a reason, a purpose. We went to Tsaile several years ago to ask about the Yé'ii Bicheii bijish [Night Way Medicine Bag] that belonged to my elder Tł'aaí who rests here and many of his things are kept here, too. And because of this, I was concerned and wanted to see these things for myself and I have seen them. What I saw was pitiful; they had become moth infested, these things which had allowed us to grow and multiply through prayers which were said for us through them. We the Dziłtł'ahnii, the Mountain Recess People.

"Based on kind faith I want to have the mirage stones (*hadahoniye'*) and the arrowheads (*béésh 'est'ogii*) returned to me. And also the sacred mountain soil bundle, the hard goods, and the Talking Prayer Stick.[10] They exist in poverty, eaten by insects, this is how I saw them. So I am here for them in the heat and other hardships, wanting to find out about them, and for this reason I am here. We are here. We wanted to find out and to know so that we may have them returned to us. There are probably rules, they were just handed over to the White Man. They [the objects] are not being taken care of. This is what I say and this is all I have to say."

In describing her feelings about Hastiin Tł'aaí's ceremonial paraphernalia stored in a special set of drawers at the Wheelwright Museum in Santa Fe, Eva was visibly shaken. When she began talking about the moths or bugs that had eaten some of the feathers she began to cry and had difficulty finishing her sentences.

For Eva and her family, Hastiin Tł'aaí is an important link to the past and the source of sacred knowledge within the clan. Tł'aaí knew six different chants (Blessing Way, Shooting Way, Navajo Wind Way, Apache Wind Way, Hail Chant, and, most importantly, the Night Chant or Yé'ii Bicheii).[11] He was well-known not only on the Navajo Reservation but also in the white (Bilagáana) world because of his important links, first to Arthur and Franc Newcomb, who ran a trading post near his home, and later to wealthy easterner Mary Wheelwright and anthropologist Gladys Reichard. His life was touched by an Anglo world bent not so much on conquering and Christianizing the Navajo as on incorporating them economically and culturally. While traders like Arthur Newcomb brought western goods to Navajo families, Franc Newcomb, Wheelwright, and Reichard, unlike missionaries who focused on conversion, were interested in understanding Navajo culture and recording ceremonies on the Navajos' own terms.

Tł'aaí befriended Arthur Newcomb in 1913 when Newcomb bought the trading post near Tł'aaí's home at Bis Dootł'izh Si'ą (Blue Mesa), now known as Newcomb. The trading post was the main institution through which Navajos were incorporated into the U.S. economy. Families sold their wool and lambs to the traders, and Navajo women brought in their rugs. In return they were given credit accounts and were able to purchase coffee, flour, pots, plows, and other Anglo items. After Arthur married, his wife, a reservation school teacher known as Franc, became a friend of Tł'aaí as well. She began to make drawings of the sandpaintings that he produced as part of several of the chants he knew.[12]

When Mary Wheelwright, a wealthy Bostonian, traveled through the Navajo Reservation in the nineteen twenties, she stopped at the Newcomb Trading Post, visited with Franc and Arthur, and met Tł'aaí (McGreevy 1993:84). Over the next fifteen years she worked closely with Tł'aaí recording the songs and myths from his ceremonies. During the winter of 1927, Franc Newcomb, her daughter Priscilla, Tł'aaí, and his nephew Clyde Beyal (who acted as an interpreter) traveled to Alcalde, New Mexico, where Mary had a house. Over a two-month period, with the help of Professor Herzog, who wrote down the music, and anthropologist Harry Hoijer, who provided transcriptions, they recorded the songs from the Yé'ii Bicheii or Night Chant (Tł'éé'jí). In October 1927, Tł'aaí, Clyde, and Mary traveled to Phoenix, where the Newcombs were spending the winter. They recorded the legend of the Hail Chant, with Arthur Newcomb and Mary Wheelwright writing down the English version

(Newcomb 1964:167–69). In 1936 on a trip to the San Ysidro Ranch near Santa Barbara, Tł'aaí visited Wheelwright and recorded some portions of the Navajo creation story (McGreevy 1993:86, Newcomb 1964:205). Over the years, Franc Newcomb made copies from memory of many of the sandpaintings Tł'aaí used in the ceremonies he performed.

In 1931, Beaal Begay, Tł'aaí's understudy and apprentice, died suddenly. Tł'aaí felt that he was too old to teach another apprentice the ceremonies he knew. The next autumn, when Mary Wheelwright was visiting the Newcombs, she asked Tł'aaí what would happen to his ceremonial paraphernalia. He replied he did not know. Mary responded by asking him if he would be willing to have it stored in a place where everyone could see it and study its use if they wished. Tł'aaí was pleased with this possibility, and Mary began plans for the Museum of Navajo Ceremonial Art, which was eventually built in Santa Fe in the shape of a Navajo hooghan. In 1932, Tł'aaí left his collection of ritual paraphernalia to the museum in perpetuity as a research collection for succeeding generations of Navajo singers (Frisbie 1987:243). He lived to conduct a traditional House Blessing Ceremony, but died of pneumonia in February 1937, nine months before the formal opening of the museum (McGreevy 1993:87, Newcomb 1964:208–20).

Although Eva was a small child during the early nineteen thirties and probably only saw Hastiin Tł'aaí once or twice in her life, she feels strongly about the contributions he made to Navajo culture as a singer and as a weaver. The day after we visited the Wheelwright Museum (Saturday, June 11, 1994) I asked her what thoughts she had about Tł'aaí.

"Yesterday we traveled to Santa Fe. And there I looked at my late grandfather's belongings and also the rugs that my relatives made. Our older relative, he was called Left-Handed [Hastiin Tł'aaí]. We looked at his rugs. One of the weavers was my older [clan] sister Daisy Nabaahii; another was Gladys Manuelito. They were my older clan sisters. The only one still living is Irene Ball.[13] I was bothered quite a bit and that's why I traveled over there. People will think, why did she go down there? They will hear that I went. A few years back, I began to think about this. I thought about it from that time on: about my uncle, the one called Tł'aaí. My mother used to tell me that he was my uncle. I was six years old when I first saw him. 'This is one of our elder male relatives and his name is Tł'aaí,' she said. He wore a headband and wore a blanket. That was how I saw him. And since then, I don't remember seeing him. Based on that, I believe we Dziłtł'ahnii, the Mountain Recess People, are continuing to exist. His late mother had been taken captive at Fort Sumner. After she escaped and returned home Tł'aaí was conceived, and from that birth we came into existence, and to this day we of the Dziłtł'ahnii clan have flourished and grown. This did not take place somewhere else. It took place here on this mountain ridge, on the **Chuska Mountains**, on this land we call **Washington Pass**.[14] This is how it is, and our relatives returned to this mountain ridge [to the top of this mountain rising up]. And so, we the Dziłtł'ahnii have since grown to maturity."

Eva mingles her memories of Tł'aaí with her strong sense of how her clan is rooted in the Chuska Mountains, placed there in a landscape that has defined them and allowed them to expand and grow. She uses the word *"diniit'ą́,"* which is associated with plant life, especially corn, growing to maturity. The metaphor of the cornstalk that is just below the surface of this description is also a metaphor of growth that is "emplaced" in a certain locale associated with members of a matrilineal clan, kinsmen, or relatives. There is an unbroken link, subsumed in the metaphor of the growing cornstalk, between 'Asdzą́ą́ Ts'ósí, Hastiin Tł'aaí, Eva's mother, Eva, and her children.

I asked Eva if she remembered any other stories about Hastiin Tł'aaí, and she replied, "My uncle was named Hastiin Tł'aaí. He was from Adobe Rising Up [or Adobe Hills, Bis Deez'áhí]. That was what it was really called, but it is also called Newcomb. Well, he got to know a white woman [Franc Newcomb, the trader's wife], and they went places together. And eventually [he made] the rugs with Yé'ii [sandpainting] figures; they were not small. There was nothing quite so beautiful. We carefully looked at them [in Santa Fe]. They were woven with Yé'ii Bicheii designs [figures of gods]. That with which he did his healing, he put back into his rugs this way. Some were called Mother Earth sandpainting rugs.

"He did not have a wife, this elder male relative of ours. He only had his nieces. He was truly a worthy man.

"They used to plant all over. At that time they didn't have tractors. They used black greasewood shaved to a sharp point to plant with. What they called 'corn food' was all that they ate back then. Also back then, on top of Mother Earth and on top of the mountains there were plants which were used for food. So that's how our ancestors were back then. To some extent, I truly believe I speak the truth, and I become worthy because of it. This is how I think of it. If all of this is forgotten, then it will be hard.

"That was my understanding of it, throughout this time and to this day. Our elder relative [Hastiin Tł'aaí] practiced our traditional chants and prayers. He existed for so many years and lived such a good life because of his knowledge of Blessing Way and other chants. Many were cured from these ceremonies, but now it seems like they have been forgotten. That is how I think about it. It is true and such a pity. That is how I viewed it. I now want some of these [ritual items] put back into my hands, even though I do not have the knowledge to use them. In my **religious**, I know my own beliefs—the same way that my elders lived [is how I live]. Whatever they were blessed with, to this day I am also blessed to walk on this earth.[15] If these things are given back to me I will carry them with respect, the Mirage Stones [hadahoniye'] and arrowheads. That is all I request. I will remember all this, and will be worthy because of it. My children will be worthy (and of value) as well.

"I have my mother; my mother was 102 years old. From the time my mother existed she told me that if I lived like this and walked in our sacred ways [according to our prayers], 'then you will be someone of value [a worthy person].' That is what she said to me. For this reason, I will not waste it [these ceremonial items] and I won't just make fun of them. These words are absolute.

"I was not raised anywhere else but around the **Washington Pass** area. On that mountain was where I was born. And to this day, I am a woman from this place, the one called **Sheep Springs**. From a certain point, the white people and the Navajo have been aware of me, and that is how I walk around. And so for that reason, my thinking has been laid down. That is how I think about it, to this day and from this time on."

Eva emphasizes relationships with her mother and with Hastiin Tł'aaí as well as with the places she refers to in English as **Washington Pass** and **Sheep Springs**. She applies the important concept of "worth" or "value" to both goods and people. Her connection to the songs and prayers of Hastiin Tł'aaí, embodied in the Mirage Stones, Arrowheads, and other items (including the Earth Bundles) that we viewed in Santa Fe, gives her and her children that value and sense of worth.

As is clear in Eva's conversation, motion is one of the most central components of Navajo language and thought. Gary Witherspoon observes that for Navajos "the world is in motion . . . things are constantly undergoing processes of transformation, deformation, and restoration, and . . . the essence of life and being is movement" (1977:48). Witherspoon also points out that the verbs associated with "going" or movement are much more important in Navajo than the verb "to be." In fact, Eva uses the verb "walking or going by walking" in the same way that the verb "to be" is used in English. Rather than stating "white people and Navajo people have knowledge of me; that's how I am," she uses the verb "to walk," which in Navajo is "*naashá*," I walk around. I translated the sentence as follows: "The white people and the Navajo have been aware of me, and that is how I walk around." In another case, with the help of my translator Carole Yazzie-Shaw, I chose a slightly more static translation, but one that flowed better in English: "She told me that if I lived like this and walked in our sacred ways, then you will be someone of value." The sense of movement would have been more apparent if I had more literally translated Eva's recollection of what her mother told her: "This is how you should walk, this is how you will walk, holding these which are called sacred; then you will be worthy."

Finally, thought is an important aspect of how Eva talks about herself. She says, "A few years back, I began to think about this," or "That's how I think about it." As Gary Witherspoon notes, thought, knowledge, word or language, and speech are four key aspects of understanding how the Navajo world works. The Holy People (Diyin Dine'é) gathered together in a hooghan and thought the world into existence. Thought is represented in the term Są'ah Naagháii (Long Life), and speech (the realization of thought) is represented in the term Bik'eh Hózhǫ́ (in accordance with Beauty or Blessing) (Witherspoon 1977:17). These twin concepts are the most abstract and important in Navajo philosophy, and they are reiterated time and time again in Navajo chants and prayers during healing ceremonies or hatáál. "Navajos believe strongly in the power of thought. The world was created by it; things are transformed according to it; life is regenerated from it. People are cured and blessed, vegetation is improved and increased, and health and happiness are restored by the power of thought" (Witherspoon 1977:29).

In addition to hinging on motion and thought, Eva's story is fundamentally rooted in place, in specific locations where she and her relatives have lived and continue to live. Birth and the spot where one's umbilical cord is buried associate a Navajo with a particular place. Just as Eva sees herself as someone who was born near Washington Pass and someone whose land is near Sheep Springs, so are her clan relatives associated with various living sites. Place or emplacement on the land in Navajo is best thought of as the stopping of movement. Land (*bikéyah*) is the place where one's feet (*hakee'*) are planted. Thus, birth, land, and movement on that land are all connected.

Dziłtł'ahnii from Bis Dootł'izh Si'ą́

When we started to make the tape recordings that are the basis for this book, we first went to the place on the mountain where Eva was born (described in chapter 1), and then we visited the winter home where Eva spent her childhood days until she was eight. Our visits to important places allowed us to see all the sites where Eva's relatives lived.

Our first excursion out from Łitso Dah 'Ask'idí (Yellow Hills), Eva's home, was to visit Rena Nelson, a clan sister who lives about a quarter of a mile west of Eva. Rena's grandmother had raised Eva's mother, Mary Sandman, so Grandma Sandman and Eva had always been close to this set of clan relatives. We went there to gather Rena's memories of Tł'aaí, since Rena is older than Eva, and we thought she would be able to remember more.

Eva and I had often visited Rena in the nineteen sixties. I first met her about a week after moving into Eva's house. Eva and I, her sister-in-law Anita, and Roslyn, Anita's daughter, had gone piñon picking. We returned in midafternoon, disappointed over a small harvest of piñons, barely a frying pan full. Rena came to visit. She made herself at home and was fixing "slapped bread" (náneeskaadí), the Navajo equivalent of flour tortillas, when we arrived. Eva added a can of corned beef to our meal of bread and coffee, and all five women chatted as we ate. Grandma Sandman joined us later, after she came back from herding her small number of sheep. Rena bedded down for the night with us, fixing a place for herself on the front room floor near Grandma Sandman. Rena had just returned from the Phoenix area where she had been with her husband Andy, her sister, and her sister's grown children. She came back early, tired of cooking for the whole crew early every morning before they went to work in the fields. Besides, Andy and two of her nephews had gone on a drinking spree. This prompted Rena to take the bus back to Gallup and she hitchhiked home from there (Field notes, December 9, 1965). Rena's comfort in Eva's home is an indication of the closeness of their relationship. Over the years I have frequently seen her when visiting Eva or when I have taken Eva over to her house on some errand. Rena can always be counted on to help contribute goods or labor for a ceremony or family occasion (such as a graduation party).

Just as we were getting to sleep that night, Rena's sister Julie arrived to take her back to Crystal so that she would have someone with whom to stay until her family returned. In January 1966, I met Rena's daughter, Rosemary, who spoke good English and was about my age. I was quite friendly with her during the next few months. In January, Rosemary had just returned from a stay in California. A year before this she had spent over twelve months in Michigan at a Bible college. She accompanied her mother, aunt, and older male cousins to Phoenix to help pick fruit in fall 1965 and left from there for California where she tried to get a job as a telephone operator. After attempting to get several other jobs, she returned to Sheep

Springs, partly because she was having periods of illness. Rena was first married to a man from Lukachukai. Rosemary and Steve were children of that marriage. She later married Andy (who was from the Red Rock area near Gallup), and they lived in Gallup for several years. Rena worked as a housekeeper for an Anglo woman, while Andy worked for a construction firm. On that day in January, I drove Rosemary and Rena into Gallup to pick up Rosemary's suitcase at the Greyhound depot; then I drove them out for a visit with Andy's relatives near Red Rock. Unfortunately they were not at home, so we drove back to Sheep Springs (Field notes, January 10, 1966).

When Eva and I visited in 1994, we found Rena and Andy in the front room. Andy was sitting on his bench, filing wood to make the legs for Kachinas, which he had been selling lately to make a living.[16] Sitting with me on the couch, Eva explained that she and I were writing a book about her life. She assured Rena that she would not reveal ritual secrets, but would describe the way the family lived in the past. "Your name will be in the book, but I will not tell everything. It's like what singers say about songs [in the Chants]. 'The songs are within you; you do not hand over all the information. Some of these protect you,' they say. And because of this you only give out surface information."

Eva went on to introduce the subject of Tł'aaí, "Well, Hastiin Tł'aaí is who we are. You know that his late mother came back from where she was a prisoner, and that was the origin of the Dziłtł'ahnii people; that is where they came to be at present. That's who we are—that is my own thinking. That is the reason we went to Santa Fe."

I started the conversation by asking Rena if she had ever seen Tł'aaí herself. "No," she replied, "I didn't see him." But she heard her mother talk about him. "There were stories told about him. Hastiin Tł'aaí was a great weaver a long time ago and also a medicine man; that's what they used to say about him. They also say he sang all sorts of chants. Back then when we were small, we used to live up on the mountain with my older sister [Mary Parkett]. My mother and father made a living together. We were still living with them when we moved up on the mountain. Up there we herded sheep. We had a lot of livestock, perhaps three hundred head of sheep. It was a large herd. We herded sheep on horseback. That's how we used to live during the summer. We were still living up there then.[17] My mother used to say, 'This land has always been ours and that down below [on the flats], too. It is called Big Water [Tó Nitsaa].[18] Our elders, including Hastiin Tł'aaí and his mother, used to live there, and we are all one clan, the Dziłtł'ahnii clan. We are all one.

"Our grandmothers and grandfathers, our mothers and our fathers[19]—back then they used to live up there on that land. Back then they selected that land for us, our elders. These included Hastiin Tł'aaí's relatives and family members and clan relatives, all of them together. That's how we lived back then. And we lived in the Tó Nitsaa area and that land was the Dziłtł'ahnii land. Now it's gone, but it's still our land and we go up there once in a while. We both herded sheep when we were very small, my little brother Daniel and me. We herded sheep on horseback back then. My older sister stayed home with her husband. She took care of the home. Then our father and mother used to come up there [on the mountain]. They used to bring us food when we were herding the sheep. Back then my mother used to say, 'This used to be our land, Hastiin Tł'aaí and Hastiin Tł'aaí's mother were neighbors.' There's a small hill in the distance and a 'male hooghan' [*'ałch'į' 'adeez'áhí*] with a cloth on top, and Hastiin Tł'aaí's mother used to sit beneath it. And they moved up there every summer. My mother told us that back then; that's how she remembered it.

"That's the place we used to move up to back then. We herded sheep until autumn and then we herded the sheep back down below, near this hill right here, near the mountain cove [*bitát'ah*]. We used to live around here.

"Back then our grandfathers and grandmothers selected the land here, all this land and that below. This is our land. In the past it used to belong to all of them. This was Bis Dootł'izh Si'ą́, the wash and further on down below. This is the land they selected, our grandmothers and grandfathers. Now today, we live on this land. Also we plant our fields here. This land is now here. That's how we lived from the past up to the present time.

"Our grandfather [*nihicheii*], Hastiin Tł'aaí, he used to live at T'iis Nídeeshgiizh [Cottonwoods Spaced Out, what is now Newcomb], somewhere around there. There were also other Dziłtł'ahnii living there; perhaps they were aunts or grandchildren. There were a whole group of clan members over there growing or increasing in number. They were all relatives.

"Our -cheii used to weave large rugs; that's what our mother told us. He used to card the wool and spin it himself. He wove for many years.

He also performed various chants and ceremonies back then. He also performed the Night Way, perhaps. He was a medicine man for many years. That's how he made a living back then, our elder Hastiin Tł'aaí. That is what we heard.

"They used to call him Tágí 'Agodí [Straight Bangs].[20] That's what they called him back then. I don't remember when he died. They never told us anything. The people just told us he used to live at T'iis Nídeeshgiizh."

After we finished talking about Tł'aaí, Carole, Eva, and I continued to ask Rena about her relatives. She remembered that her mother's mother, a woman who had been blind all her life, took

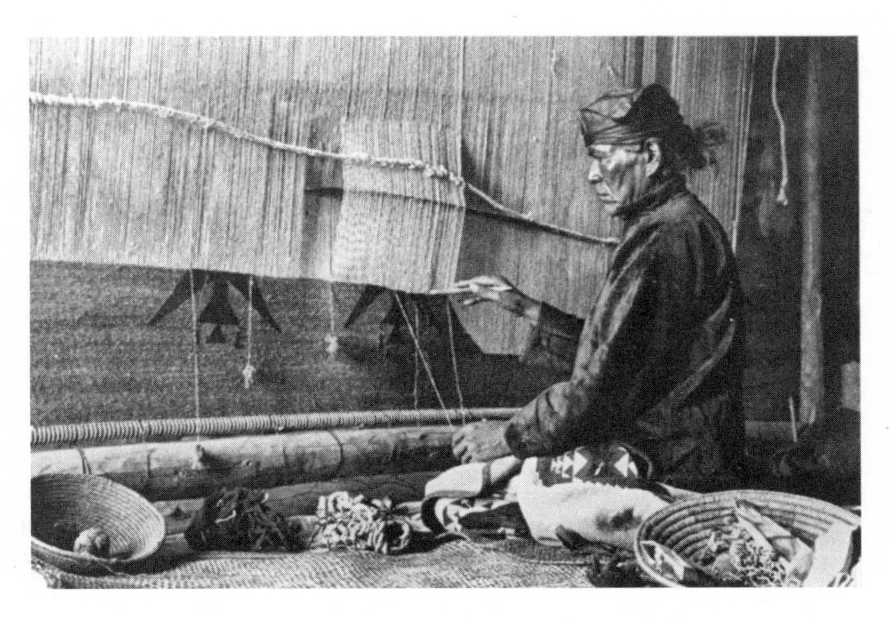

FIGURE 2.3 Hastiin Tł'aaí weaving one of his sandpainting rugs.

COURTESY OF WHEELWRIGHT MUSEUM OF THE AMERICAN INDIAN.

care of Grandma Sandman and Ben Bimá, after Grandma Sandman's mother died. Grandma Sandman had three siblings: her sister, Annie Foster, a brother called Dziłtł'ahnii and a brother called Sam Gould. When the mother died, Grandma Sandman was given to Rena's grandmother, while Annie Foster, Sam Gould, and Dziłtł'ahnii were raised by Hastiin Tł'aaí's mother. Later, Sam Gould moved to Crownpoint and married there. Dziłtł'ahnii died in adulthood without children. Annie Foster married a man known as Hastiin Yázhí and moved to a home two or three miles northwest of Eva and Rena's residence groups.

When we left Rena's we went to look for the hooghan where Grandma Sandman was raised and the hooghans near Bis Dootł'izh Si'ą́, (Blue Mesa) the family's ancestral land. We found the first site just to the north of Rena's home: the ruins of a hooghan and also a little house where Grandma Sandman may have grown up. Then we drove on a long dirt road south and west toward Blue Mesa where we located the ruins of the house where Rena's uncle and father had lived. Later that day when we were sitting under some trees on the mountain talking about Eva's family history, Eva told me a little more about the significance of the place, which was not only a clan residence, but a sacred location. "This morning, that place where we went at the mountain, long ago, at that place medicine men used to travel to the top at Blue Mesa where they would make offerings of hard goods."

Tł'aaí's Home

From Blue Mesa we drove over to Newcomb, hoping to find Tł'aaí's old home. We drove down a dirt road west of the Newcomb Trading Post and Eva pointed out the home of her clan brother, John Gould. His mother, Daisy, one of Tł'aaí's nieces, became a famous weaver, making some of the finest rugs in the Two Grey Hills style. We looked for a little hill on which the house may have been located, and we took one picture of a foundation that may have been what was left of the house.

We have to rely on historical documents and photos for a sense of place.[21] Franc Newcomb describes it in her book *Navaho Neighbors*:

There were five hogans on Klah's [Tł'aaí's] homestead, four or five corrals, and two or three sheds which were roofed shelters with pole and brush sides. At the time of which I am writing, his sister with her youngest daughter, Daisy, and three granddaughters, Lucy, Carole, and Evelyn, occupied the largest hogan.

These three younger girls were the children of her eldest daughter that had died during the flu epidemic, and whom Klah had immediately brought to his home where he and his sister could care for them. Klah's cabin stood a little distance from the others and was a square room with a large fireplace in one corner, a wide stone chimney, stone walls, pole beams in the ceiling, and a plank door that could be closed and locked when he was away.

Here he kept his valuables—his medicine bundles, ceremonial blankets, baskets, buckskin robes, furs, prayer-plumes, and trunks filled with masks, dance kilts, rattles, and sacks of plant pollens. From the ceiling-poles hung large bundles of reeds, yucca spikes, and herbs of various kinds. This cabin was where he slept when he was at home, and it was where he made preparations for the ceremonies he was called upon to conduct, but all of his meals were served, and all the cooking was done in his sister's hogan.

Klah's mother's hogan was a small log structure located near the largest sheep corral where she could hear any unusual noise made by the dogs or the sheep during the night. Just outside her door there hung the iron blade of an old plow and beside it lay a metal fire poker which she could use as a gong to summon the family at any time of day or night. Two of Klah's sister's girls had married brothers; Hanesbah [Gladys] had wed Sam Manuelito, and Althbah [Irene] had married his younger brother, Jim Manuelito. The two young couples had built their hogans not far from Klah's so all of their sheep could be herded in one flock and the younger men could oversee the irrigating and farm work together. [Newcomb 1966:179–80]

FIGURE 2.4 Hastiin Tł'aaí, his sister Ahdesbah, a niece (possibly Daisy), and three of his sister's granddaughters.
COURTESY OF WHEELWRIGHT MUSEUM OF THE AMERICAN INDIAN.

FIGURE 2.5 Hastiin Tł'aaí, probably in front of his home, which appears more like a round stone hooghan than the square "cabin" described by Newcomb.
COURTESY OF WHEELWRIGHT MUSEUM OF THE AMERICAN INDIAN.

Eva has a vivid memory of Tł'aaí's summer home near their own in the Chuska mountains. "When I was small, I would herd sheep with Ben.[22] I was quite small. Right here was Tł'aaí's horse corral, they used to say, at Dził Ditł'oi, below Ben's mother's house. There were big logs laying in circular position there. Now they are probably gone. 'This is where they used to live,' my mother would say. At that time they did not haul wood. And last summer the one we were looking for and couldn't find was the house that belonged to a man named Hastiin Bitsii' łigai [White Haired Man]. It was still there."

Tł'aaí as Nádleeh

Hastiin Tł'aaí never married, and some people called him a nádleeh. "Was he nádleeh?" I asked, recalling that once, thirty years before, Eva had used that term in describing a Navajo to me. It was a few days after I started living with Eva in 1965. We took a trip to the Two Grey Hills Trading Post so that Shoemaker's Wife, who lived with Eva, could buy her some meat, chili, milk, and pop using her credit at the store. Eva pointed out that the woman sitting on the couch was really a man. She said he wore a skirt, just like a woman, and she wanted to know if there were any white people like that. She said he was called nádleeh in Navajo (one who is in the constant state of change). Since then I have read about nádleeh and other categories of Native Americans now referred to as "two-spirit" or third gender people (Jacobs, Thomas, and Lang 1997).[23] I was interested to see if Eva thought of Tł'aaí as a nádleeh.

"Yes, nádleeh means half-half . . . half lady and half man. So he don't want to marry anybody . . . that's what it means."

"Does someone choose that for themselves?" I asked. "How does that happen?"

"They're born like that. They are probably born like that," Eva repeated in Navajo, and then switched to English to emphasize her point, **"They're born like that."**

"And then, when . . . how do they know they're nádleeh?" I asked.

"Only his mother would have known that he was a nádleeh," Eva said, "This would have been evident at birth and the fact that he made rugs was evidence that he was a nádleeh."

Carole had a different interpretation. "I don't think he was born that way. Well, eventually . . . I guess he was born as a normal child, but when he became a little older, he wanted to do what women used to do, weave rugs and stuff like that. And that's why they think that he was half woman and half man, because he can do a woman's job. He did a lot of cooking and he did a lot of weaving. So, people used to say that he's a nádleeh because he knew how to weave. And of course, you know, when he was weaving I guess he did everything himself in order to weave a complete rug—he even carded, he even spun it. He even got the warps ready and everything. . . . Maybe that's why people called him a nádleeh. But as far as I know, he wasn't born half woman or half man."

"So he was born like a male?" I asked.

"An ordinary man, but later in the future when he grew up he wanted to become a rug weaver."

"Did being a nádleeh have any influence on his being a hataałii?" I wondered.

"They only called him nádleeh because of his womanly ways, his weaving, it had nothing to do with his learning." Carole had more to add. "Then my grandma used to tell me that Hastiin Tł'aaí used to wear those real silver jewelries that he used to get from I guess Mrs. Newcomb when he went on trips with her. Remember those real thin, round bracelets that came about so many years back? Remember how they were just round?" Carole asked me. "He had a bunch of them that he had on his arms all the time."

"So are the bracelets like the ones only women would wear? Is that what he had?" I wondered.

"I guess he liked that, you know," Carole thought. "He wanted that, or Mrs. Newcomb might have given it to him, stuff like that."

Carole and I went on to discuss the fact that Tł'aaí dressed in men's clothing. She remembered that in one of the historical photos of Tł'aaí he is wearing a Navajo blanket completely draped over him. "We don't really know how he's dressed underneath that.

Mrs. Newcomb is the one that made his wardrobe . . . white pants and the shirt that goes over like a velveteen shirt."

Eva explained, "They used to say that when you had a nádleeh in the family that this brought wealth, soft goods, and the same with a handicapped child, this also brought wealth, horses, sheep. This is what my father used to say, and my mother also used to say this. . . . And that is why you shouldn't laugh at that kind of person."

Carole amplified this idea. "In our tradition, you know, nádleeh is respected and also a retarded person is respected, too."[24]

Other Dziłtł'ahnii Kin

Beginning with 'Asdzą́ą́ Hashkéhí, the Dziłtł'ahnii lived in the Chuskas in the summer and in the winter, at the base of the mountains on the flat lands (*halgai*) near Newcomb—near Black Rock Standing (Łizhin Deez'áhí), at Yellow Hills (Łitso Dah 'Ask'idí), and on Blue Mesa (Bis Dootł'izh Si'ą́). Other clusters of Dziłtł'ahnii lived near Crownpoint at a place called White Rock (Tsé Łigai), at Lukachukai (Lók'aa'ch'égai), and near the Chaco Wash close to Sheep Springs.

Eva's mother told her that Tł'aaí's mother came from White Rock (near Crownpoint). "It was my uncle who went over there. 'Sam with tied hair' [Sam Bitsiiyéél] was what they called him. He was my mother's sibling. Many lived over there. My mother and Cross Hills Lady used to travel by horseback. They just said that they had relatives from the Dziłtł'ahnii or Mountain Recess Clan, so they went over there—my mother and Cross Hills Lady" (who was Kiyaa'áanii and was also from White Rock). There are two other significant clusters of Dziłtł'ahnii clan members. One is located across the Chuskas near Lukachukai where Ray Winnie, a hataałii called Dziłtł'ahnii Yázhí, lived. His mother and Mary Sandman were sisters. Ray Winnie (Dziłtł'ahnii, born for Kiyaa'áanii) originally came from Where Waters Cross east of the Sheep Springs Trading Post, and his sister (Rita Berland's mother) and her children form another cluster of Dziłtł'ahnii clan members there. He was born in 1906 and became a Night Way singer in 1972. He also knew Blessing Way,

Evil Way, Navajo Wind Way, Female Shooting Way, Stargazing, and Mountaintop Way (Faris 1990:96–97). He participated in the transfer of Hastiin Tł'aaí's jish and ceremonial items from the Wheelwright Museum to the Navajo Community College in 1977 (Frisbie 1987:328, 341–44). Faris reports that Tł'aaí's Night Way jish was transferred to Juan Shorthair and some masks were remade by Fred Stevens, Jr. Shorthair was born in 1918 and is from Piñon, Arizona; he is Táchii'nii, born for Ts'ah yisk'idnii.

Eva added some more information about Dziłtł'ahnii Yázhí or Ray Winnie. "They have only aunts over there at Lukachukai. His mother is gone. She and my mother were siblings [came up and out together]. From here they moved across the mountain. Dziłtł'ahnii Yázhí is really from 'Áhidiidlį́ [Where the Waters Cross]. Rita Berland's mother and Ned Kiyaa'áanii were siblings and that's where they are from as well."[25]

The Navajo concept of kinship embodied in the term *k'é* connects all of these Dziłtł'ahnii. K'é has been translated as compassion, cooperation, friendliness, unselfishness, and peacefulness. It embodies all that is positive within relationships. The term k'éí means "a special or particular kind of k'é" (Witherspoon 1975:37) and applies to all those who are related through clanship. Shik'éí are "my relatives"—those connected to women of the same matrilineal clan, that is, descended from a common female ancestor where the actual genealogical links are not traced. K'é is anchored in birth, since it is through birth that a baby becomes affiliated with relatives on both the mother's and father's side. First, every Navajo is born *of* a woman (coming up and out of her womb). Birth affiliates a child with her or his mother and the mother's relatives or clan. Second, each Navajo is "born for" their father. This notion of being "born for" affiliates each child, male and female, with the father's matrilineal clan. Third, each individual is further related to those their father was "born for," that is, the father's father's clan (*dashinálí*). Finally, the individual is also affiliated with the relatives his or her mother was "born for," that is, the mother's father's father's clan (*dashicheii*). Some clans are "related to each other" and hence those in these clans address each other by kin terms and assume relationships based on k'é.

K'é and clan relationships are the primary way in which Navajo people locate themselves within the social universe. If possible, Navajos address one another by kin terms rather than names. When Navajos meet each other for the first time, they introduce themselves in terms of their clans and their fathers' clans. At public meetings it is now customary for each speaker to make brief introductory remarks stating their four clan affiliations. Thus members of the audience will know whether the speaker is a relative or not, and whether he/she is related to one's own or one's father's clan. Clan relationships also regulate marriage. A Navajo is not supposed to marry into his/her own clan or the father's clan. Clan members often visit each other, extend hospitality, or go out of their way to help clan relatives, particularly if a clan member asks for help in putting on a Navajo curing ceremony (hatáál), a puberty ceremony (Kinaaldá), or a Native American Church meeting.

As Eva talks about the history of her relatives, she associates them with particular places. Individuals are conceptually located on the landscape, and they are rooted in those places through the burial of their umbilical cords. There is an intimate connection between place and matrilineal kinship. For any individual there is a web of four sets of clan connections, and of course, for spouses and other in-laws there are additional webs of affiliation that fan out in four directions. The metaphor of the cornstalk and of a plant growing and spreading is an apt one for this connection between kinship and landscape.

Eleanor's Memories

The importance of Hastiin Tł'aaí in Eva's own life did not emerge until I talked with Eleanor, Eva's older sister, on October 15, 1994. Eleanor walked across the road from her house to visit Eva. We were in the middle of an interview, and Eva and Carole invited her in to talk about her remembrances of Hastiin Tł'aaí. Because Eleanor was eight years older than Eva, she had a vivid picture of him.

"He had white pants, moccasins, black socks. His forehead was tied with a sash. His hair knot was also tied with a sash. He had earrings, a necklace. His shirt was open with no buttons. This was how he dressed. When my older brother was burned, my father had a bad dream two days before. So it was then that her grandfather [Tł'aaí] performed the Blessing Way, an all-night ceremony, for Eva at Łizhin Deez'áhí [their home]. This is what I remember.

"And then he also performed the Chiricahua Wind Way for her, too. Where was that? I don't remember—was it here? This was how he performed the ceremony for her. This is what I remember of the story. Eva probably doesn't remember . . . she was small—maybe four, maybe three years old—about this big. I was maybe eight, yes, because there was one between us. He was my little brother. He also died up there, [that brother] who was born between us.

"According to what my mother told me, Tł'aaí was born on that mountain range. He was born four years after they returned from Fort Sumner. Right there at Mountain with a White Neck [Dził Zéé'asgai] was where my aunt used to move. There is still evidence that there was once a very wide, large, sheep corral there. Remember? That is where they say she lived, the one they call Tł'aaí's mother. The wood had turned gray and was falling, and over here was the sheep corral like this. I guess there was a whole lot of them [sheep]. And this was where Tł'aaí's mother lived, my mom told me. And then somehow, after they were born, they moved to a place called Newcomb [T'iis Nídeeshgiizh]."

At the end of this account, Eleanor reiterated something that Eva had told me many times. "My mother, she never told us the way things were. She didn't tell us anything—only my aunt from the Flats, Annie Foster. She told us some stories about the way things were. Yes, I remember the stories she told. My mother, she never said much about the way things were."

The story of Hastiin Tł'aaí's role in curing Eva after the fire brings us into Eva's childhood and to the next chapter, where we will hear Eva's narratives about the nineteen thirties.

CHAPTER THREE

"I Used To Herd Sheep All Around Here"

Eva's Childhood, Sheep Herding, and the Trauma of Stock Reduction

EVA SPENT HER CHILDHOOD, LIKE MOST NAVAJOS LIVING near the Chuskas, in a series of different seasonal homes—a house at Black Rock Standing ("on the flats") in the winter and a summer place at Mountain with a White Neck ("on the mountain"). The importance of place in Navajo life is reflected in Eva's decision to begin her life story by showing me these two homesites. On my first trip from Albuquerque to Sheep Springs in 1994 to begin recording Eva's memories for this book, we went to both childhood homes, looking them over for signs of old hooghans, sheep corrals, and fields, to prod Eva's memory and provide a context for the telling of stories about her childhood. Probably when Eva was five or six, Eva's parents moved to a new winter home at Yellow Hills and some years later began using a new summer site at Deep Valley.

Navajo live in scattered clusters of hooghans, houses, and sheep corrals rather than in dense villages like the Pueblo peoples of Arizona and New Mexico. In the last chapter Eva talked about her clan, the Dziłtł'ahnii, growing and spreading over the landscape, using the metaphor of corn plants growing to maturity. Her discussion of her Dziłtł'ahnii relatives and Rena Nelson's memories of her family history located kinsmen at named places. These clusters of hooghans, houses, and corrals, often called "residence groups" by anthropologists, are usually inhabited by an extended family, though sometimes only a nuclear family.[1] In the past, residence groups went through a developmental cycle. As children grew up and got married, the new couple usually built a hooghan for themselves. Navajo daughters usually continued to live with their mothers after marriage, so in the first half of the twentieth century, many couples lived matrilocally (with the mother) or, in more technical language, uxorilocally (with the wife's relatives). If the wife's mother had died or the husband's mother needed help with herding or agricultural work, the couple might live with the husband's mother, that is, virilocally (with the husband's relatives). Eventually, after children were born and became old enough to help with herding and other chores, a couple might establish a new residence group, usually a half-mile or so from the parent site. As their children married, the cycle started over again.

When Eva's parents were living at Black Rock Standing, they were at the independent phase of their residence cycle, having established a place away from their mothers' relatives. Their married son, Frank, and his wife, Anita, lived with them, since she had no mother or siblings with whom to live.[2] While they were at Black Rock Standing, Mary Sandman, Eva's mother, also briefly cared for her husband's mother and sister (two very elderly, blind women) before they both died.[3] At their summer home at Mountain with a White Neck, Eva's nuclear family and her married sister resided with a larger group of kin. They were part of an extended family that also included Mary's clan sister, Ben Bimá (Ben's mother), her husband, and children. Since Mary's mother had died in childbirth, she and Ben Bimá (who was the daughter of another Dziłtł'ahnii woman) were raised by Rena's grandmother, also of the Dziłtł'ahnii clan. In Navajo kinship terminology Mary and Ben Bimá were "sisters" since they are both from the same clan and of the same generation, but they also grew up together just as biological sisters in Anglo culture would have been raised. Given this history, it is no surprise that Mary and Ben Bimá would have spent the summers together, jointly cared for their flocks, and spent the days weaving side by side.

In writing about Eva's childhood, I have organized the narratives so that they focus on the three residence sites: Dził Zéé'asgai (Mountain with a White Neck), Łizhin Deez'áhí (Black Rock Standing), and Łitso Dah 'Ask'idí (Yellow Hills), where the family moved when Eva was five or six. Much of this chapter centers on Eva's relationship to her mother, her mother's sheep and goat herd, and her weaving, while much of the next chapter concerns Eva's father, the fields he planted near Yellow Hills, and his practice as a hataałii, or singer. These chapters cover the period from Eva's birth in 1928 until her Kinaaldá and marriage in the early nineteen forties. I have woven into each of these chapters narratives about relationships and events that emanated from the white world but shaped Eva's childhood such as her relationship with a white couple at an oil pumping station, her early schooling, and the drinking practices of Navajo men, including her father, as well as the impact of U.S. government programs on the family.

Navajo women are often associated with their sheep through the notion of motherhood. As Werner and Begishe note, the Navajo often say, "Those called the fields are your mother, those called sheep are your mother, sheep are life" (Witherspoon 1977:92). Through the nineteen fifties, women were often responsible for herding, the birthing of lambs, and care of the flocks, although children also herded sheep much of the time up until they began attending white schools (see Lamphere 1990). Eva's summers were spent with her mother, her aunt Ben Bimá, and Ben taking care of the flock and learning how to weave. In contrast, Eva's father is associated with the irrigated cornfields. He met Mary Sandman's family when he helped plant and harvest the fields sometime between 1900 and 1910. During Eva's childhood, he remained at Łitso Dah 'Ask'idí in the summer months rather than migrating to the mountains. His teachings were crucial in shaping Eva's philosophy of life.

Eva has taken something from each of her parents. From her mother comes her ability to care for her small herd of goats and the skill to make her intricately woven Two Grey Hills rugs.[4] From her father she acquired her considerable expertise in growing corn, squash, and melons. One can also see how his knowledge of herbs and traditional Navajo teachings, part of his role as hataałii or singer, has its parallels in Eva's practice as a diagnostician or handtrembler, a traditional Navajo role, and healer in the tradition of the Native American Church, a newer set of activities (see chapter 6).

Dził Zéé'asgai

On Thursday, July 7, 1994, I traveled to Sheep Springs to tape some of Eva's life history. It was a bright summer day, very hot down on the flats (halgai or white stretches out) where Eva's home is located at Łitso Dah 'Ask'idí (Yellow Hills). A trip to the cool mountains to see Eva's birthplace and to have a small picnic was a perfect way to spend the day. Before we turned off of Highway 666 toward the mountains, we stopped to purchase tamales and Pepsis from a Newcomb man who sells them from the back of his pickup.[5] The road from 666 and the Sheep Springs store to the top of Washington Pass is now a paved, two-lane road. In the nineteen sixties it had taken me a full hour to drive my Volkswagen bug up the steep, ten-mile road over rough gravel and around many curves. In 1994 it took less than ten minutes to make the trip to the dirt road at Oak Springs (Chéch'il Yaató). Turning north we passed clusters of summer homes, many left vacant as fewer and fewer families move up to the mountains for the summer months. Many cornfields stood empty. I saw perhaps three or four planted fields that day and only one or two herds of sheep grazing on the mountain. A single individual tended even these while others in extended family residence clusters remained on the flats, closer to wage jobs and access to the stores of Gallup and Farmington. Even the summer Chapter House, the scene of many community meetings in 1965, sat empty.

We passed Na'aldzisí (Deep Valley) where Eva used to live in the summer months, now abandoned, its houses torn down, although Anita Sandman (Eva's sister-in-law) and her married children have erected a two-room cabin across the road. The land had eroded badly since the nineteen sixties, with gullies across the road and deeper washes cutting down the mountain. About a quarter of a mile on, we turned right and headed down a narrow, seldom-traveled road to Ben Bimá's place, Eva's childhood summer home. At times I could hardly see the track and I had to be careful not to catch the bottom of my car on the road's high center. We finally rounded the bend, and I could see a small, hewn-log cabin with a roof that leaned out from the side of the house to create a shady overhang. I remember coming here in the summer of 1966 when Ben Bimá was still alive. She spent summers there with Joe Denetdele, her second husband, herding sheep and planting corn in the nearby field.

When I visited in 1966, Eva and Carole had just moved to a "shade" (*chaha'oh*) near a large ceremonial hooghan so that Carole could be a patient in an Enemy Way ceremony, which was to last three days. We traveled down the same rough road with a high center in my Volkswagen Bug and found Ben Bimá and Joe along the way. They were looking for three sheep that had strayed from the herd. Eva asked them for jewelry that Carole could wear during the ceremony: bracelets, rings, a turquoise necklace, and also a woven red belt.[6] Ben Bimá called the request over to Joe and he approached the car and offered three rings and a bracelet to Eva. We drove Ben Bimá further down the road to her small cabin. In those days it had a

FIGURE 3.1 Eva looks at the stones that indicate where her parents' summer home used to be at Dził Zéé'asgai (Mountain with a White Neck).

PHOTOGRAPH BY MARGARET RANDALL.

lived-in look with a sheep pen nearby, a field full of corn, a "shade" for cooking, and bedding slung over a wooden rail outside. Ben Bimá gave Eva a necklace and also offered the silver, bow-shaped buttons from her velveteen blouse. They went into the house to remove them, and then, with the buttons, necklace, and Joe's jewelry, Eva returned to the Enemy Way site to give them to Carole.

In 1994 we turned left at the cabin, headed up a small slope, and stopped near three tall pines. Getting out of my tan Nissan wagon, we began to look for evidence of Eva's parents' hooghan. We found the stones from the structure, and then walked near an abandoned cornfield to a small clump of oak trees. Eva's mother and father had constructed a chaha'oh under these trees. Eva told me that she was born there, in a ramada or shade (chaha'oh) that had been built for outdoor living during the summer months. It was here that her placenta and umbilical chord were buried. She bent over and took some of the earth and blessed herself with it.

FIGURE 3.2 Eva takes some of Mother Earth from her birthplace in a grove of oak trees to bless herself.

PHOTOGRAPH BY MARGARET RANDALL.

We went back toward the car, spread out my blankets, and ate our lunch of roasted chicken from the Gallup Safeway. Afterward Eva recorded her thoughts about being back at her birthplace and explained why she had blessed herself with the earth. "I remember it so. This Mother Earth, you put it on like this; then you will live a good life. And when it rains, you put that on your body or you bless yourself with the rainbow. And early in the morning you have to bless yourself [with corn pollen]. These are holy places. I am very glad I have returned to my birthplace. I am very grateful. There is where I was raised, the place I was born. If you just forget and go any old way, I don't think you will last long that way. You won't live very long. You must return to your birthplace and say prayers for yourself and state how you will be and how you will live. These days, babies are born in hospitals. What did they do with that thing that comes out with the baby [the placenta]? What do they do with that now? They probably burn it and then trash it. Not me. They say you should roll around on the dirt on the place where your placenta is buried. They would say, 'Go back over there and roll around the area where you were born.'

"They say that the horned toad is our grandfather. They say that when he is born, he rolls around in the dirt. Just like him we do the same. And also the horned toad is made sacred. So when you come across one, you must pick it up and place it on your heart and make a prayer, or if you have corn pollen, make a blessing. 'Stand in front of me with your hands. Protect me and speak for my protection.'"

Knoki-Wilson says that burying the placenta is done so it can "become one with Mother Earth again" (Schwarz 1997:138). The baby's umbilical cord is even more important. The parents or grandparents often bury the cord in a location considered to be beneficial to the child's future. A boy's cord was usually buried in a sheep, cattle, or horse corral, or in the family fields when it was desired that he be concerned with livestock or farming. Likewise a girl's cord might be buried in a sheep corral to ensure that her thoughts were with the livestock, or inside the hooghan so that she would become a good homemaker. Another place where a girl's cord might be buried is where the loom is erected in the hooghan if the family wishes her to become an expert weaver (Schwarz 1997:138).

Eva continued to build a picture of what the area looked like when she was a child.

"Right here is where I was born. It's like I am six years old and this is how I remember it. My aunt [Ben Bimá] had a hooghan over right there; our hooghan, a round one, was here and right over there was a sheep corral back then.[7] And then over there in that cluster of trees was the water [a spring]. And over there was a road, but there's none there now; another goes over there. And then over there was the water for the sheep. And that's how I remember it. My mother and father were around here. Ben's father was right around here. And my mother and father were here, living in a wood house with rock underneath [a rock foundation], hurriedly put together. It was a round hooghan, and there were some wooden boards with flour sacks sewn together and laid on top. And here was where they all used to live. And here there was a rug loom underneath two pines standing together.[8] And that is how I remember it.

"Back then there were a lot of sheep. But there weren't any stores. Around here there were no stores, nothing. The only one nearby was the Two Grey Hills store over there. We didn't have any vehicles then, not even any wagons either. We did have donkeys to use. When they finished weaving, they would ride the donkeys to Two Grey Hills. And from here that former road goes down and way over there is Fuzzy Mountain [or Mountain Covered with Vegetation—Dził Ditł'oi], and nearby was Hastiin Tł'aaí's hooghan, and his mother and sister. And also they moved over to Newcomb. . . . To me it just seems like yesterday."

Before we left, we hiked over toward the rim that looks down the mountains at the flats. We were searching for the hooghan of Hastiin Tsii' Łibai (Mr. Gray Hair), a neighbor who also knew Hastiin Tł'aaí and his mother. We had no luck finding evidence of the house or the sheep corral; Eva suspected that someone had carried the wood away. The place looked abandoned and overgrown. The old fields were choked with sagebrush. Yet the tall pines, the occasional stand of oaks, and the open, hilly area evoked a time when there had been more grass, when the sheep could have grazed peacefully within a short distance of water. Later that afternoon, Eva told me stories of how she herded sheep with her cousin Ben all over this area.

FIGURE 3.3 While pointing out the place where her parents' house once stood, Eva tells Louise what the area used to look like at Dził Zéé'asgai (Mountain with a White Neck).
PHOTOGRAPH BY MARGARET RANDALL.

Łizhin Deez'áhí

Our trip to her winter home, two days later, provided a great contrast. Down on the treeless flats, Black Rock Standing (Łizhin Deez'áhí) was a hot, dry place in July even at 8:30 in the morning. But the sunny, southern exposure must have been a warm place in the winter. The Black Rock Standing is actually a hill of black gravel or a coal-like substance sticking up in full view of the highway.

The residence group itself was slightly north and east of the hill. We found evidence of the stone hooghan where Eva's parents lived as well as some rocks from the hooghan where Eva's father's mother and aunt stayed while Eva's mother cared for them. Eva also showed me the rocks that were all that was left of a small corral perched against the hillside that had been used for lambing.

Eva had described the location of her parents' residence group in relation to others who lived out on the flats between Black Rock Standing and the place where the foothills rose toward the Chuskas. This description locates neighboring Navajos on the landscape, placing each residence group in a locale with a name. Most are relatives connected to Eva through relations of k'é. To an outsider this is just a list of names, but for Eva, it speaks to the social universe surrounding her parents and the specific kin connections in her network.

In the early nineteen thirties there was no one living at Yellow Hills, where Eva currently lives. "There were no people around. No one lived here. There weren't even any sheep to be seen. There was a woman by the name of Shoemaker [*ké'íít'iní*]. She was Diné Chíí's late mother. They were only two—she and 'the woman who holds her head up' ['Asdzą́ą́ Dégo Yániil'ą́ní]; that was Paul Gould's late grandmother. That's it. Over at Blue Clay Sitting There [Bis Dootł'izh

FIGURE 3.4 Łizhin Deez'áhí (Black Rock Standing), a hill of gravel or a coal-like substance, rises above the flatlands and a dirt track leads to the house where Eva spent her winters as a child.

PHOTOGRAPH BY AUTHOR.

FIGURE 3.5 Eva stands near the rocks that formed the family sheep corral in the nineteen thirties, pointing out where distant neighbors lived to the south at Łizhin Deez'áhí (Black Rock Standing).
PHOTOGRAPH BY MARGARET RANDALL.

Si'ą́ní], there was Hastiin Tłááshchí'í.[9] These were the only ones that lived around here in separate hooghan clusters. From somewhere, others moved here. Hastiin Yázhí's wife [Annie Foster, Eva's mother's sister] lived out on the flats. She rode her horse over here and she made the sound of 'Yííiiyá' when she rode in. My mother and father lived at Łizhin Deez'áhí, over there where the rock is pointing up and it looked like an outcrop of rocks. My late cousin Diné Chíí'—his mother had a tent made from flour sacks sewed together.[10]

"There was nothing. No one lived around here [near Eva's current house]. Over here, from these rising hills there used to be a road [just behind Eva's house]. From there they traveled to Shiprock by wagon. There was nothing. Over there [Black Rock Standing], I was small. I don't know how old I was, but I still remember it well. The house was made of sandstone layered rocks, which my late father had built for us.[11] And then my late older brother [Frank

Sandman], somehow he was building a fire with the coals still in there. He poured white gas on it. It made a 'ts'ibag' sound, and he caught on fire. That is how he became like that. He became crippled, and his ligaments burned on one side. Most of his hand was burned, and that is the reason why his hand was like that. He was in critical condition when they transported him to the hospital in Shiprock. He was on the edge of death. That is what they were saying. Somehow he came back to life. That is how I remember it.

"When he was in the hospital and I went over to the hospital to pay him a visit, there were small, tiny spiders that were all over his body. And that's probably what brought him back; they made medicine on him. That's why you're not supposed to kill spiders, because they make medicine.

"As for me, someone threw me out of the hooghan and I was standing outside. Over there someone grabbed me. The fire just went up. I was crying. At that time they didn't have cars, but the only person that had a car was Hastiin Bitsii' Be'estł'ǫ́ní [Mr. Tied Hair]; he had a Model T. That's how they took him to the hospital.

"When Frank was about Aaron's age [eight years old] he was a normal person. He was riding a ram and it bucked him off. He broke his hip, and in those days they didn't have operations or a hospital nearby. It healed back that way, so he always limped.

"My mom used to take care of my –nálí [*shinálí*, my father's mother] over at Black Hill Rising. There's another one, Peter Begay's mother's mother.[12] They are both from one family, my paternal grandmothers. They were sisters. They're both blind, and they can't walk. They just crawl and I have seen those ladies when I was small. . . . Two more days, and she's gone. She was just crawling around and talking. And my mom says [to my father], 'Take your mom and her sister back to Newcomb. I cannot take care of someone's mother.' So we took them down with the wagon and the next day one of them died. I don't know when the other one died."

Eva remembered their days at Łizhin Deez'áhí as a time of prosperity for her family. "We had a **whole bunch**; we had a lot of goats, three hundred, maybe four hundred.[13] We would herd them down to the water. The water had been there for a long time. There was a donkey with a tarp on his back among the sheep. When it begins to rain, we would run underneath the canvas. That's how we herded the goats toward the water. . . ."

The Oil Pumping Station

In the narratives thus far, Eva has described her childhood as tied to two places, each associated with her immediate nuclear family and extended kin. The wider social world included other important relatives related to both her mother's and father's clans, but there were also ways in which the area was tied to the larger capitalist world, and there were important relationships that developed with non-Navajos during Eva's early years.

There were two white people (Bilagáana) out on the flats at a place that was once called Metal Lying Down (Béésh Sinil). Eva talked about her connection to them. "There were two houses like this which they stayed in. From somewhere they would get oranges about this big. And when we would herd our sheep over there, they would milk the goats into a pail about this big, which they would fill with milk. They probably drank it. And for this, they would give us **oranges** and **apples**. There is something on him right here about this big." Eva cupped her hand to the side of her face, describing a growth that must have been very large and disfiguring. "And so we called him Niida'achaaní. He was very old. The people looked to him, giving things like pails or pots and pans [they traded with him]. Then suddenly he had a heart attack there. 'Niida'achaaní's heart has stopped,' they said. They said, 'He died.' I don't know where they took him, maybe they just left him there. That's what happened over there."

Eva went on to describe what must have been an oil well. "There used to be oil coming out. There was a pump like this. It made a 'bo bo wo wo' sound like this. A huge house or building was there. . . . He [Niida'achaaní] used to help my father out because he had a car. He hauled water for him, and my father gave him a goat; I remember it well." When Carole, Eva, and I drove over to Béésh Sinil, we could clearly see the foundations of the oil pumping station. We picked up nails, stones, glass, and other artifacts.

Niida'achaaní and his wife evoke gestures of reciprocity—goat's

FIGURE 3.6 Louise and Eva walk over the ruins at Béésh Sinil (Metal Lying Down) looking for nails, glass, or other signs of the oil pumping station that embodied the intrusion of an industrial economy into the pastoral/agricultural life of the nineteen thirties.
PHOTOGRAPH BY MARGARET RANDALL.

milk in exchange for oranges and apples, a goat for the hauling of water—but the pumping station itself is evidence of the intrusion of a capitalist economy into Navajo life.

Poking through the scattered pieces of nails and glass that we found at the pumping station site made me aware of the ways my family and Eva's were part of the same world, and even closely connected by the discovery of oil and gas on the Navajo Reservation. Urban white families in the West during the nineteen twenties and thirties were in a very different economic class and social position than the Navajos. Beyond the obvious differences in language and culture, white people were more upwardly mobile and had much more access to consumer goods, wealth, and even power. Nevertheless, both Navajos and white westerners (including European immigrants) were encompassed by the same political economy.

My maternal grandfather, Herman C. Bretschneider, was born to an immigrant family in Leavenworth, Kansas, in 1885, about the same time Eva's mother was born. When the depression of 1893 forced the family to sell the business, Emil Bretschneider moved his wife Rosa and his four children, including my grandfather, who was eight years old at the time, to Denver, Colorado. Five more children were born in the family between 1893 and 1909. My grandfather, who spoke German during the first six years of his life, attended public schools and learned English. Although he attended high school and received high marks, he never received a high school diploma, and I never found out why he left school.

He married my grandmother, Louise, a third-generation German-American, in 1908, and my mother was born in 1909. After clerking for the Colorado and Southern Railroad in a small Hispanic town in Southern Colorado, he joined the Midwest Refining Company and moved his family to Casper, Wyoming. He learned something about geology and participated in the development of the Salt Creek oil fields near Casper. By 1920 he had returned to Denver and was prospecting for oil on the Navajo Reservation. I can still remember looking through a book of photographs showing my grandfather and several other men posing by a car on a Navajo Reservation road with Ship Rock in the background. Lawrence Kelly's account of the early leases on the Reservation tells us some of what happened in those years. Geologists were combing the Four Corners area beginning in 1921 hoping to find oil. Evan Estep, head of the Navajo Agency at Shiprock, reported that neither he nor the Navajo wanted the prospectors around. "It has been with considerable effort that we have been able to restrain the Indians from taking vigorous action against such prospectors," he wrote in January 1921 (Kelly 1966:48). Something happened over the summer to change their minds, and Estep called a council of all adult males in the area on August 13. At this meeting, the San Juan Navajos granted Midwest a lease of forty-eight hundred acres on what was known as the Hogback structure. On September 24, 1922, Midwest struck oil on the Hogback, which led to a situation of the area being overrun, according to Estep, "by all kinds of classes of speculators, fly-by-nights, bootleggers, and other forms of criminals" (Kelly 1966:55).

The history of leasing on the Reservation is a complicated one, but it resulted in the formation of the first Navajo Tribal Council (under a form prescribed by Estep) in July 1923 and eventually in the Indian Leasing Act of 1927, which guaranteed that royalties would be paid to the Navajo for oil found on Reservation land. Leases continued to be approved in 1926 and 1927, but many did not result in oil. Overproduction and a drop in oil prices resulted in a decline in the number of wells on the Reservation. By 1935, when Eva was seven years old and after Stock Reduction had had a devastating impact on her family, there were only thirty-three producing wells on the Reservation. Perhaps one of the wells that persisted that long was the one at Metal Lying Down.

Moving to Łitso Dah 'Ask'idí

Eva was pulled from the burning hooghan in the fire that burned Frank Sandman. This was when Hastiin Tł'aaí performed a Blessing Way for Eva, who was about four years old at the time. Eva's father had a prescient dream about the fire two days before it occurred. The fire prompted the family to move from Łizhin Deez'áhí to Łitso Dah 'Ask'idí. Clearly the bad dream and the subsequent fire meant that the place was dangerous (*báhádzid*), not somewhere the family should rebuild and stay. A new place would be hózhǫ́, not filled with *hóchxǫ́'í* (evil, difficulty, unpleasant conditions), but blessed, harmonious, balanced, and beautiful.[14]

Stock Reduction

The family moved to Łitso Dah 'Ask'idí and established a residence group about three hundred yards north of a large, yellow mesa just east of a small yet elongated yellow hillside that formed a backdrop for the new hooghan and sheep corral. This is the location where Eva's mother lost half of her large herd of goats in the Navajo Stock Reduction Program.

Eva told me this story twice, once the day before we first visited Łizhin Deez'áhí in July and then again on October 15, 1994, when I returned to conduct more interviews. Eva remembers herding the goats when they lived at Łizhin Deez'áhí, but later, in response to my insistent questioning about where they lived when the goats were taken, she says that they had already moved to Yellow Hills.

"And then he herded a lot of goats over here—maybe three hundred, maybe four hundred. There were so many. And then there was a man named John Collier who was around then. 'Bring the goats in, bring them in,' he said—about **half**, even more than that . . . all of them. My late mother was really crying. The goats were all herded away. And then the next morning, they herded them into a very large sheep corral at Sheep Springs. And the people were butchering, taking out the intestines and cooking them. It wasn't just them; it was all the people who had livestock. The one they called Old Man's Grandchild [Hastiin Sání Binálí], he was among those with John Collier. My uncle [Frank Sandman] rode his horse over there and brought back a whole bag full of goats' heads in burlap sacks hanging off the back end of the horse. He dug a large trench for them, where he cooked the heads. We had the heads, nothing else. We were not paid any money. There wasn't anything." Later Eva said, "Maybe my mother had been paid. I don't know. They were all crying. The goats were just herded away. They were just herded away and then butchered. That's what happened to them."

When Carole finished translating, I explained the version of Stock Reduction I remembered reading about. I told her about the early period of reduction and the killing of several thousand sheep or goats. As it turned out my dates were off by a year or two, and I underestimated the number of goats bought or destroyed.

History tells us that in 1930, the Navajo had almost a million sheep and more than three hundred thousand goats. Indian Commissioner John Collier first met with the Tribal Council in the fall of 1933 and got them to agree in principle to Stock Reduction, citing the damage to Boulder Dam from soil erosion. The first sale of sheep in early 1934 resulted in only a small reduction in total herd size. By July, the Tribal Council agreed to accept the sale of one hundred and fifty thousand goats and up to fifty thousand sheep. The sale, completed in the fall of 1934, was badly mismanaged. "Agents in some areas," according to Aberle, "put heavy pressure on owners, and often on small owners, to sell. It proved impossible to deliver all the goats to the railhead. So some were slaughtered and the meat dried and given back to the Navahos; others were shot and left to rot; still others were shot and partly cremated with gasoline. To the Navaho this waste was appalling, and the attitude toward their valued resources was incomprehensible. Criticism and opposition, especially from women owners, was intense" (Aberle 1966:57).[15]

Eva's own narrative emphasized this same theme: the devastating impact of Stock Reduction on the women who not only owned many of the sheep but cared for them as well. "My mother, she was just crying when all her goats were herded away. So that was what happened. We were taking care of just a few of them, and they just kept getting less until they were all gone."

Eva suggested that her mother might have agreed to reduce her herd when agents first talked with her, but the actual shock of having the goats herded away was overpowering.

"Yes, I remember when the goats were taken away. There were two white men. And then I guess my mother agreed. A few days after she said yes, they came back, and they led them all away by horseback. They called him Hastiin Sání Binálí. He was on horseback; he traveled with the white men. 'Take half' [he said].

"And then my mother was crying. My older brother rode his horse over there, beyond Sheep Springs over where the corral was. That was where they had corralled them. And there they were butchering them. Like this, with their heads scattered around. My brother brought back the whole heads, in a sack, all of them in a straw sack, hanging behind him and one up front. He brought them back, and then he dug a pit, and they built a fire, and they put them all in the pit. I remember that. And we ate the head[s]. After that I did herd sheep . . . that happened first when the goats were taken.

"I was about twelve years old, maybe, nine or ten or eleven.[16] And then my aunt's [Ben Bimá's] livestock and my mother's—we combined and herded them together. Those that were left over then gave birth, and they became many once again. And that was what we herded. There must have been three hundred or more, **a whole bunch of it**. And after they were herded away, we combined what was left, and they reproduced and multiplied again."

Herding on the Mountain Near Dził Zéé'asgai

Eva's stories about herding are mainly about the summertime, when she and Ben took care of the sheep and goat herd together. Although there were others in the residence group, the stories revolve around Mary Sandman and Ben Bimá, maternal cousins who were raised together and were "sisters." They took primary responsibility for the herd and also wove rugs together while supervising their young herders Eva and Ben, whom Eva called *binaaí* (older brother). Sometimes Grant, who was eight years older than Eva, also herded with them.

Eva first talked about herding with Ben when we visited Dził Zéé'asgai. Eva portrayed Ben as a "rascal," someone who took his frustrations out on her and on the sheep, certainly a very different image of him than the one I had in the nineteen sixties when I met him. By that time, he was married, had several children, and was a Navajo policeman, a symbol of law and order. Thus he was someone Eva turned to if there was a family quarrel that needed mediation and whom she, in turn, helped during ceremonial occasions such as planning a hatáál for Ben's daughter and later her Kinaaldá.

But I could see in Ben's demeanor the mix of humor and mischief that Eva remembers from his early pranks. One January morning in 1966, Mary Sandman, Eva, and I went to see if we could help out with Ben's daughter's Kinaaldá. Rena came along to find out if Ben knew anything about her ten-year-old son who had run away from a nearby boarding school.[17] Ben was just about to eat breakfast, still in his undershirt. He spoke to me in English and wanted to know how I liked Navajo country and what I was doing. Then he told me, "When you were first around, everybody wanted to know what you were doing. So I told them that there was some man in Argentina who had sent you as a spy. He was going to have you practice on the Navajo Reservation, and then send you someplace else." I jokingly accused him of spreading stories, but it was apparent that Ben thought the whole thing was a big joke (Field notes, January 7, 1966).

Ben's pranks always elicited hearty laughter from Eva, but these stories of impetuous behavior and teasing also reveal the hardship that they suffered at the time. As children, Eva, Ben, and their clan brothers were incredibly resourceful. They lived on wild foods and small animals, accepted important economic responsibilities, and struggled on their own without adult assistance. These themes were repeated time and time again in Eva's stories of this period.

Looking around Ben Bimá's summer place and remembering how she and Ben used to take care of the flock, Eva said, "There were a lot of sheep . . . a whole lot which they herded, three or four hundred. From here, we would let the sheep out, Ben and me. We herded the sheep all over, from here to there. In the morning, we would take them out toward Fuzzy Mountain [Dził Ditł'oi] and then bring them back from the other direction."

Eva often focused on how little they had to eat and how she and Ben had to use their own ingenuity to obtain food during the day. "And there were no potatoes back then. All we had was flour and sugar and salt and lard. When they went to town, they would only divide up a small amount. Then they would return saying that they had gone to town. We would be herding sheep with very little, and we would carry a small, beat-up can. We would spread out a blanket, when the goats were calm, and we would milk them. We carried a small bag of flour with us, and we would build a fire and put the flour in the milk."

There was always the threat of discipline, but little in the way of meat and food from the parental generation. "And then when they would butcher sheep, there would be a lot of ribs and intestines. They will not share with you, only a very **small piece,** and then they would tell you to go and follow the sheep. The whip would be sitting over there, and you are never told twice. You take off the first time you are told. They will not ask again. If they have to ask again, they will whip you. They used a fire poker."

Ben always wanted to have Eva go with him when he was assigned the chore of herding. He used to call Eva, drawing out the word for "little sister" and calling plaintively, "Shideeeeezhí," asking her to help, but then often harassing her when she was herding with him. "Sometimes my older brother Grant Tsosie [they were born one after the other, Grant Tsosie and Ben], he would herd sheep sometimes. I really hated him [Ben]. I hated herding sheep with him. **It sure made me cry**. He would make me cry, and I would be crying among the sheep. And then I would herd the sheep back home.

I would tell his mother and his father. And then his mother and his father would whip him.

"They called me 'Daa'diłtł'ohí.' **I don't know** [what this word meant]. My hair knot was tied up this small, right here, that was probably what he meant. 'If you tell on me, I will make you cry, so don't tell on me,' he would say. And I was so afraid of him, and wary of being around him, and sometimes did not want to follow them. And then his late father would whip him. And he would say that he would never do it again. And they would do it to me again. He would make me cry. When the sheep took off, they would follow them. I would stand behind a tree afraid of them. I was also afraid to even follow the sheep. I would look to where they were and when they went after the sheep I would follow my sheep. And with the birds that fly, he would make a slingshot. That is what he would do."

More of Ben's Pranks

Ten days later we spent the afternoon of July 16, 1994 (Saturday), and most of the day of July 17 (Sunday), sitting on a blanket near the mountain summer place at Na'aldzisí not far from the summer Chapter House and Eva's first husband's family land. It was a pleasure to sit on a blanket among the Gambel oak and ponderosa pine, eating a picnic lunch and talking. On Saturday, we were pleasantly interrupted by Rosalyn (Eva's brother's daughter), who was looking for her cows and stopped long enough to share some watermelon. On Sunday, Valerie, Carole's daughter, and Duane, her boyfriend, returned early and took Carole and Aaron, Carole's youngest son, off to visit Rosalyn and her children. Later a trip to the nearby spring gave us a chance to get good mountain water for our coffee.[18]

In such a spot, it was easy to imagine what it might have been like to herd sheep and goats in the summers during the nineteen thirties with only a few hooghans in the mountain area, no cars or pickup trucks, far from the trading posts at Two Grey Hills, Newcomb, and Sheep Springs, and from the dirt road between Gallup and Shiprock.

Ben was five years older than Eva, and in these stories Eva

reiterated her feeling that Ben behaved badly. Eva reported that Ben's mother, "used to whip him when he was small. Like about fourteen years old, I think. Because he was very naughty . . . spending most of his time making a slingshot. Chasing me after the sheep. They were running around like crazy. Hating them, he would herd them together. Then he would grab one of them by the leg and take them into that hooghan that we were trying to look for that was there at that time. This is how the hooghan was. It had a door and he would throw four or six of them in. And then shut the door.

"Then after we returned over there to Dził Zéé'asgai, we put the sheep back in [the pen]. And then the sheep were crying. Then my mother and my late aunt would run over there. 'One is gone,' they would say. And then they would go after and look for them. They would look for the one that had run away.

"They looked in vain, yes, they looked in vain. For two days they looked in vain. And then he told. 'Don't you tell them,' he said to me. 'There at that hooghan is where I threw them and locked them in. Don't tell about them,' he said to me. I don't know how many days they were there, maybe six. It wasn't until then that he told. He was really laughing.[19]

"And then Ben said, 'Let's go over there' to his mother and my mother, too. He took them over there. The sheep were really crying—at the hooghan we were looking for them unsuccessfully."

Eva continued her story, telling of another incident when Ben got mad at the sheep. "And then over at Fuzzy Mountain [Dził Ditł'oi], there was a fearful amount of sheep that Grant Tsosie [Eva's older brother] was herding. From up top Ben was sitting. He was really mischievous. The sheep in front [the sheep that was the leader of the herd, the 'black sheep'], he was sort of wild. As the sheep walked past the edge of this big rock he threw things at it; he stoned it to death. The sheep fell over dead. 'Don't tell on me. You Devil, if you tell on me, I'll make you cry.' This is what he said to me. And then we carried it back. They tried just asking him what had happened to it. He said, 'I don't know, it just died.'

"And then I herded sheep with him, all the way down to 'the gray area.' No, there wasn't any food—nothing. All we carried with us was a small sack of corn flour, tied up in a piece of fabric. We picked up one of those cans lying around. Some of them were rusted. And then the goats would run under the shade when it got hot. Then we would catch one of them and milk it, making about this much milk. In the morning we would smear sheep manure on the goats' teats so that the baby goats don't suckle. And then when the teats swell up with milk, we would milk the goats while we were herding at Saltbush Place [Dik'ǫzhítahdi]. And then we would build a fire. Then we would boil the milk and then add the flour. We would milk a lot and share the drink, milk."

During her translation, Carole explained to me how Ben and her mother would mix a dough out of water and flour, with a little salt, and roll it up. Then they would bake it in the hot ashes. It was called "łeę' yist'iní."[20]

I Used to Herd Sheep All Over the Place

Eva summarized her knowledge of the mountain area. "I used to herd sheep all over the place, on this mountain. I know where to go from there Zéé'asgai over this way to Oak Springs [Chéch'il Yaató]. It's called the water, Oak Springs right there, over there between that. There's a flat right there, on that side. Away from it, there's a road. And you chase the sheep all over the place. And this side is piñon grove [*deestsiin dik'ą́*] way over there. Up on top of the mountain [dził naa'áhí bighą́ądi] I herded the sheep to the water with Ben."

She even went to stay with Gladys Manuelito and herded with her clan brothers, Gladys's sons. "At that time Dennis and Ira Manuelito and Harry Manuelito—and they were young kids, too. We used to play and get together, and we used to eat those squirrels . . . gray squirrel [dlǫziłgai dóó tsin dit'inii]. We roasted it in the oven and ate it. It tastes like piñon nuts. Dennis and Harry lived over at Aspen Grove [T'iisbáí shizhóódí]. And their mom and dad were living over there. And we used to visit him and herd sheep together. And sometimes I would stay over there at their mom's place. Their mother was Gladys Manuelito, Hastiin Tł'aaí's niece.

"Then in the morning when we were herding sheep, after we let the sheep out, we were riding horseback. They saw a little bear. They caught him. They roped him with a rope. We carried it around, that little bear. He was crying. And we told Dennis's mom. She got mad at us and whipped them. Whipped us. I was about April's age [about twelve years old]. I was that small. I remember that there was water there. For this we carried a gun and we would shoot it—the black squirrel and the gray squirrel. And then we would cook them and then we would eat them. We eat . . . we roasted the gray squirrel and the one that has a long tail."

Learning to Weave

Ben Bimá and Eva's mother often spent hours weaving in the summer. Eva's first description of Dził Zéé'asgai includes the image of a loom strung between two pine trees. The two women taught Eva—and even Ben—to weave. I was curious about the fact that Ben could weave.

"Yes, and he also used to weave, Ben. He really strung the loom for me himself.[21] It was very small. It was about this small.[22] He sure set up the loom under a pine tree, right here. So **my mom** and my aunt were **teach**ing me. So I was really weaving. We completed the rug. And then it was taken to town for us, at that time. It was this small; it was probably this small. There was sugar. Sugar was all they brought home for us. 'That was all it was worth,' they said. And then with powdered flour, powdered flour . . . he would put it in a frying pan." Carole explained in translating this that Ben wanted to mix the sugar and the flour in a frying pan to make candy. "It made sort of a candy like taffy."

Eva said her first rug was "very small." "I was about April's age. It was striped." The rug was all different colors, in stripes straight across. Navajo girls usually are taught to do their first rug with stripes. "And then afterward, after you learn, you use your own imagination and create one accordingly."

Ben's weaving was not completely innocent. He was still a "rascal" and not above playing a prank on his mother and aunt while they were at work on their loom.

Carole described one incident as told by her mother, "When he was about fourteen years old, they got hold of some goofy clothes—old, old clothes. And they dressed up, you know, with the hat. And

Grandma . . . they both couldn't recognize who they were. And they got so scared. And then they had a loom over there, where they were weaving. And every now and then, you know when there are mosquitoes; they used horse manure and put it in the can. And then you start burning that, burning it to chase away the little mosquitoes. And I guess she had a can sitting beside her, where they were weaving a rug. And Grandma was so scared that she was ready to hit him with the stick. But eventually they wanted to tease their moms, and both of them were weaving. And they got a hold of a cherry bomb. From where she doesn't even remember. They placed that cherry bomb in the can where that manure was burning. Then all of a sudden that bomb went off, and my grandmother fortunately was really, really mad and upset with the boys, because that's how they used to tease her."

Stories from Dził Zéé'asgai are centered around Eva's mother, the sheep herd, and weaving. The summer residence group was very much in the orbit of the Dziłtł'ahnii relatives; Eva spent hours with her clan brother Ben and then other times with Tł'aaí's niece and her sons. While Ben's mother and Grandma Sandman were always together on the mountain in the summer, Eva's father remained down on the flats.

CHAPTER FOUR

"This Is Your Land"

Eva's Father, His Teachings, and Coming of Age

Eva's Father Baa Jiicha Binálí

EVA'S FATHER WAS A CENTRAL FIGURE IN HER LIFE, FIRST at their home at Black Rock Standing (Łizhin Deez'áhí) and later at Yellow Hills (Łitso Dah 'Ask'idí). I associate him with these two residence sites, on the flat plains at the base of the Chuska Mountains, because he remained there during the summer months to plant and tend the crops near Yellow Hills. He also set off from there for several weeks at a time to conduct sings for patients in other Navajo communities.

In the fall and winter Eva's childhood focused on going to school at Newcomb. While this experience was vastly different from herding sheep at Dził Zéé'asgai during the summer, both winter and summer were marked by persistent hardships and the need to rely on local plants and animals. At the end of this period, Eva had her first and second Kinaaldá, ushering her into womanhood and making her eligible for marriage. About this same time, her sister Eleanor divorced and left home for wage work in agriculture. Finally, her parents also divorced. All of these events transformed the residence group and Eva's life at Yellow Hills.

Eva's father was originally from Turning Mountain (Dził

Náhoozííí), near Newcomb, where his mother and siblings planted their fields. His clan was Tł'ááshchí'í, the Red Bottom People, and his clan relatives played important roles in Eva's life. Eva's paternal grandfather's name was Baa Jiicha Biye' (Son of Crying for Him), and Eva's father was called Baa Jiicha Binálí (Paternal Grandchild of Crying for Him).

Since Eva's father died before I met her, I know him only through Eva's narratives and Carole's memories of him when she was a child. In 2000, Eva received a photo of her father from a distant relative. She framed the photo and put it on a shelf in her bedroom. Carole could hardly remember him, since she was only six or seven when he died. But she did have a vivid image of his appearance, confirmed by the recently discovered photo. "I can still picture how he used to look. He used to have long, shoulder-length hair. . . . And he used to have his hair put behind [his head], and then he used to wear a headband like a medicine man. . . . And I can picture that because that was how I remember him." Eva's father was a singer (hataałii) who knew a number of Navajo ceremonies and often traveled to distant communities to perform them for patients.[1]

In Eva's narratives, her father comes across as the person who instilled in her many of the values that direct her adult life: the importance of cooperation, an attachment to the land, and a respect for Navajo tradition. On the other hand, he had a difficult relationship with Eva's mother, at first tying her up when she refused him as a young bride and later leaving after he discovered her affair with her sister's husband.

"My mother and my father . . . this is what my mother used to say," explained Eva, speaking in the words of her mother, "'When I was small, when I was about twelve years old, so then [your] father, he had already become a man, I was given to him.' This is what she used to tell us. She said, 'And so I was afraid of him, and I didn't want him.'

"So she was left by herself with him, and he would tie her up next to a pole and wrap the rope around her so that she wouldn't run away from him. 'He did that to me,' my mother used to tell me. 'That's how it was.' And somehow she finally got used to him."

Even before he came to live with Mary Sandman, Eva's father's

FIGURE 4.1 Eva's father Baa Jiicha Binálí (Paternal Grandchild of Crying for Him) who was a hataałii (singer) and agriculturalist. This is Eva's only photo of him.

COURTESY OF EVA PRICE.

family was associated with farming. He had an older brother Tł'ááshchí'í Bidághaa' (Red Bottom Clansman with Mustache) and a sister named 'Asdzą́ą́ Naagháhí (Woman Who Walks Around). His mother's name was 'Asdzą́ą́ Tł'ááshchí'í. "Turning Mountain [Dził Náhooziłii] was the name of the place over there by Newcomb, over there was where my father was really from, where Mary Woods now lives. That was where his house was. From there they planted; and from . . . around that area was our land."

Carole also explained, "My grandfather used to help people, you know, plant along this area [near Yellow Hills] and that's the way they got to know who he was . . . when it's time for planting in those days people used to get together. 'Someone is planting over there,' they would say. People used to have respect for each other, and they used to plant together."

The Tł'ááshchí'í Relatives

The most important group of Tł'ááshchí'í relatives were a cluster of three siblings: Diné Chíí's mother, Shoemaker's Wife, and Shoemaker Begay. Their mother was 'Asdzą́ą́ Tł'ááshchí'í's sister. Diné Chíí's mother and Shoemaker's Wife were Eva's *bibízhí* (paternal aunts) and they were married to the same man, Shoemaker. The brother, Shoemaker Begay, would have been Eva's paternal uncle (bibízhí or *bizhé'éyázhí*—"little father"). Shoemaker's Wife had eight children, six of whom had died by the mid–nineteen sixties. In the late nineteen forties Eva, her mother, and her sister-in-law began using the summer area where Shoemaker's Wife had lived, a place called Na'aldzisí (Deep Valley). When I first went to stay with Eva, Shoemaker's Wife was living with Eva. Eva explained to me that she was the same clan as her father. She told me then that Shoemaker's Wife had a daughter who was a good friend and that when the daughter was in the hospital, Eva went to see her and talked with her for a long time. The daughter told Eva to take care of her mother as long as the old lady lived. Eva said then that she had been taking care of Shoemaker's Wife for around seventeen years, that is, since 1948 (Field notes, November 30, 1965).

In 1994, Eva told me more details of how she came to take care of the old lady. Shoemaker's Wife and her daughter Elsie used to live at Diné Chíí's house, that is, with her sister (and co-wife) and son. Eva's father went over there and found that Elsie was sick. He told Eva's mother that he was going to bring them over to their house (at Yellow Hills) and have them stay with him since they had no one to care for them. So he took his wagon up to Diné Chíí's house and brought them back. Elsie got sicker, and she used to cry a lot. They finally took her to Rehobeth Hospital near Gallup, the only hospital in the area, and she died there overnight. The old lady, Shoemaker's Wife, continued to stay with Eva's mother and father.[2] Eva and Carole said that Shoemaker's Wife moved around with Eva's mother and father. "They were never left behind."

When Shoemaker's Wife was really old, and Eva and Carole did not want to be responsible for her anymore, they sent her to Minnie Barney, who was her granddaughter. She had pneumonia when she died.

In 1965–66 when I stayed at Eva's house, Grandmother Shoemaker slept on the floor near Grandmother Sandman at night. I often provided her with transportation to the store or other places. On that November day in 1965 when I first arrived at Eva's, I took Grandmother Shoemaker up to her brother's residence group, over a winding dirt road that led from Yellow Hills on the flats into the foothills or Gray Area. Her nephew Philip Begay, at only thirty-two years old, had just died of pneumonia and she went to visit the grieving family including Philip's mother and wife. In Navajo tradition, relatives of the deceased are supposed to stay at home for four days after a death. They receive visits and help from their relatives during this period. Eva was particularly critical that very few of the relatives (neither his mother's Bit'ahnii kin nor his father's Tł'ááshchí'í kin) had come to help cook and care for the family. This lack of assistance was something Eva always noted, particularly because of her father's lessons about the importance of cooperation (Field notes, November 1965).

Father's Teachings

Eva's father often talked to her about the importance of helping others and of taking care of the land. When Eva told me the stories of Ben herding sheep and tricking his mother and aunt, I asked if her mother or father ever gave her any teachings. "Just only my father. He talked to me. That was when I was older. Some children will continue to sleep next to their fathers even when they are too big to do so. Well this was also a lesson they taught. He told me, 'You are now too old to be sleeping next to me, my child. You must now sleep alone.' He told me that because I used to sleep next to him. It was in their teaching."

Eva's father stressed the importance of hospitality and cooperation, indicating that being a good Navajo woman meant behaving in a way that was respectful as well as generous. "'In your future, wherever you go from here on out, don't do negative things. Wherever you go, be respectful. This is the kind of woman you must be. One of these days, when someone comes to visit you, even if [you have] only a single cup of coffee, you must give it to him. This is how you should be and with this will come good things. This is why you must be kind,' he said to me."

Eva acknowledged that her mother never talked to her about such things. But her father did. "And he also told me not to ask for too much, 'Accept whatever that person has to offer.' This is what he taught me."

The Farming Community at Łitso Dah 'Ask'idí

Just in back of the yellow ridge of hills behind Eva's home at Łitso Dah 'Ask'idí, there are a number of agricultural fields, watered by a ditch system that collects water from the spring runoff. This system was created by a government project in the nineteen thirties, and the fields were allocated to local Navajo families. Eva described how her father had an important role in creating these fields and in participating in the cooperative work arrangements that they entailed. "That water has been coming up for a long time. And around here there were no fields. It wasn't until several years later that these fields came to exist. My father, Helen Joe, and the late Lena's father [Helen Joe's husband]—they were the ones who started the farm here. When planting long ago back then, it was done with a **stick** [*díwózhii* or greasewood], **sharp like this knife**.[3] Like this they did it. Like this, they put in **corn**. Anywhere there were wide open spaces, where water would stand, that was where people would plant. And from that time on, this land was issued out, and then **they move to** here."

Eva remembered how the neighbors who held plots in the irrigated area helped each other with planting and agricultural work. "Twelve, at that time twelve [horses] would be hitched together and they would follow each other. People did not say, 'buy me gas' or 'give me money.' It was more like what we did this morning. A goat was butchered and made into stew and the meal was their payment. The people planted upward from here."[4]

Eva emphasized the reciprocal nature of the cooperation. "They used to help one another. They didn't ask for payment. They didn't say, 'You must pay me this much.' With the horses hitched up, they plowed a large area within a short time, going upward toward their hooghans. That's how they planted for years. And when they planted and harvested, it was the same. They did not think that, this is none of my business. They hoed like this and helped one another.

FIGURE 4.2 Eva hoeing corn in the fields where her father used to plant. He instilled in her the importance of the land.

PHOTOGRAPH BY MARGARET RANDALL.

"And then during harvest, there was no need for a **freezer**. The corn with its husks still on was carried underground with a **gunnysack** and a lid covered the open ground. They had food to cook until spring arrived.

"When the cantaloupes and watermelons were harvested, the skins were peeled off and the fruit was strung along a hanging piece of wood. Corn food [corn mush] was set right next to them and they would dip into it with the [dried] cantaloupes. That was how it happened throughout time. Watermelon was done the same way."

Cooperation and reciprocity were an important part of life for those that lived at Łitso Dah 'Ask'idí and the surrounding residence groups, the scattered clusters of hooghans that utilized the new fields. "Yes, at that time everyone thought of each other as coming from one household. This was how they all got along. When things ran out, then you are told to go over and borrow some things from a neighbor. This was how people used to be. They did not eat alone."

Given his role in the agricultural life of his family and the local area, Eva's father was particularly articulate on the importance of taking care of the land, evoking the connection of the land with kinship and sustenance, and speaking of the land as both "your mother" and "your father." As Eva recalled, "He said, 'Your land is here. With this land, you will exist forever. It will become your mother and your father. You will feed yourself from it and eat off the land. You will exist like this without interference from anyone else. This is how you shall live. Planting corn for food, with this you will grow. This is how you will live,' he said to me. Well, he lived off this land here. By successfully watering and planting hay and harvesting a lot of corn, he sometimes would bring out twelve loads [of harvest]. I don't know where Eleanor [Eva's older sister] was. It was as if she had just defeated her mother's and father's wishes, moving about, never really coming home. She was about eighteen years old when she was given a husband."

The Role of Alcohol in Eva's Father's Life

The couple at the pumping station and the trading post at Two Grey Hills were only two of the manifestations of white civilization near

Yellow Hills. In addition, contact with the larger political economy brought another element to the Reservation: alcohol, both in the form of "home brew" and bootlegged wine. Eva's father made his own alcohol but only on one occasion. "At that time **wine** did not exist. I remember that well. My late father used to plant corn this tall—maybe cane [*'akaz łikaní*]. They were tall; they looked like **corn**. And also lots and lots of cantaloupes and watermelon were harvested by my late father. So then there were no white men around, no **stores**. My late father sometimes used to drink occasionally when an event took place. They did not drink the same way that people drink now. My late father had a fire going outside, right there. And then he gathered some copper pipes, like the kind **gas** runs through . . . hollow copper tubing. He had several of these tubes going in, and he had a fire underneath, and it was boiling. And then here was the corn and watermelon, cantaloupes, and corn syrup ['akaz łikaní], and he also brought home yeast from the **store**. Then he put in the yeast and it was sure boiling, about **one whole day**, with the foam bubbling over. There was a bottle underneath, **underneath here** and from here there was a piece of metal sticking in and in here it was dripping, in here. So I don't know how much he made. **About this much** was what he made, **one gallon** that is. And then he drank it, and I saw him do it. I was standing there so I know about it. So he drank it and it began working on him. He got **sick** and went to lie down over there [on top of the hill]. After walking back, he said, 'My stomach hurts, my daughter. I drank it.' I think it was called 'gray water' [*tó łibáí*]."[5] In translating this, Carole explained that her grandfather had had diarrhea, and that he told Eva he had made the alcohol wrong. So he never attempted to make it again.

About the same time, Eva went on to tell me, "There was a man from Gallup named 'Mancisco.' He was a Mexican from Gallup who became acquainted with my father." Carole thought he might have had a Mexican name like Martinez, but his first name may have been Francisco. Eva explained that the men would be gathered in a hooghan, waiting, and say, "Here comes Mancisco driving in." Several of Eva's father's neighbors, Tséhootsohnii, Jay Gould, Gol Yázhí, and the husband of 'Asdzą́ą́ Dégo Yániil'ání (The-Woman-That-Raises-Her-Head-Up) would be waiting. "All of them used to sit around in the **middle of the night waiting for the Spanish guy to come in and bring in that wine, what kind of wine I don't know**. Way past **two o'clock, one o'clock**, he would drive in. They would hand over a sheepskin to him [in trade]. All around there were **bottles** scattered about. So, then they would pour it in **those big barrels, those big**—they were this big. **They would fill up two gallons.** There was no such thing as **shit**, no such thing as **goddamn**, none. They used to drink nicely back then. The men . . . **they don't get mad, don't fight, they don't do nothing**." Eva emphasized this using English swear words and putting her last sentence in English. Then she continued in Navajo. "From there they only learn chants from one another. They taught each other. **'Sing right,'** they said. And they all used to get enraged with each other. 'This is how you bring out the songs,' they claimed. So it was like that back then."

Liquor in the nineteen thirties seemed to be less disruptive than it became in the late nineteen forties and fifties. Drinking was a male activity integrated into the long hours men spent singing in Eva's father's hooghan. It was probably a rare pastime, since liquor was not easily made nor easily obtained. It took three days and nights for Mancisco to drive his wagons out to Yellow Hills. In the larger Anglo-American society, Prohibition in the nineteen twenties drove drinking into homes and private clubs. It became more acceptable for middle-class women to drink hard liquor as part of sociable "cocktail hours" or at private parties. College fraternities and social events surrounding football games, picnics, and dances encouraged drinking among middle-class youth. While working-class alcohol consumption reemerged after Prohibition as a primarily male activity in public bars and saloons, middle-class alcohol consumption continued to flourish in the private sphere.

Eleanor, Eva's older sister, remembered sessions the men would have when they were gathered in the hooghan. She emphasized their ability to look into the future and predict what would happen to Navajo culture. "And also my paternal grandfather Hashtł'ishnii Nééz used to come here. She [Eva] probably remembers, but maybe not. She was about this small. His name was Many Goats from Deez'áhí; he was very good at singing for bears.[6] Tséhootsohnii and Kiyaa'áanii Tsoh from Tsé dahóyéé,' they used to visit my father in the circular stone house. And in there they would tell stories, tell stories. A sheep would be butchered. My mother would butcher. She would cook, never being lazy about preparing food. There was corn. They would eat with cornmeal mush. It was as if something very important was going on—with all the meat they ate—and then they told their stories. I don't know how many nights it took for them to talk, four nights or five nights. And so I would sit there; I was fairly tall. This is what I remember.

"I don't know how old I was, eight or nine maybe. I rode sitting behind a man, Hashtł'ishnii Nééz. We herded sheep. And so when they told their stories in front of me, they never told of bad things such as that which is called witchcraft; they didn't talk about any of this. They only spoke of good things, and then they would sing. They just went like that, one or the other. Probably just stories? That was probably how they did it. And there I sat. And so my paternal grandfather [Hashtł'ishnii Nééz] used to tell me. They saw the way things are today way back then. So how are things today, do you see? Things are not good at all these days. The winters are not what they used to be. The summers are not what they used to be. That is what they talked about, and that young women will not wear their long skirts. They will just wear scanty clothing from between their legs, he said. You see? People will no longer wear the hair knot. It will be gone, they told one another. In the end, there will be only one spoken language, the English language. When this happens, time as we know it will end. This is what they said. This is what I remember. I was present when they said this."[7] Many of these prophecies (changes in clothing, the dominance of the English language) would come to pass as a result of the Anglo-American educational system, a system Eva experienced firsthand.

Eva's Years in School

Certainly, the white institution that had the biggest impact on Eva was school. She first attended the boarding school at Toadlena, about twenty miles from Yellow Hills, her home. She was there only a few months before her mother put her in the Newcomb day school. Under John Collier's administration in the nineteen thirties, the BIA built day schools for those Navajos who were close enough to roads that could be traveled by truck or bus. In this period, both boarding and day schools were designed to instill white values such as hard work and discipline, and to teach English.

Eva remembered little of her first school experience. "I was there for only a few months at Toadlena. The old building was torn down, just one or a few are still standing. At that time it was a boarding school. And there was a girls' dorm and a boys' dorm. Then my mother went over there. I was put at the day school so that I would return home every day. I was there only a few months, maybe two." She knew three other girls at the boarding school. These were the daughters of her older brother, Allen Sam. "Lillian Togasalla, and Sadie, and Susie were there. They had already become women and were way ahead of me. I attended school with them and my late mother used to say, 'Take care of her.' That's what they were told. And they brought watermelons to us over there, so I wasn't scared. **Ben Watchman** was **in school**, too." Ben was Eva's clan brother who teased her so much during the summer months. With his presence and that of the girls who were her cousins, she was not scared at all.

Her mother transferred her to the Newcomb school because it was much closer. There were no school buses in those days. They were transported in an old pickup truck, "**an old, old, old-fashion pickup**. The late old man Sam, the late Sam Manuelito, he was the **bus driver** at the time.[8] Back then when it snowed, no one came to pick us up. We stayed over there in the hooghan [school building]. There used to be **two** hooghans, over there, one for boys and one for girls. That is where we slept. That's how they took care of us. A woman named Lula—she's from somewhere over there—and Willie Frazier and the late Phillip Monroe [worked at the school].[9] That was at the **school**, and the bus didn't come for us, so we slept there. They used to take our sheepskins over there. Back then there were not many children, nothing. Just a few. **About twenty something**."

When I first asked Eva to describe her experiences in school, she talked about the teacher. "The **white** [man], they used to call him all sorts of names, like 'The Man With the String up His Rectum.' That was his name. He had the kind of pants that you buckle up here [overalls]. He used to really whip us. Where can you find a **teacher** like that now? He was meaner than mean. He used to make us stand on our heads like this—Daisy . . . Daisy Sherman. He used to do that to her. She spent maybe **an hour** like that." Students were punished for not listening or for making the other children cry.

Later, Eva recalled this man's English name, "Yes I remember, he was an old man named Elison. He wore suspenders, and also his wife, she's kinda old, that was my teacher. Underneath the stone building were cement vents from which heat flowed from a main fire source; there was no heater. The tall ones were separated from the small ones. There really weren't any grades at that time, just two groups."

Eva remembered more about the physical facilities and the food and the clothing. These aspects of her school stood out strongly in her mind, partly because they conveyed the hardships of going to school, although she said she learned English easily. "Then there was no food at Newcomb, nothing. **Beans** and **corn, yellow corn bread** really, that's all we ate. Also, **brown sugar**, about this much. They were in sacks or bags and a piece would be broken off. 'Here,' they would say, and they would hand you a piece. That is all we ate."

They also gave out clothing and shoes to the children, but much less than Navajo children now get through the funds the Navajo tribe allocates for new school clothes to parents of young children. "They are now handing out clothing from the **Navajo Tribe**. But then we got nothing. There were some shoes with pointed toes. She [meaning Louise] has probably seen them around somewhere where they are on display. The heels . . . the toes were curled upward. They were laced from here to there. That's what we wore, and they were given to us. Those were our shoes.

"The clothing was made out of fabric and it was sewn together from here to there. That's how we wore our clothes back then. Holes were cut out of the cloth from flour sacks. They were fixed up [the best they could be]. That is how we wore our clothes; that's how it was." Carole added that the flour sack dresses, with simple holes for the arms and head, were dyed black.

Eva was quick to contrast her schooling with that of children in the nineteen eighties and nineties. "They didn't mention any laws.[10] Like right now they have laws [about what teachers can do]. Right now there are laws. It was true that it was frightening. 'Here's what you will learn,' that's what they told us. Our noses were pressed into it.[11] That was how school was run back then. Now it isn't like this any more. Everything now is **'They go for their own.'** They make the rules for themselves [nobody obeys]."

After eight years, Eva's mom kept her at home. Her sister and brother had different experiences. "Eleanor was kept hidden. She stayed home. That's my mom's fault." Grant, her older brother, went to boarding school. "He went to school; he went for a long time. He went to Toadlena. He became an adult there; that was where he went to school. I don't know up to what grade he completed. . . . He didn't start going to school until he was fourteen or fifteen. Ben also went to school at Toadlena. . . . They used to run away a lot, yes, the police used to ride horses. . . . They used to hunt the boys down, sometimes chasing them all the way up on the mountain."

Hard Times in the Nineteen Thirties

While Eva was going to school, she often had to fend for herself. She remembered one time in the fall when her mother was away for two or three months.[12] **"I remember it. They had piñons over at Crystal. I think they lived over there. And we came back from Newcomb school. And we had nothing to eat.** Nothing. Chickens were all that were running around. Hens. **I think that Don Foster caught the chicken.**[13] **We were going to boil the eggs. He put his hand in the chicken's stomach, like this, and pulled the eggs out. And we boiled them.**

"Pierce Peter, Rosalyn's son, that was his name.[14] **We went to school** with him, **me and Don.** We were brought home by **bus**, so there was nothing. **No one was taking care of us. Just only us.** Pierce was older, **maybe about JR's age** [sixteen years old]. **We had nothing to eat. There's nothing and we didn't know how to cook. In the morning, the pickup came and they took us to school. We ate at school, but only cornbread and beans.**

"Sometimes we crawled in the window. We climbed through the window and we took the **flour**. We got only **flour**. **We put** the pan on the **stove** and then **we roasted it** [the flour] **in there; we**

made it yellow. Pierce boiled **coffee** and we would put it in and add **sugar**, too, and then stir it. **It tasted good like that, too. We put it in a bowl, like a corn mush. It tasted good anyway.** You stir the coffee in and then it **tasted good**. We called it yellowed flour.

"That's how we ate in the evening with **Pierce**. And if we didn't have that, we had corn. **You roasted the corn.** You cooked it good, roasting it in the frying pan. **And we put water in there, and put salt in there. It tastes good like that, too, when you roast the corn. It's not fresh corn, but it's dried.** That's how you cook it; and then you put water in it and salt. It tastes good."

I asked Eva if everyone had left her. "See," she replied, **"I have a hard time. I don't know where my sister is, at that time**. . . . Grant was in school somewhere. My older brother Allen Sam was at Roads Passing Over [Bitis 'Adeetiin] where Emerson's mother [Frances] lived.[15] **She was alive at that time and my brother [Emerson] was a younger boy. So sometimes, they took me home over there. And I stayed with them for one night or two nights.** 'Asdzą́ą́ Bitis 'Adeetiin was Lillian Togasala's mother. She [Frances] had a hooghan there; she was married to Allen Sam then. **She brought the wood from where the hill is,** juniper. **You had to chop them about this small. She ground the corn** . . . ground it and ground it. She made Tanaashgiizh [cornmeal mush] for us. **See, we had a hard time when we were being raised, Louise."**

The family had to be resourceful in terms of getting food. "And the **prairie dogs**, when it rains . . . when there hadn't been rain and then it rains very hard . . . **there was a whole bunch of prairie dogs. When the rain, the water's running . . . we** [would] **get the shovel with Leonard Sandman, and the water goes in the holes . . . and the prairie dogs** [would come out]. **And we killed them. We got the bucket, and we put it in the bucket. In two buckets or three buckets, we would take it home. We would build a fire outside and roast them.** You take it out. You roast all of it and gut it. **You cut it in the stomach right here; you take out** the intestines **and clean it. . . . We put the sharp stick in, we make the sharp stick** about this size and you pin it on **like a safety pin**, and open up the **fire** and put them in there and **cook it in there about an hour . . . with the skin on it. The fur**—you clean it off with the fire and **roast it. You**

know, you throw it in the fire, and, like the head, you clean it off, and leave the skin on and put it in the ashes **and cook it and roast it. And you take it out about** one hour later **and it tastes good.**

"Yes, I tasted it, I ate it. At that time, they didn't say it was not good. There was probably nothing wrong with it, so they also ate rabbits—**jackrabbits and those big rabbits. You can eat the same way, too. We got nothing to eat but that. We get up and go hunting for rabbit. We always kill one, and bring it back."**

Eva also had to work hard for her parents. Besides herding sheep, she was taught to process food, particularly corn. "We used to grind corn. They would roast the corn and they told us to finish it. And it's a whole bunch of corn in the bowl. Oh, it's hard to grind it, make it into flour. And when you finish that, then you can eat. That's what we were doing all winter."

"Was it hard work?" I asked. "Yes," Eva replied, "I think that sometimes I was crying. I don't know for sure. My mom was after me. My dad was after me to do those things. They're lucky, this new generation over here."

I asked Eva if her parents ever butchered any of the sheep. **"They were stingy with it,"** she said. **"They didn't do it, just once in a while they butchered. They didn't give you a whole bunch of meat, just a little piece of bread."**

"Why do you think your parents were so stingy about feeding you?" I wondered.

"At that time, they didn't have anything," Eva replied. **"They didn't have anything. No potatoes, no lard.** And then at another time, they were given commodity food; my father went to **Newcomb** for this. **They give you a commodity food, oranges or either any canned stuff.** That is how we were raised."

Eleanor's Marriage

While Grant was in school at Toadlena, Eleanor, who was six years older than Eva, was married, which eventually took her away from the residence group. In an interview with Eleanor, I asked her when she was married for the first time. "I had a wedding.[16] There was a wedding basket. I was unaware of what was going on, as they were making plans for me. And this one [Eva] probably doesn't even remember. There was Hastiin Yázhí, my aunt, my mother. My father also probably did not know what was going on, probably because Hastiin Yázhí and my mother wanted to get together. So then probably this man Kin łichíi'nii [Red House Clansman], as they used to call him, from over there, Irene's paternal grandfather used to come from up there. They made plans with him. What's his name Harry Brown? Maybe [by now] he died from old age. They asked for him, Harry Brown."

As in Eva's parents' case, the marriage was arranged and the bride was very young, probably just after her puberty ceremony. Eva was only seven or eight years old when her sister married. The marriage was held in the summer at Dził Zéé'asgai, and Eleanor and her new husband began living there. The family probably lived at Yellow Hills during the winter. The arrangements were made between Hastiin Yázhí (married to Grandma Sandman's sister) and Grandma Sandman, on the one hand, and Harry Brown's relatives on the other.

Eva told me about the ideals surrounding an arranged marriage. "Women were not as they are now. It was very much so that when a woman had girls, **fourteen or up, fifteen, sixteen, or seventeen**, they were incredibly overprotective of them. They weren't even allowed to go off a short distance by themselves; this is how they were taught. 'You will not waste your life on any man who becomes interested in you,' they were told. This is what they were taught. And so from somewhere . . . a man notices a beautiful woman, and so back home money is collected, also sheep, cattle, or horses, and a sash belt, and beads to be traded for this woman. You must pay for her. He [the groom] is told, and he goes over there, and plans are made. He is told that he and his people will be fed this much."[17] In the early part of the century, it was customary for the groom to offer a number of horses to the bride's parents as a form of bride price, along with other gifts. I asked Eva about her own marriage and about that of her mother, and in neither case could she remember any bride price of gifts from the groom.

In an arranged marriage, the wedding is usually held at the hooghan of the bride's family. The groom's family are the main guests, all crowding into the hooghan, the men sitting on the south side of the hooghan, the women on the north side. The groom sits to the right of the bride and both are at the west side of the hooghan facing the assembled relatives. Eva described what happens as the ceremony begins. "And there inside the round hooghan in a clockwise direction, it is called, starting from the entrance, a man will carry in the water. It's his [the groom's] uncle, it is like that—his uncle carries the water for him, places it on the ground, and then pours some on his [the groom's] hand and he washes his hand like this **wash**, so then the woman moves over and the man sits there. Then over there a basket, like this—a basket called *ts'aa'* is put down. A mixture of white and yellow corn like this, inside a small pot of mush, is made like this.[18] Then beautifully like this, it is poured from the four directions and also down the middle. And then the corn pollen: whoever is to bless the hooghan does it when a couple is being married in this place.

"And in this basket, from the east they take out some of the mush. Each does as the other, taking out the mush. Also the water in the same way, they drink the water like this. In this way, these two people are married. When he marries the woman here like this, there is something special for them from a bird, a blue bird and its mate. A small child or someone will catch them, so then they shake corn pollen off of them and with this they do the blessing so that wherever the couple goes, all the way to old age they will continue to travel together; they will not separate."

The couple feeds each other taking mush first from the East, then the South, West, and North parts of the basket. Finally the couple eat from the center of the basket of mush; this guarantees that they will have children. The basket of mush is passed to the visiting guests, who eat out of the basket as well. A meal of stew, fried bread, coffee, and other foods is then served. After the meal, the groom's relatives and the bride's relatives that have now joined them give speeches encouraging the couple to care for each other. In the nineteen thirties the wife would have been told to cook for her husband, while the groom would have been exhorted to chop wood for his bride and get water for her. Both would be told not to get mad at each other, not to talk back, and to do what the other asked. They would be told *hazhǫ́'ǫ́ sooké* (or stay together nicely or well). These specific injunctions reiterate fundamental Navajo values of helping out, cooperation, and reciprocity (Lamphere 1977:71).

Eleanor was very afraid of her impending marriage. She first found out about the plans for her future from one of her clan sisters. "So my older sister and I herded sheep over at Rock That Stands Up [Tsé 'íí'áhí]. Just then she told me. 'This is what they are saying,' she said. And then she said, 'No my little sister, it will be all right.' I decided to run away down there, to my aunt's house. Ben's mother's was where I would go. Then my older sister said no. She said it would be all right.

"At that time something happened to my mother's foot—it swelled up this big. They did many sings for her. Maybe someone had implanted something in her foot. Back then there was no Peyote religion. There was no one to remove objects from the body either, so she just sat there with her foot like that. So then I guess that they probably made plans for this man.

"They began to build an arbor [for the ceremony] over there. They made a shade. They were planning to make a mate for me there."

Eleanor was only thirteen and didn't even know what a "mate" was. She was only thirteen years old. (She used the term *biką'*, which means a sexual partner.) Harry Brown was a much older man. Eleanor thought he was probably dead by now, since she hadn't seen him.

"What are they called, those plants up on the mountains, *déélʼdaa'*. They were lying like this. That was it; they were just lying like this. Inside the hooghan they had made for me, the déélʼdaa' lays. Hastiin Yázhí was running around—my older brother Donald, too. It was OK with them. Then they probably said *now* and the people came. I don't know what, who made the corn mush. I don't even know that. The corn mush, well it was put in a wedding basket and then corn pollen was sprinkled across like this—corn pollen. I don't know who sprinkled the corn pollen across. I don't even remember.

"Well, then the one you are betrothed to takes some of it out and then puts it in your mouth, and likewise you take some out like he did and put it in his mouth. Just like this, from all four sides, all the way around. This is what they mean by eating corn mush.

"And then I don't know how many years I spent with him. Maybe three, maybe two, I don't remember. Then he went away on his horse and never came back to me."

Eva remembered that Harry Brown was from Two Grey Hills. He was Kin łichíí'nii or Tó'aheedlíinii. Eva continued, "She had a daughter. To this day she would have probably been like Katherine Morris [about fifty years old]. She was pretty big when she died, this tall, about twelve years old maybe. Somehow she got some menstrual blood in her mouth, and this is what killed her. In the Navajo way, it is very dangerous, in the Navajo teachings. They used to say that a woman's menstrual blood is very dangerous. If you swallow it or it somehow warms up to you, it will cause your back or your bones to break. This is what happened to her. She just walked on it. This is why it happened. She was just with her grandmother."[19]

Kinaaldá

One of the most important events in a young girl's life is the coming of age or puberty ceremony, which the Navajo hold when a girl first menstruates. It is called the Kinaaldá and replicates the ceremony first held for Changing Woman, the most important female Diyin Dine'é or Navajo supernatural. The days following the onset of her first menstrual period are particularly important since the young girl is in a holy and vulnerable state and what she does with her mind and body will influence her later life and the kind of woman she will become. There are four important parts of the ceremony, which lasts for four days. First, the girl is dressed in traditional clothing and jewelry on loan from family members. These goods are blessed during that time by virtue of their contact with the young girl. Her hair is tied by a woman relative who represents Salt Woman, who first helped at Changing Woman's ceremony (Frisbie 1967:359). This woman also "molds" or vigorously pulls, massages, and stretches the kinaaldá girl's body. This strengthens her limbs and shapes her body, assuring a strong, straight body during the remainder of the girl's life.

Second, the girl runs toward the East three times a day, at sunrise, noon, and sunset. Each of four days she runs a little farther, often accompanied by younger children who yell to notify the Holy Ones (Diyin Dine'é) that the ceremony is taking place. The running assures that the young woman will not be lazy or idle and that her body will be strong. Third, corn is ground, a corn batter is made, and the cake is poured into a husk-lined hole in the ground where it is baked overnight. Fourth, a singer conducts an all-night sing, chanting songs from the Blessing Way (joined by elder women and men often from a wide range of neighboring families). Near sunrise, the girl washes her hair with yucca soap and runs one last time in the dawn light. The corn cake is cut and passed out to the singer and those who participated in the all-night singing, as well as others who have helped. The girl is again molded, and she in turn molds older relatives and little children, since her special powers can help heal aches and pains and keep the bodies of young children growing (Frisbie 1967:29–62, Schwarz 1997:190–200).

During the four days of the ceremony, the girl must not eat sugar or salt. Nor can she eat her own cake. These activities will cause her teeth to decay and fall out. She must not sleep during the day, and she must work hard, grinding corn and obeying her elder female relatives. She is enjoined not to be lazy or stingy. She should not be mean or quarrel with her sisters and brothers (see Lamphere 1977:43, Keith 1964, Frisbie, 1967:350–57, Schwarz 1997:201–22). Many of these rules restate the importance of hard work, generosity, and cooperation, and all assure that the kinaaldá will live a long and fulfilling life.[20]

We were sitting in Eva's house at Yellow Hills the day after we had visited her birthplace at Dził Zéé'asgai when I asked about her Kinaaldá. She said she had had two ceremonies, as was her generation's tradition, one at her first menstruation and one during the second. Both ceremonies had been held there at Yellow Hills during the winter months.

"It was right here that I made my cake. Over there where the post is standing, there was a hooghan there, not at the mountain. Right there, that's where the hooghan once was. Right over there I made my cake, **two** times. **And Anita Sandman she tied my hair. And Diné Chíí'** molded me. The one that used to sing the Wind Way Chant, James Peter's late father [performed the ceremony]. He was an old man who sang the Wind Way Chant and the "house songs." His name was Wind Way Singer.[21]

"Then at that time they were saying, 'See that kinaaldá girl is running far.' **They told her not to do it.**[22] . . . With one single song, with that you leave from here as the song is begun, run, run, and turn back with the song still being sung, and then just **by the fire you go out again and run this way, they're still singing. You come back, the same old thing. You go in, by the fire. Go this way. I did the four ways."** Eva explained why the kinaaldá is not supposed to run a long way. "And when you do Kinaaldá, you are not supposed to run far, just a short distance. **You get some, this kind of stuff.** If you run a long distance, you will not receive goods. **You wash your** hair first and then you run. That's what I did."[23] In other words, by running a shorter distance, a more plentiful life is assured, one where others will be generous and bestow on you food, clothes, and things that are needed.

I asked Eva if they told her about some things she was not supposed to do during the Kinaaldá. She replied, "Yes, **not to eat** . . . one is not allowed to eat sweets, **pop, no nothing, and don't chew the hard stuff. And don't go sit like this. They told me to sit straight.** And you are not allowed to eat your own cake, or your teeth will all fall out.[24] Don't get mad, and do as you are told. Be courteous to everyone. You are taught to be respectful; you are supposed to follow directions quickly and not be slow in getting things done. Cross Hills Lady and Helen Joe helped with the cake and also, Elsie Joe. And Ben Bimá and Eleanor Chee.

"The reason they did this [helped with the cake] . . . **it's very important to you, when you make the first cake and the second one, Mother Earth**, you do this to tell her 'thank you.' And that is why you put the corn down there. **Make your life. When you make those cakes, you last long, that's what they told me.** You will live a long time. And then the buckskin that your hair is tied with, right here, I still have it.[25]

"And when you lay down, **when you lay down, you can't go like this and lay down just straight.** You lay down nicely. **No pillow, no nothing. So you don't have a hunchback. My mom taught**

me like that. That's why I can sleep on the ground anywhere I want to sleep. They told me I'll last long like that, too.

"You also have to lay down straight. You need to sleep on something hard. You are supposed to get up every morning during the four days and run. That means that later in your life you'll be an early riser."

This emphasis on the body and on practices that will build strength and endurance is part of a young girl's and also a young boy's growing up. The most common practice is having children run at dawn to the East and having them wash in ice water or roll in the snow. Eva embraced these habits and felt they were important to teach her own grandchildren.

"And also you shouldn't sleep all morning. You can't sleep. You see, my mom and my dad told me. Don't sleep in, early in the morning. You have to get up by when the sun rises. When it's dark, you get up and walk around. There are good things around, good food, money. All this comes to you when you walk early in the morning. And then at dawn, the sun comes from over there; the dawn is beautiful, all red. You have to bless that dawn with yourself—put it on yourself [bring it toward you]. If you lay down and sleep and don't get up until nine or ten or eleven—my father and my mother told me not to do this."

Eva went on to explain what would happen if you slept in. "You get old right away. You're not doing anything. You get sick right away, and you're not going to be strong. You won't be strong. You must run. Run early in the morning. In cold weather."

Eva described running early in the morning when she was young. "I even brought ice back from Paul Sherman's house. Ice. We had no water. We only had ice. A sack—we put ice in it and carried it back, and then you put it by the fire and melted it into water. So this is how we were raised: 'rise up at dawn!' 'the horse ran off, go get it!' 'let out the sheep!' . . . that's [hard]. . . . I didn't even have shoes. Just moccasins. Shoemaker was his name. My grandfather, Shoemaker, he made my shoes, small moccasins. And the ice had to be broken up. It was hard, about this thick ice. You can't heat it with something like this. Oh, yes it was cold. I bet we were crying. We went over there with Leonard [Sandman] and Emerson. We were the same age as Leonard. We only had greasewood for firewood. You would have to carry a rope with you and then take the greasewood and **chop it this small**. And then string the rope across. You would put the greasewood on and tie it together and put it on your back. It was a long ways to where we live now. We had to get greasewood near Rebecca Allen's house."

Her sister Eleanor had a much different story. She told me that Eva often pretended to run. "That one [Eva] is small.[26] . . . And then I would run from where the hooghan is. I was told not to sleep, just as she told you before. Over there at Paul Sherman's hooghan I would run up, at night while it's still dark, and then back again. Then I would wash where the water is and then back again. And she [Eva] will be standing there waiting for me, a short distance from the hooghan, over there under the circular stacked rocks. And then she would go inside pretending to have outrun me."[27]

In the years following Eva's Kinaaldá several events happened that changed the composition of her family. Eva's parents were divorced and her father moved to Crownpoint, Eleanor left to do agricultural work and live in Gallup, and finally Eva herself was given in marriage.

Parents' Divorce

As is the case in many matrilineal societies, marital bonds among Navajo couples are relatively weak (Aberle 1961:165). Divorce is very common, especially among young couples and in the early years of a marriage. Kluckhohn said of the Navajo in the nineteen forties and before, "It was highly unlikely that any man would reach old age without having been married to at least two different women. A great many would have had three wives and a considerable number four or more. A fair number of women would have only a single husband up to the age of 60, but many would also have had two, three, or more. Most fertile men and women who lived to the age of 60 would have had children from at least two different spouses" (1966:353).

Eva's parents' divorce was precipitated by the relationship Eva's mother formed with her brother-in-law, Hastiin Yázhí (Little Man).

Eva, being only a child, had only a vague sense of what was happening. "Hastiin Yázhí probably used to ride his horse over? At that time I was unaware of what was going on. I must have been about that small. He would sure ride his horse over, and right away every time when my mother was home alone. He was doing this for your grandmother; adultery was being committed against my father. He [my father] was out performing sings, going places, like Aneth, Utah. He would pull a horse behind him. So when he was asked to perform a ceremony, he would leave and sometimes would be gone for a month. And then he would bring home an incredible amount of fabric and baskets and things like that; they would be sticking out like this, and he would bring it home on the horse. And here there was Hastiin Yázhí. Grandma was cheating. I don't remember very much, just this little bit."

The divorce left Eva's mother more impoverished and the extended family with fewer resources. "My father knew about it. He knows what's going on. Then after that my father just left the sheep, and they diminished, and also the horses diminished. Then he left us and went to a place called White Rock [or Stony Butte, Tséłgai] over there that was where some of his relatives lived. 'Asdzą́ą́ Tł'ááshchí'í [his mother, Woman of the Tł'ááshchí'í clan] was her name; he went back to her. Here we had nothing and then after that it was all gone, nothing. Then Guyman barely kept seven horses together.[28] And so Tł'ááshchí'í Bidághaa,' he knew something about what was needed for the sheep, the horses, and the material goods, and so did my father."[29] Eleanor left her daughter in the care of her mother and went to work as an agricultural laborer near Gallup. As Eva told me, "She had a **divorce**. She ran off to Gallup and from there, I don't know what she did. From somewhere a truck arrived over here. It was a big truck. It was from Grants, they said, over there at Blue Water, from **Blue Water**. Back then they used to plant **carrots** and other things I'm not sure about over at Blue Water. It's been a long time. They went over there and they worked over there. In summer she never came back over here. Since she went back, she met Johnny K. Yazzie's father and she got to know him. From there she stayed in **Gallup** and was not around here."

Eleanor's leaving indicates the powerful pull that the regional cash economy was beginning to have on Navajos. Trading posts, the commercialization of weaving, and the sale of wool and lambs through traders had brought Navajos into the U.S. economy beginning in the eighteen seventies. There had been relatively little wage work, however, even in the Depression when CCC (Civilian Conservation Corps) jobs provided only a little relief from the devastating effects of Stock Reduction. The changes introduced by World War II would bring Navajos, including Eva's family, even greater change.

CHAPTER FIVE

After the War

Things Fall Apart

FOR EVA, THE EARLY NINETEEN FORTIES SEEMED TO RECApitulate the life of her mother, but then the changes accelerated by World War II brought both family disorganization and attempts to cope with change in a positive way.[1] Beginning with her arranged marriage to Aaron Curley, there are echoes of Eva's mother's and older sister's narratives in her own account: not knowing how the marriage was arranged, being scared and running away, but eventually going through with the ceremony. Eva avoided her husband for several years, but finally became pregnant in late 1947. With more automobiles and hospitals, Eva, unlike her mother, attempted to have her baby in a hospital. Carole was born in the back of a pickup, indicative of the unreliability of transportation in the nineteen forties and of the change that was coming to the Reservation. When Carole was still a baby, Eva's marriage fell apart, and she formed a relationship with Joe Price, a veteran of World War II. New drinking patterns and off-reservation wage work distanced Eva's generation from the life of herding and farming that their parents still maintained.

Grandparents like Eva's mother were often the link for children to the more traditional Navajo livelihood. Thus Carole's childhood was much like that of her mother, herding sheep in the mountains, visiting the trading post, and watching her grandmother weave. But the expansion of education and the missionary activities of the Mormon Church took Carole in new directions, leading her off-reservation. While in Eva's day, Anglo-American customs and institutions (drinking, oil exploration, schooling) penetrated the Reservation, their impact was much more extensive after 1945.[2] Off-reservation experiences (agricultural labor, the relocation program, railroad work, the Mormon Church's Placement Program, and boarding schools) were deeply transformative and led to new dilemmas and conflicts, pulling the family apart.

Eva's Marriage

Eva's first marriage, to Aaron Curley, was arranged when she was only a teenager, and like Eleanor's, her mate was a much older man. (Aaron was probably twenty-six or twenty-seven years of age.) As Eva described the situation, "I was married to this one's father [Carole's father] like that. People ate in our honor, this one's father and me. I don't know . . . only my mom and dad knew about it. It was my mother who actually did it, not my father. Well, he [Aaron] was with another woman, Betty's mother. Betty's mother passed away. She was Ben Yazzie's daughter. And then, so many years . . . I don't know how many years they were together. And then I was told that I would be given to him. 'You'll be given to him,' they told me." She said she was **"about twelve or thirteen. I was scared of him—for four years.**[3]

"Yes, I was afraid of him, and they were saying that I should marry him. And they cooked and prepared food and I was told to take out some cornmeal mush in the four directions, and so I ate some. Then people spoke to me."

"Did you live in a separate hooghan?" I asked. "We just lived in the one round hooghan," Eva replied. "Did you cook for him, how did that work out?"

"I used to run away from him [and stay with a relative]. Her name was Elsie. She was Shoemaker's Wife's daughter, the youngest one. We would go around together. In the summers, I would herd sheep with her. 'Why did they do that to you?' she asked. So I would run away from him. Sometimes I would even spend the night over there."

Grandma Sandman was a close companion of Cross Hills Lady ('Asdzą́ą́ 'Ałnáos'áhí), a Kiyaa'áanii woman. Both women had ties to the Crownpoint area so it seems likely that the two women arranged the marriage between their children: the recently widowed Aaron and the young Eva.

This was how Eva characterized her marriage, "I was scared. He told my mom . . . he told my mom and his mother Cross Hills Lady ('Asdzą́ą́ 'Ałnáos'áhí) that he was not wanted by me. That's the reason for it . . . **I was not used to him**." Later, when I asked how long she had been with Aaron, she said, "Four years, maybe, no it was not four years." Eva emphasized, "A man . . . he had already become a man. **He was a man.** I was just a child.[4]

"At that time, my older brother Grant was in the army, **World War II—1940, '41, and '42.** That is how I remember, when he came back, he really got mad at my mother. 'Why did you give her away to a man? Are you crazy?' he scolded her. 'You should have let her go to school.'"[5]

It is likely that Eva stayed away from Aaron for at least four, or perhaps even five, years, since she did not become pregnant with Carole until late 1947 when she was nineteen and a half years old. Eva told me about Carole's birth during my first week with her in 1965.

> Carole was born at the side of the road near Buffalo Springs. There were no pickups around at that time and she started getting pains fairly close together, so they decided to try to catch a ride to the hospital in Fort Defiance. Her mother and Shoemaker's Wife went with her. Her mother hailed a pickup and told them the problem, so they all got into the back; however, the pains came closer and closer together and finally they had the people pull over to the side of the road, where the baby was born. Instead of going to the hospital they just went back home. [Field notes, December 2, 1965]

I heard two other accounts, both from Carole, concerning her own birth. Her most extensive description came in 1996, when we sat in her mother's house at Yellow Hills on a cold January day, after I had decided to conduct a series of interviews about her childhood. Carole first explained, "They never had a nearby hospital, and the only hospital that they had was in Fort Defiance . . . and I guess my mom was in labor with me for maybe like almost two days . . . She tried to give birth to me . . . and I guess what happened was it scared my grandmother. I guess she tried to wave somebody down. . . . So, so she just waved these two [people] down—a man and a lady. They happened to be coming by in a truck. They helped my mom get into the truck and then on my way to the hospital, right by Buffalo Springs on the roadside, about two miles from that old Buffalo Springs Trading Post . . . it's a highway department now . . . two miles north of there. That's when I guess I was born.

"I guess I was really ready to come out when the man eventually stopped. . . . He stopped and that's where my mom gave birth to me on the roadside. . . . And my placenta, they were telling me that it's buried over there. . . . And they're always teasing me and saying that, 'OK, that's where your, your land is.'

"So, I was born in the back of a pickup truck, yes. . . . And, instead of takin' my mom all the way to the hospital, I guess, they just turned around and brought my mom back over here, and that white lady that delivered me with my grandmother came back several years ago and stopped along here. I guess they remembered that this was the place where they helped my mom. And several years back, they came back to see how old I was. . . . You know, they came back to check on me.

"And I guess what my mom was fed was nothin' but herb. Every time when you have a birth of a baby you have to drink herb. . . . It's called *'awéé' biyaałéí yilbéézh* [baby placenta herb boiled].

"And what they used to do, many years back, was when you have a baby, they tie you up . . . right here, on your tummy with a real wide sash belt in order for you to keep your tummy in . . . so that your uterus will contract. . . . That's what I was told, so every time when I had my kids, I either had to wear like a big enough girdle that I used to keep my tummy in and my mom, or my grandmother, used to say you heal better that way."[6]

Eva explained that after she was taken back to Yellow Hills, "**Medicine** was prepared and I drank it. The medicine has the healing power to cure at that time. When the baby first comes out, you cannot feed it milk right away. **You had to put** corn pollen into the baby's mouth. **You pray.** And the pollen nourishes the baby. **They bless with corn pollen** [*tádídíín*]. When the baby first comes out, it is washed over there and corn pollen is placed in its mouth. **We bless it with** tádídíín." Eva explained that they take the baby outside when the sun comes out. "At that moment they communicate with the baby. The baby will be like this and like that. Even though the baby doesn't understand, they talk to her/him and give him/her the assurance of their love."[7]

Carole said that her grandmother was the one who fed her tádídíín and took her outside and talked to her. "And eventually they talked to the baby. . . . My grandmother, she used to talk to mostly all of the kids. And she did that with all of them." Carole remembered her grandmother had told her how she had performed these activities for her grandson, Walter, who was only a year older than Carole.

I asked Eva if she had used a cradleboard for Carole. She replied that she did not remember it, but yes, Carole did have a cradleboard. Carole expanded on this, "I think when I was . . . a baby, the person that made me a cradleboard was my dad. My dad . . . was like a carpenter, at that time. And I think I had a cradleboard that used to belong to him, 'cause my dad used to make, weaving items—utensils—for making a rug. And I know that, he made me one. But I don't recall what happened to it. . . . If somebody had brains enough, we'd keep it in the family."

Divorce from Aaron

Sometime after Carole was born in 1948, Aaron started a relationship with Margaret, a young woman who was about sixteen years of age, although Eva thought she might have been much younger. Certainly by 1950, Aaron was living with Margaret and bore a daughter that year, when she was eighteen years old.[8] "I was told that he would work hard to support me. Where did he take care of me? There was nothing. He just went to another woman and ran away to her. He had built houses and provided a wagon, but he took it all back. I didn't even get a chance to say what was mine, and he took it away. . . . He did the same thing to her. She was about twelve years old, maybe eleven."

I wondered if he was mean to her. "Yes," she replied, "I don't know how many times he hurt me. That is why I let him go.[9] It was OK. He was given to me, even though I did not want him. At that time there were no laws." Eva explained that her parents did nothing. Her father had left the family to live in Crownpoint. "He [Aaron] would tie me up or he would lock me in." Eva went on to explain that her sister Eleanor was in Gallup with her husband and two young sons, Johnnie and Paul. Her older brother Allen Sam was living with his wife and children at Bitis 'Adeetiin about three miles away. Only her older brother Frank and his wife Anita were living nearby.

I asked Eva if Aaron left her or if he was pushed out. She replied, "He ran away on his own. He was going over to see the other woman at that time. I guess he was married, so he would go over there and no one bothered him about it. My father told me, 'No, my baby, you must not cry after him. You should not be jealous. No, leave it alone. It is embarrassing. It is poverty and hunger,' I was told. 'You should not be jealous,' I was told. 'Let it go.'"

When I first went to live with Eva in December 1965, her story contained more details, focusing primarily on the use of the Navajo Tribal Courts to get a divorce, something that in the nineteen fifties was a relatively new element in Navajo life. My field notes from then state,

> Eva mentioned that Carole was Kiyaa'áanii yáshchíín [i.e., her clan was different than Joe's clan and hence she had a different father] and then she started telling me about her marriage to Aaron Curley. She said her mother had taken her out of school and told her to marry Aaron, that he would take good care of her. However, she said that Aaron drank and he used to beat her. They used to live at her mother's place at that time. Finally, she ran away to Farmington where

her "brother" Dan Foster lived and worked.[10] She stayed with him and his wife and took care of their two children.

Eva said that Aaron placed a complaint against her (that she had run off with some boys) and the police came to get her. So there was a court hearing about the situation. Eva told them that Aaron had beaten her and that she didn't want to stay married to him. The judge gave her a divorce, for which she paid $10, the standard fee. Eva said that Aaron had bought her some furniture and a sewing machine, but he took it all back over to his mother's. The judge said that she should go over and get them, but Eva said that since he'd already taken [them] away, she didn't want to go over and claim [them]. If a man buys something for his wife, she said, he is supposed to leave it for her if they get divorced, not take it away. Eva continued that Aaron was still the same way—getting drunk, and that he had married Margaret when she was real young. She insisted that Margaret was 'behind her' [younger than she was] . . . and that Aaron treated her the same way. [December 3, 1965][11]

In writing down Eva's story of her divorce, I could not help thinking about the history of divorce in my own family where it was a secret in both my mother's and father's life. The anthropological literature on the Navajo suggests that while first marriages were arranged between families, they often broke up, and that second and third relationships were consensual and not marked by any ceremony. Although divorce or separation goes against the main Navajo injunction that a couple "stay together with care" (hazhó'ó sooké), it happens frequently as I noted in the last chapter when discussing the divorce of Eva's parents (Kluckhohn 1966:353). Among white Protestants (in my case, a family of German and Scots-Irish heritage), monogamy was prized, but not always attained, especially since gender relations were changing in the nineteen twenties and thirties), and partnerships that strayed from the norm were carefully hidden.

My mother and father were ten and fifteen years older than Eva. My mother graduated from East High School in Denver, Colorado, (the same school I would later attend) in 1927 and entered the University of Colorado that fall. Pictures show her and her friends dressed in flapper fashions, that is, short skirts, short, curled hair, cloche hats, silk stockings, and high-heeled shoes. She joined a sorority and her scrapbook is filled with invitations to teas and dances, crushed and dried flowers, and photos of picnics in the mountains featuring cars with wide running boards.

At the end of her sophomore year, she "ran away" and married a young student from a small town in Nebraska. He had just graduated from the University of Colorado and had been accepted to medical school at the University of Nebraska in Lincoln. The marriage lasted only a few years and ended, I think, because her husband had an affair with a nurse at his hospital. My mother graduated from the University of Nebraska and then returned to Denver. My grandfather noted in his diary, "Miriam returned home today; that's over." No one ever spoke about this marriage within the family, and I only found out when I asked my mother why some of the hand towels were embroidered with a "K" (for her first husband's last name) rather than an "L" (my father's initial). After returning home to live with her parents and finding work in a lab at a local hospital, my mother decided to become a medical technologist and enrolled in a program in St. Louis. While living in a boarding house there she met my father, another boarder who had just moved to St. Louis to join a patent law firm. He too had been divorced, from a woman whose name I never learned. It was perhaps unusual in the nineteen thirties that both of my parents were divorced when they met; however, divorce was becoming more common among Protestants in the nineteen twenties and thirties with the advent of "companionate marriage" as the ideal. Since both marriages ended before children were born, it was much easier to erase these relationships from the family history. My own sense is that there were more family secrets (divorce, abortion, alcoholism, illegitimacy, and mental illness) among the middle classes in the nineteen twenties through fifties than most families let on.

Class differences were also an issue in white American marriages. Although my father had attended the University of Idaho and George Washington University (where he received his degree in patent law), my mother was certainly "marrying down" to a man from a small town rural heritage, clearly a far cry from the place my grandfather had carved out for himself within the oil industry in Colorado. My parents were married in 1939 and I was born in 1940, probably just about the time Eva had her Kinaaldá.

Unlike Eva and Carole's family, my family and extended kin network were largely unaffected by World War II primarily because of the way historical events intersected with the timing of each generation's young adult years. The generations in my own family were spaced so that the men did not serve in either World War I or World War II. My grandfather was in his thirties during World War I, and my father and my uncle (my mother's sister's husband) were both too old to be drafted in World War II. So my own memories of the war are confined to the victory garden we grew in St. Louis where I was born and the ration tokens we used to buy sugar and margarine after we moved to Denver, my mother's hometown, in 1945. There are no war stories that are part of the family history, and no patterns of interaction or important male friendships that were shaped by the war.

After the War

By the time Eva divorced Aaron, World War II was over, the veterans and war workers had returned home, and the Navajo economy had collapsed. The sources of income that had sustained Navajo families from the armed services and war industries dried up and the pastoral economy—diminished through Stock Reduction—could no longer support families.[12] Most sources emphasize the impact of the war on Navajo veterans and indicate that veterans became important advocates for increased educational opportunities for Navajos (Thompson 1975:77, Locke 1976a:460, Parman 1976:288). Certainly their close contact with other Americans soldiers, their immersion in American culture as practiced in the military, and their increased sense of the importance of knowing the English language changed their cultural orientation (Bailey and Bailey 1986:223–30, Vogt 1949:17–18). Most of the men in Eva's life—her brother Grant, her brother's son Leonard, her clan brother Ben, and her new husband,

Joe, were all war veterans. In the early nineteen fifties new influences from Anglo capitalist economy—primarily wage work and drinking—transformed Eva's daily life. The routine of sheep herding and weaving was replaced by excursions to Gallup, binge drinking, and trips to pick agricultural produce. These activities and Joe's work on the railroad emerged as key components of Eva's narratives.

On the surface, my family enjoyed the era of postwar prosperity like many other middle-class Americans. By 1945 we had moved back to Denver so we could be closer to my mother's parents and had purchased a three-bedroom brick bungalow in East Denver about ten blocks from my grandparents' home. My father established a patent law practice with a partner, and my sister and I spent the late nineteen forties and fifties in a very middle-class neighborhood. We saw this period as one of stability and increasing prosperity, not one of rapid change. That came later, with my father's death of a heart attack in 1954. But even that change was largely personal, in contrast to the broader changes brought to Eva's and Carole's lives by increased contact with public education and Christianity.

Joe Price Enters Eva's Life

Shortly after Aaron and Eva were divorced, Eva started a relationship with Joe Price. "I came to know him and then we had children: four. We don't do anything traditional, no, nothing," indicating to me that they did not have a traditional wedding. Carole interjected, "But to my understanding, when Joe came into her life, Joe was a serviceman. And when he came back from the service, you know, that's when she met him. And that's how, you know, life started. So they never had a traditional wedding or nothing. They just got together."

Joe built a house for them, but this may have been after Eva had given birth to her sons, Timothy (born in 1956) and Randa (born in 1957). This was the house where I stayed in the fall of 1965. It was a two-room log cabin that had a sloping roof over the kitchen or front room. As my field notes state, "Eva said they had built the back part about seven years ago [1958]—she and Joe and Carole. The front part was about three years old. They had just gotten the electricity a year ago from NTUA [Navajo Tribal Utility Authority]. It cost $170 to have the house wired with several outlets" (November 30, 1965). The front room of the cabin held the small woodstove where Eva cooked meals for her kids and for Joe or me when we were around. There was a metal-legged table and a few chairs where we sat to eat our fried bread, potatoes, and coffee, occasionally supplemented by the pork chops or chicken that I would bring when I came from Gallup. Grandma Sandman and Grandma Shoemaker slept on the floor on sheepskins, using several heavy blankets to cover themselves. In good weather, the bedding was aired on a wooden rack behind the house each morning. In the back room there were two double beds. Eva always gave me a bed to sleep on and then slept with Randy (her two-year-old) and Ruda (her five-year-old) on the other bed. Randa and Timothy slept on the floor on a pad between us.

Eva told me much more about her relationship with Joe on that first day in 1965 than I learned in 1994.[13] My field notes describe our discussion.

> During the morning Eva and I had a long conversation about her marriage. She said Joe was in the service for four years. He had a wife in the Gallup area [near Pinedale] and then one at Crownpoint [at a place called Smith Lake].[14] At Crownpoint he had a nice house and cows, a real pretty place. But when he came back from the service his wife had a baby from someone else. Eva said they had a Squaw Dance for Joe at Sheep Springs after he came back.[15] His wife was there then and Eva saw her. However, they soon separated, and Joe just stayed at his mother's.
>
> Apparently Eva and Joe started going around with each other, and then Joe came and asked her to cook for him. She said OK, but her mother didn't like it, so they ran off to Colorado (taking Carole with them) and stayed there for several weeks.[16] When they returned they stayed with Eva's mother.
>
> Eva said that she used to drink . . . Joe too, up until about two years ago. They used to run off to Gallup, and she didn't take care of the kids. They had no car, no nice

things at that time. They spent all their money on drinking. [November 30, 1965]

Navajo Drinking Patterns in the Nineteen Fifties

Joe's and Eva's drinking, as described in her interviews, contrasts with that of her father. Rather than individual experiments with tó łibáí (a home brew made from corn), or the drinking of bootleg wine in a hooghan among several older men who practiced their Navajo songs as they drank, Eva and Joe traveled to Gallup, bought liquor, and consumed it in public places.[17]

Levy and Kunitz characterize Navajo drinking as "male, peer group binge drinking" occurring in public places among groups of males of approximately the same age. "Frequently it takes the form of a binge where large quantities of liquor and, more recently, wine are consumed as rapidly as possible. The drinking continues until the participants pass out or the supply is exhausted" (Levy and Kunitz 1974:76). This pattern is analogous to drinking on skid row during the nineteen fifties and sixties and to fraternity drinking in the nineties. Levy and Kunitz did not discuss women in their book, which was based on research during the nineteen sixties. It is clear from my own observations, however, that women often accompanied their male partners (boyfriends or husbands) to bars or other drinking settings such as back alleys, behind trading posts, or in pickup trucks.[18]

Eva's drinking meant that Grandma Sandman basically raised Carole. As Carole described it, "All these years, I always think that she never really had enough careness for me because Grandma was always the one that taught me a lot of things. . . . And of course in my younger days, my mom was just an alcoholic after she met Joe, and I was always afraid to stay with them . . . and, to tell you the truth, I went through a lot of hardship when I was young, so I don't want my kids to have that kind of a life when my mom and my stepdad were drinking. We used to have this great big corral right here behind the house, over here. You can still see the sheep manure there . . . and when these guys were drinking over here. . . . This was just a one-house building over here—one room, and when they were drinkin', me and Grandma would just take our stuff out in the evening, and we would sleep among the sheep, in the sheep corral.

"Right in between there . . . that's where we used to go. I remember that they all used to get together when I was a little girl. Eleanor and her husband, Leonard Sandman, of course, Grant Tsosie. Everybody used to start havin' a party and that's the time . . . it was time for us to find us a place to sleep. That's what we used to do is sleep in the sheep corral."

Relationship with Grandma Sandman

Carole's memories of her relationship with her grandmother, like Eva's memories of her own childhood, revolve around herding sheep on the mountain at Na'aldzisí (at Shoemaker's Wife's summer place), learning to weave, and spending time with her brother Paul (Eleanor's oldest son who was about Carole's age).[19] Paul used to tease and harass Carole in much the same way that Ben used to make life difficult for Eva.

"And then I lived here with grandma and during the time when summer would come around we had a lot of flocks of sheep . . . maybe like close to two hundred and that was the most important duty that we had to take care of. I remember my brother Paul K. Yazzie, the late Paul, we used to [chase] after the sheep and we would be herd[ing] sheep at all times.[20] And at times my brother Paul would get really jealous because I would get the most attention from my grandma. He would make me cry. And my grandmother taught me how to weave real small rugs. She used to show me how to do it. And several times, she would weave a bigger rug and then I would weave a small rug. But we used to make our strings [from] the regular natural wool that we used to have coming off of the sheep. And we did that ourselves. We used to dye it, and we had a natural color brown that we used to use all the time too, and white. And I used to make maybe like a small rug. I know it didn't cost a fortune, but at times we used to sell it to [the] Two Grey Hills [Trading Post] and of course at that time my grandmother used to trade up there. And the only thing that she would bring home for me would be maybe some candy and soda pop, enough for me to get by. And, it's always a thrill. It was always something precious for me when I used to finish a rug, even though it took me maybe like three weeks to finish a real small rug."

"So how big were they?" I asked.

"They were sort of like twelve by twelve," Carole continued, "You know, the small ones. And during the summer, we used to herd our flocks up toward the mountain. And at times my mom used to tell my grandmother that I couldn't go with her. And boy, that made me feel real bad because I was always Grandma's tail. And at one time she started herding her flocks over the hill here. And I cried so hard to where I ran after her. And she was herding the herd [on] horseback. . . . And she told me come on: *Tį́'*. And I ran after her and she put me right behind her back, and we would herd the sheep all the way up to the mountain. And it took several hours, just herding the sheep. Maybe like five to six hours. And we would go get to our summer camp. . . . And at that time, our summer camp was just a small chaha'oh, a small shade house. That was over . . . where we used to live."

"This way from Chéch'il Yaató?" I asked.

"Yeah," Carole continued. "And at that time, we had another grandmother here, Shoemaker's Wife. . . . We used to have somebody take her out there. And we all lived together. She used to have a lot of sheep."

"Did you have both Shoemaker's Wife's and your grandma's flocks together?" I wondered.

"Yeah, they were combined together. So it was always something very precious when we had to herd the sheep up there."

At another time, Carole reiterated much of the same feelings, though in this case she was describing a time when she herded with her grandmother near Ben Bimá's place, at Dził Zéé'asgai (Mountain with a White Neck).

"When I used to herd sheep with Grandma . . . up in the mountains, we used to herd sheep way down below there, Dził Zéé'asgai. . . . And that used to take us maybe like all day, and she would hide from me.

"'Cause we had a whole lot of sheep and goats all together. She would be on one side over there and I'd be over here on the other side. . . . And whichever way the goats would start going, we would just follow them on the side, and more likely at times she would hide from me. And I would stand at the edge of a cliff trying to holler, 'Shimásání eeee' ['Grandmother,' dragging out the last syllable]. . . . And she'd be standing behind one of the trees there when I'm trying to call her, and I would start running and try to look for her and next thing you know she would start laughing and she would come out from behind a tree. . . . We had our good ol' times together. She used to tell me not to holler that much. I don't know how many times I've walked this trail, up to the mountain with her.

"I don't know how many times we walked that trail. But I don't know right now, if I'll be able to do it. . . . But, it was like one of those things where it was a must when you have to take the sheep up there, and, the only person that used to take our stuff up would be Kenneth Dinetclaw [a close neighbor]. And he would leave the stuff up there for us, with my mom. And we would, you know, put up our tent. We had a tent and a hooghan. . . . I don't know if you saw that hooghan."

"No," I said, "The only thing that's still standing now is Ben Bimá's house, but the hooghan that was there is now just a few rocks sort of in a circle."

"Was that hooghan still up there when you were there?" I asked Carole. Carole wasn't sure but she remembered another hooghan at Na'aldzisí. There was a round hooghan there that Mr. Tree took down, and that was where Carole had her Kinaaldá.

Rivalries with an Older Brother, Paul

Both Eva and Carole had told me about Paul's childhood. Paul was the oldest son of Eva's sister Eleanor. As a mother's sister's son, Carole called him "older brother" in Navajo. He was born in Gallup to Eleanor and Tom K. Yazzie's older brother. Carole explained, "Many years back when Paul was a baby—he was about three months old, I believe—he was brought back from Gallup. And then he was fortunately raised by Grandma Sandman. And Eleanor stated that she'll be back in two days. It took her weeks and months to come home. And she never did. She never came back for Paul."

Eva remembered that Paul also was ill after Eleanor did not return. "It was a week and later a month. He was pitiful and then he became ill. Just my mother and I took care of him. He got a stomach ache that wouldn't go away, so they got a medicine man who gave him medicine, and he got well. It was just his grandmother that raised him, and I also took care of him as time went on. So over at Intermountain [a boarding school in Utah], that was where he went to school. Paul went there and graduated from there. So when he came back [from school], he told her [Eleanor] that she wasn't his mother. He said this to her until he passed away. He said that his grandmother was his mother. This is how we raised him."

Eva recalled that Carole and Paul didn't always get along, "At that time, [when] this one [Carole] was small . . . I don't know how tall he [Paul] was. She remembers her grandmother then. When payments from welfare first came about and her grandmother received payments, they would fight on the way to Two Grey Hills."

Carole amplified this statement in her translation. She said that Eva "stated that when Paul was a teenager, him and I used to fight quite a bit. And at the time . . . when Grandma started receiving her monthly income, we used to take turns to go to Two Grey Hills with her. And she would appoint who's going to go. So when it was my time for me to go with her, he would get mad in the morning. He would get mad, and he would start making me cry. He was probably about five or six years older than I was. And he used to hit me with rocks. And I'd run behind Grandma Sandman. And he was like a pester. . . . He would make you cry all the time—hit you, or whatever. And I'll never forget that time. Those were our younger day[s]."

"So he was going to school at Intermountain in the winter?" I asked.

"During the summer he would return," Carole explained to me. "And that was the time where he used to do that. He used to make me cry, 'cause we used to have a fight about it. And the only thing that Grandma Sandman used to offer him, when he used to herd sheep. . . . Remember the square Bull of the Wood[s], tobacco? . . . You know, they were square at that time. And they didn't have any Skol then. It was Bull of the Wood[s]. And every month, that was his treat. 'Cause he would chew that Bull of the Wood[s] while he was herding sheep. And Grandma Sandman used to bring maybe like three or four squares [of] Bull of the Wood[s]. And she would only give him one. And at the time when he finishes one, she would give him another one. And constantly he would have that Bull of the Wood[s]. And I don't know if he had that Bull of the Wood[s] when he was in school. . . . But that was, more likely his treat."

Carole Attends Her Mother's School

When she was six years old, Carole went to school. Like her mother she knew only Navajo when she began. "I remember when I went to school I went to Newcomb Day School and it was like we used to catch the bus every day. [I would] come home in the evening. And . . . I used to have a teacher by the name of Mr. Whilder. . . . And, at that time . . . it was not like the school that they have now to where they have seven classes . . . that they have to change. No, it wasn't like that. We used to have one class a whole day."

Contrasted with Eva's stark stories of students being forced to stand on their heads, Carole found important teacher-mentors at school and eventually a second family through her escape to Utah via the Mormon Placement Program. School and the English-speaking world had a longer lasting and more transformative impact on Carole than on Eva. Like others in her generation, she became bilingual and a participant in American teen culture.

"With one teacher all day?" I asked.

"Yeah, one teacher all day. And I remember my book *Spot*."

In an earlier interview Carole and I had laughed over the fact that both of us had read *Dick and Jane* books at school in about the same period. In telling about her mother's schooling she remembered her own, "Because when I was in school I remember . . . we used to have these books I used to hate it so much, we used to read it all the time."

"So what were the books?" I wanted to know.

"The books were called . . . there was a name there that popped my mind. Jack . . . "

"You didn't do *Dick and Jane*?" I said, incredulous.

"*Dick and Jane*, yes!"

"'Cause I did *Dick and Jane*, too, everybody did," I replied.

"Everybody did," Carole agreed. "That was the beginning of every education I guess, *Dick and Jane*."

"But you didn't care for those?" I interrupted.

"No," Carole replied. "It was like every day you had to read that over and over and over. I don't know how many books I went through."

"'Look Jane, look. See Spot, see.'" I parroted the sing-song like quality of the phraseology. "They weren't really even sentences . . . just like these five words."

"Five words, 'Jump Spot, jump.' Something like that. 'Dick play and run.'" Carole's memory was better than mine, when it came to recalling the simple sentences.

My concluding thoughts were, "Right. They were pretty weird books. I guess that's what they taught everybody between about 1945 and 1955."

Carole and I had much the same reaction to *Dick and Jane* readers: they were boring. But they also communicated white, middle-class culture of the nineteen fifties. Though separated by class and racial positioning, both Carole and I, and other *Dick and Jane* readers, nevertheless were presented with a model of American girlhood.

Although I was eight years older than Carole, it is instructive to explore the ways in which public school functioned very differently in our lives. For Carole, school was an assimilating experience, an exposure to a new language and a white, hegemonic culture that must have seemed very foreign to a young Navajo in the nineteen fifties before TV, American toys, and video games became such a presence in Navajo households. For me, education buttressed the class and racial position I occupied in the dominant culture. Yet there were implicit gender, beauty, and popularity norms that were difficult for me to adjust to and feel comfortable with. I attended an all-white public elementary school in East Denver with children whose mothers all stayed at home and whose fathers worked in a range of jobs, from mover with a long-distance company, to a druggist, minor bank officer, dentist, IRS accountant, airline pilot, baker, and dairy truck driver. We skipped rope, played on our swing sets, roller-skated down the sidewalks underneath the elm trees, and played on the "rings" at school. As girls we learned to dress properly (in the days when all girls wore dresses), wear curly hair, and wish we were blond. I can still remember roller-skating with Judy Mason, who lived two blocks away, and being envious of her blond good looks, like a child version of a movie star. Having my hair curled with foul smelling, scalp-burning permanents at the beauty shops was a routine I came to hate. By sixth grade, I was also overweight, a condition that made me even more sensitive about my appearance and my inability to climb the ropes or be chosen for the winning team in gym class. Our activities included "Bluebirds" (part of the Camp Fire Girls), Sunday school, Vacation Bible School, and swimming at the local YMCA. The grade school curriculum not only taught us how to read, print, then write, and do arithmetic, but also inculcated notions about whiteness, male and female roles, and American nationalism.[21] These same themes were part of the Navajo school experience as well.

I was interested in how much English Carole might have known when she went to school and if she had found it difficult to learn a second language. "Did you know English when you started school?" I asked.

"I started learning a little. But not . . . not too much. It was like Navajo all the time. But I think that's where I started learning my English when I started school. But now-a-days, you know, like these kids here they know their English right from the time when they're born. . . . Yeah, that's where I started learning my English, was when I [read] with those [*Dick and Jane* readers]. . . . After that I attended school over here in Newcomb until I was the age of eight or nine and then after that they had these LDS [Latter Day Saints, or Mormon] Placement Programs.[22] So after that, you know, I was placed on a placement."

Carole recalled a Black woman teacher who wanted to adopt her in the years she was in grade school, before she went on the Mormon Placement Program. "My mom was pretty well what you would call an alcoholic. And she really didn't care much for me. And I used to go to the day school over at Newcomb. I was attending kindergarten, and I was attending first grade . . . and I believe . . . people used to feel real sorry for me. And there was an elderly colored lady . . . I often wonder if she's still alive. She almost adopted me. Just because of the situation that I was living through . . . that I was never cared enough for. And I believe . . . at times I would go to school without my hair being braided. And at that time I used to have long . . . pretty long hair. . . . I guess she asked my mom if she could adopt me and take me just away from here. But my mom refused and she stated, 'No.' She didn't want to. But one time I went to Santa Fe with her [the teacher].

"And we took a trip out there. She wanted me to meet her family out in Santa Fe, and we took like maybe three to four days. And I remember, we were on the train. I guess I fell asleep and after I fell asleep . . . I was in the bunk by myself. When I woke up I was alone, and I started crying. She came back and told me not to cry. And I remember we went to Santa Fe. I really don't remember what we did over there, but as far as I know the most exciting trip I ever had in my life was going on the train trip."

"How old do you think you were in school?"

"I was probably about eight years old at the time when I went down there. And she wanted to adopt me but my mother refused. So I wasn't ever adopted."

The Mormon Placement Program

Carole went on the Mormon Placement Program, where young Navajo boys and girls are sent to various towns in Utah to live with Mormon families and to attend school there.

"So as far as I remember, when I was about eight years old I wanted to go on the Placement Program. See, at that time we had the sisters, the LDS missionaries. They used to come around and teach us the gospel, and I got baptized into the church. I have my baptism record somewhere, and that showed what year and what day I was baptized into the church of LDS. After that I wanted to go on the Placement Program because of the struggle and mess that I was going through. Finally I decided to pressure my mom for her to sign the piece of paper. I went on placement . . . the LDS Placement Program for like maybe two to three years.

"My first family that I used to live with was Ethel and Myron Cardinal. I still remember who they are, and I had one foster sister and her name was Sharon Cardinal. And Myron had a lot of respect, and he taught us a lot of things at the time when I was up there. And of course I was up there with Bernice and Mabel.[23]

"With the foster sister, there was four of us. And when it was time for us to leave we used to gather over here at the LDS church . . . and, either late in the evening and we would travel all night and get to Provo, Utah to where we had to depart there at the mission home, and that's when, they called our foster parents. I guess they select who they want to pick, so, we got picked because they thought we were all from the same family . . . Mabel, me, and Bernice. And that's how I got to live with them. And then we used to have a foster grandfather, too, that stayed with us. And he passed away the second year I was there. He lived with us. He was an old man, and he passed away.

"That's where I was raised among the Mormon people. Of course, they have to be LDS people in order for them to take in foster kids." Carole thought she was in Utah about three years.

"The fourth year I decided to stay back down because, I don't recall what year it was, but I've been trying to get a hold of Sharon. When I was up there my foster dad, Myron, he used to work at the airport called Hillfield Airforce Base. And one day on a Saturday, I think he had to work or something like that, and he wanted for us to go to the airplanes that were right there in the field. He wanted for us to observe it and take a look at what he does there. I recall that they took our pictures when we were in the airplane because when we were sitting in the helicopter and they even took us for a ride around. I was so scared. I think that was the first year I was there. I was so scared 'cause I had never been in an airplane in my life, and I was crying 'cause I was holding on to my sister Bernice, and she was just laughing about me. She says, 'Don't cry!' and here she was younger than I am. I remember 'cause it was scary . . . first time when you get into a helicopter. And I know that they took our picture. I'm trying to get a hold of my foster sister. I'm trying to get the pictures from her."

Carole's Kinaaldá

During one of the summers when she was back in Sheep Springs, having returned from school and the Mormon Placement Program, Carole had her Kinaaldá. She remembers that she was with her Grandma Sandman and Shoemaker's Wife, living on the mountain at Na'aldzisí.

"I was told to run early in the morning. And I know we had that hooghan, and I ran about a half mile. That's where I used to turn around. And I remember I was doing that for four days, until my cake was finished. And I know my Aunt Eleanor was there most of the time, and my sister, Ethel. And we were told we weren't supposed to eat sweet stuff.[24] And she used to give me candy on the side. And she used to hide it. And we never got caught. She did that because people were always eyeing us when we were together. I know she used to hide candy for me and I used to eat it. And nobody knew about it. I'll always remember that. We cheated on the rules at times."

I wanted to know if she remembered any other rules about what she could not do during her Kinaaldá. "We weren't supposed to be lazy. We were supposed to be very active, run. We were told that for our own self, later on, when we grow up to be a woman. Of course that is like forty-something years ago that I am talking about. I don't remember who gave the blessings that night."[25]

Carole was very glad that she had participated in a Kinaaldá, but she did not tell her grandmother about her second menstrual period and thus did not have a second ceremony, which was the tradition in Eva's generation.[26] "I'm glad that I did that, but I didn't want to do it with a second time. I just totally hid it from everybody else, and I never told anybody that, my second time around. But at first when I received it, I know I cried. It scared me. Because when I was becoming a woman, I was never instructed on how to take care of myself. And the only person that would inform me of these things was my grandmother, Mary Sandman, and I would ask her questions when we were herding sheep, during the summer, and when I became like that, she would inform me. She was the one that told me. Well, my mother was an alcoholic then. She wasn't paying much attention at the time when I was becoming a teenager. And up to this day, I still wish my grandmother were here. I could have learned a lot from her."

Missionaries to the Navajo

Missionaries played two very different roles in Carole's life and mine, yet they were crucial intermediaries in our cross-cultural experiences in the nineteen fifties, illustrating how religion was just as much a crucial element as the economy in integrating both of us into the same regional system of interaction and dominance. For both of us, missionaries provided the impetus for travel: Carole from the Navajo Reservation to Roy, Utah, and for me from Denver to Tuba City, on the western edge of the Navajo Reservation. Carole remembers two Mormon "sisters" who were undoubtedly on their two-year mission to the Navajo Reservation. One of these was herself Navajo, Sister Néich'íshii. Carole described how they "used to come around and they used to teach us the gospel and I got baptized at a church." She recalled that Sister Néich'íshii composed and sang several songs, including one called "Go My Son." "She just sang it in the English. So that's how I remember who she is. But the other, the other one, was a white girl, but I never knew who she was. I really didn't pay much attention, because I guess, she was an Anglo, but with the Navajo lady, you know . . . after she finished her mission she stopped at the house several times . . . just to say hello and see how things were and stuff like that."

The missionaries also organized activities for Navajo children. "They had what they call Youth Nights, and we used to play games, volleyball, or activities. Or we used to do a little artwork, and that's how I got interested. They used to pick us up and we'd go over there.[27] At that time late Ella Ann Tsosie was around, she's about the same age as we are . . . Mabel and Ethel, Walter, Johnnie and Paul used to go over there.[28] And of course we didn't stay out there that late, you know, we had a limited amount of time, to where we had to be at the house by eight o'clock, and it was just a two-hour thing."[29]

I was also introduced to missionaries in my grade school years. Our church, the Montview Presbyterian Church in East Denver, Colorado, supported a Presbyterian mission in Tuba City, Arizona, more than one hundred miles from Carole's home in Sheep Springs. Mary, the missionary whose last name I have forgotten, used to come to our Sunday school classes. I still have a very vivid image of her. She was short with dark, brown hair, tied in a traditional Navajo bun. She always wore a velveteen blouse and three-tiered skirt, just like most Navajo women of her age. I do not remember the content of her talks to us (though initially I must have been ten or eleven years old), but I believe she showed us pictures of Navajo life, stressing that they lived in hooghans and herded sheep. The women, she explained, wore clothes like she was wearing and wove rugs. Her trips were undoubtedly to report on her missionary efforts and to continue to solicit financial assistance from our church. Despite it being a time when three-tiered skirts and Navajo-like blouses with rickrack trim were fashionable and turquoise jewelry was popular outside the Reservation, the Navajo seemed both exotic and in need of our help and charity.

When I was in junior high school, a dynamic young minister named DeeDee Harvey arrived at our church, along with his Hollywood starlet wife. He held special services on Sunday for young people and organized a number of youth activities, including "sock hops" in the church basement and informal outings. By the time I was in high school, a summer trip was being planned to Tuba City to help build a storage shed for the mission there. I volunteered as a cook for the trip and we spent weeks planning how we could feed fifteen or twenty young teenagers mostly with canned food, since Tuba City did not have a supermarket, only a trading post with limited supplies. There was much discussion about the route we would take since the roads across the Reservation from Window Rock to Tuba City were unpaved. Several parents and DeeDee drove cars, including some station wagons. In the end we chose to take the dirt road going to Tuba City, and a paved route through Grand Junction, Colorado, on our way back. There was a sense of going off to a strange and even slightly dangerous place, with the possibility of running out of gas or having a flat tire in the "desert." I remember the long, dusty road across the Reservation where cars needed to be carefully spaced so they wouldn't "eat the dust" of the vehicle ahead in the long caravan. I recall lying in the back of one of the station wagons (in the days before seat belts) during a hot, dusty afternoon, glancing out at some strange mud villages that we passed just before we wound down a long hill, crossed a flat valley, and drove into Tuba City. These were the Hopi Villages I found out much later, but they seemed like glimpses into a foreign and unknown life.

As teenagers we were much more interested in our own relationships than in finding out about Navajo life. Given the nineteen fifties notions about the gendered division of labor, the boys constructed the storage room with cement cinder blocks, while the girls cleaned and painted, and four of us prepared the meals. We slept in the basement of the community center in our sleeping bags, except for one night. Then we took a "camping" trip to a place called Ghost Mesa where we watched a full moon rise over a hauntingly beautiful canyon. I remember seeing a number of Navajo families around the Mission church and Mary's small house. We spent time walking through Tuba City, examining the BIA boarding school buildings, and visiting the old trading post; however, we never connected with Navajos as individuals or even got a glimpse of the more widely known aspects of Navajo life such as sheep herding or rug weaving. Our sense was that we were in some exotic and interesting place doing "good works" for the needy, who were seen as distant yet completely "Other." Carole's experience with the Other was in great contrast to mine.

As Carole has already emphasized, contact with missionaries persuaded her to enroll in the Placement Program and three years of trips back and forth from the Navajo Reservation to Salt Lake and then on to Roy, Utah. When I asked if she went to church every Sunday, she replied, "Every Sunday. We weren't supposed to miss a day, and we used to have a Wednesday night evening get together, like MIA. It's called, Mutual Indian Activities. . . . And that's where we used to do the same thing, like artwork, teaching of the gospel, and at times we would get selected to do a speech or a talk on Sunday morning. To prepare they would appoint you, what you did a few days before Sunday. Several times I was told [to do this]. I don't know what I spoke about, but I stood in front of the church, and the church—the one that I used to go to—was a *big* church. I got used to it though, after I did that once. I took a little bit of piano lessons. I was in a lot of activities at the time when I was in Utah, like I was on the volleyball [team], I was on the basketball [team], but to tell you the truth, the most boring time was when you used to get homesick. There were times when I felt that way. I used to think a lot about my grandma, cause she's the one that didn't want me to go. But I told her, 'It's best for me to go.'"

In discussing school, Carole at first emphasized how different it was, but soon, in answer to my questions, gave an account of how quickly she adapted. "It was like you walk into a totally strange place, and down here when I went to school, all we had was just one big classroom, day after day, but when I went to school up there it was just like, we had to switch classes, six or seven classes. And then, the cafeteria—and it was a *big* cafeteria. And down here, on the Reservation, all you see is a lot of Indians teaching classes, or teachers' aides. But in Utah it was totally different where a lot of Anglo . . . and it was all you would see."

Mabel and later Bernice, her sisters, were the only other Navajo children in her school. At first, she found the material difficult. "Well the first week it was . . . and then the second week, I got to know the school very well. I had a little problem in reading, but later on, I caught on. And, of course, homework was what I had to bring home every evening. It was more in Utah than it was down here."

I asked her if her classes were harder in Utah. "It was about the same. There wasn't much difference. It was the same, it was just they emphasized a lot of learning for you to do . . . just not teaching you much. You had to do a lot of reading and learn."

Unlike my brief foray, Carole's experiences were longer and more in-depth including everyday life with a Mormon family, activities at the church, and three years of schooling. When she speaks of this time, she usually emphasizes how she adapted easily to the expectations placed on her and participated in a range of new experiences. Once in a while, she suggests how strange the encounter was at first and how much she continued to miss her grandmother. We both traveled away from home to experience the Other: Carole to Roy, Utah, and me to Tuba City, Arizona. Carole's connections were much more transformative, while mine were brief, reinforcing a sense of the exotic, but perhaps planting a seed that eventually led to my choice of anthropology as a profession and field research on the Navajo Reservation in the nineteen sixties.

Frank Sandman's Death

During the three-year period when Carole was away, two significant people in Eva's life died: her father and her older brother Frank. Both deaths were connected to drinking and indicate how far alcohol had penetrated into the family. Eva told me about her father's death one day in December 1965 when I was asking her where various family members had been living so that I could reconstruct residence histories for my dissertation.

About six or seven years before my time in Sheep Springs (sometime in 1958 or 1959),

> they got a phone call from the people at Tsé Łigai [White Rock, near Crownpoint where Eva's father lived], saying that Eva's father was sick and that "You should come and take care of your daddy." So they went over there to get him. Eva said he had fallen off a bed when drunk and had hurt his head. Anyway, he was paralyzed on one side and couldn't move (possibly from a stroke I suggested). They brought him home [to Sheep Springs] for two weeks. Eva said it was really hard to take care of him, as they had to turn him over in bed every few hours. They finally took him to Shiprock and then the Shiprock hospital sent him to Albuquerque. Once, Eva said, they went to visit him, but he didn't know them, so they just went back. Two days later, they received a call from the hospital that he had died. Apparently his body was sent to a Farmington funeral home. Eva said they bought clothes for the body and a blanket and quilt (for $160—she still remembers how much it all cost). They paid $100 and something for the casket. He was buried at Shiprock and they were going to have to pay a gravedigger, but they explained that they had no money. However, Ben Watchman was a

policeman at that time, and he arranged that three prisoners from the jail would dig the grave so that the family didn't have to pay. [Field notes, December 7, 1965][30]

Frank's death was much more tragic and resulted in a complete reorganization of the living arrangements of Eva's extended family, basically breaking one extended family residence group into two new ones. Eva's description in 1965 gave a much more detailed account than Carole was able to give me in 1996, primarily since Carole had been in Utah when he died.

According to my census records, Frank died on September 15, 1960.

> Eva said she went to Gallup that time to do washing for her mother, who was in the hospital in Shiprock. She came back and saw Frank sitting by the side of his house, drunk. (Frank, Anita and their kids were living in a two-room house about a quarter-mile from Eva's. Also in the camp were Eleanor and Tom Yazzie, possibly in Eva's mother's house.) Eva and Joe were in their house asleep, along with Paul K. Yazzie, when Anita came to the door around 11:00 p.m. and said their house was on fire. Joe went over there (along with Eva) and knocked down the door. It was all burning inside. Joe said he saw Eva's brother on the bed—just his feet, as everything else was burning up. Eva said they didn't know what had happened. Perhaps Frank had turned over a kerosene lamp while drunk and that's what started the fire. She said Leonard (Anita's oldest son) and Louise (Leonard's wife) weren't helping any. (Also Eleanor and Tom were drunk, and not of any help.) Eva was mad at all of them, possibly because they may have been to blame for the fire. (Frank's children were sleeping in the other room—and weren't hurt by the fire.) [Field notes, December 7, 1965]

My field notes go on to describe how the family handled the tragedy.

Eva and Katherine (Anita's daughter) hitchhiked to Newcomb to talk to Ben, Eva's clan brother, about the fire. The first car they stopped was driven by Mexicans, and was heading toward Sheep Springs [the opposite direction from Ben's house]. Eva told them the trouble and told them to stop at the trading post to talk to the trader and tell them what happened. The next vehicle was a diesel truck who gave them a ride to Newcomb. She told Ben, and he radioed to Shiprock and Farmington. The police apparently arrived on the scene, and took measurements, asked questions, etc., to try to determine what happened. Efforts to put out the fire failed, and apparently it just burned until most of the house was destroyed. Eva was going to file a complaint and have Louise, Leonard, Eleanor, and Tom put in jail, but then her brother Ben told her not to, since they were poor and didn't have any way to help themselves.

Eva said they next drove up to łibátah [the "gray area" or foothills] to tell the people up there what had happened and ask for help. . . . They also asked all the people who lived around them, and they all helped. She said during the next few days and weeks people brought blankets, dishes, clothes, and food to help out. They also helped to build a new house for Anita and a hooghan for Tom and Eleanor. . . .

They went up to Toadlena [about twenty miles away] to a lady Anglo missionary whom Eva knew and had the casket made, just out of boards. Then they just gathered up ashes and other remains of the body and put them in the box. They also bought clothes and blankets to put in it. They buried the body over the hill (relatively near the old residence group). Eva said they also shot the horse that Frank used to ride all the time. [December 7, 1965]

When Carole was telling me about her Utah experiences, she remembered that her uncle had died. "And that week, I guess they called my mom, or my mom called up there when Frank . . ."

"Oh," I interjected, "You weren't here when he died?"

"No. No," Carole replied. "But I recall, you know, that they were all . . . having a great ol' time at the time that the house started [on fire].

"But I understand, you know, they were saying that he . . . he was drinking, and some of them . . . like Leonard Sandman was drinkin' also at the time. He [Frank] tipped over the kerosene lamp. And the only person that was in there with him was his daughter. . . . Elizabeth was young at the time, 'bout four or five. And I guess the only thing he said to her was, 'Run out. Get out' while he was tryin' to find his way out through the door, I guess. . . . I think he was pretty drunk at the time. He didn't make it out. That's what they were telling me when I came back. And when I came back people didn't live over here. See, I left when people were over here, against this hill—real nice horse corral and houses and everything.

"See, what had happened was there was a two connection of a house. . . . OK on this side that's where Leonard Sandman used to [live]. It was two houses that were built together. On that side that's where Anita used to live, that was her kitchen and then just a little ways from there, that's where that hooghan [was] . . . the one that my uncle burned in. It was one of those they call it a male hooghan.[31] . . . That was [what] he was in. And then a little ways from there maybe like just a walking distance, that's where Eleanor had a one big house, just like this one here—a one-room house. People used to live there when I left.

"So, when I came back from Utah, things were a little bit different then they used to be. People used to tell 'em, 'You can't live over there.' Everybody else just moved across [to the other side of the highway]. And then over here . . . I guess Joe didn't wanna move this house. He just wanted to stay here . . . so that's how we stayed. We were a little distance from where those people were, see? So, we stayed to where they used to say, 'It's gonna affect you guys or something later in the future' . . . but it hasn't affected anybody yet."

I asked if Carole's mom had telephoned her in Utah and asked her to come back after her uncle died. "Yeah," she replied, "But then I couldn't have come back 'cause they figured that if I came back I wouldn't go back up there to go back to school. They figured that I might stay down here, see? Because of the way my mom was, they didn't want me to go, and they told me that the funeral was the next day. I think it was during the spring, I'm not sure. It was right after I went back up because that . . . that's during the fall. Sometimes during the winter, I think. I'm not sure because nowadays you have funeral for people, OK, just like the way we're planning it for Grandpa Virgil. Then, you know it was like they couldn't find any pieces [of him] left, except right here, they just found the bone. There's nothin'. So, where they predicted that he was laying . . . that was just nothin' but ashes, and my other uncle, Allen Sam, was the one that . . . up and made a casket for his brother out of lumber. And I guess that with the help of Mr. Fred Berland—'cause Fred Berland used to hang around with my uncle Frank, a lot . . . and I guess Mr. Berland was the one that provided a Pendleton blanket for him. They put that underneath, and what they did is they just bought him some clothing and they just put him away. And they put him away over on the other side of the hill.

"So they buried him. No, it was just a wooden box. Well, maybe he made [it] . . . by thinkin' about him. That's probably . . . how high, wide, and how small he made [it].

"I didn't come down for the funeral, or I didn't come back down for any memorial services. But, [at the] end of the school year, that's when I came back was during the summer. And that's when Old Grandmother [Mary Sandman] was telling me what happened to my uncle.

"I did go back the next fall. That was the second year when I was up there when my uncle died. But the third year I went back up and I went to school again up there." Finally, she returned after three years in Utah. Carole, in some respects, regrets not having stayed in Utah. "That time, I guess my mom didn't want me to go back, but I always think I should have stayed up there."

Carole's years in Utah and Frank's death represent the nadir of Eva's family life. Drinking had a very disorganizing effect on the family, bringing about Carole's movement away from the family, the death of Eva's father, and her brother. In the meantime, Eva had three young children, born in 1956, 1957, and 1960. Over the next few years, Eva herself became ill and had several experiences that allowed her to transform her life and pull herself out of a cycle of drinking and disorganization.

CHAPTER SIX

Eva's Conversion

Regaining a Place of Blessing

THE DECADE OF THE NINETEEN SIXTIES WAS A PERIOD OF transformation for Eva and her children, including Carole, who entered her teenage and young adult years. During this time, Eva converted to the Mormon religion and began attending meetings of the Native American Church or Peyote religion. She added these religious traditions to her own traditional Navajo beliefs and continued to participate in Navajo healing ceremonies. She also gave up drinking. Carole attended a school in Durango, Colorado; the BIA boarding school at Fort Wingate, New Mexico; and the public high school in Shiprock, New Mexico. She interrupted her schooling twice: once to take care of her baby brother, Randy, when her mother was hospitalized with a pelvic infection, and later when she became pregnant with her first child. It was also in this decade that I got to know the family.[1] I carried out my dissertation field research in 1965–66 and lived with Eva for several months. By the end of the decade, Eva and Joe had also ended their relationship, and Joe had returned to live at his parents' residence group.

Drinking

During the late nineteen forties and fifties, the male members of Eva's family got more and more embroiled in drinking activities. Both Eva and her sister, Eleanor, became drinkers as well. Levy and Kunitz discuss Navajo drinking in terms of two patterns. The first, as noted earlier, is male peer-group binge drinking in public where large quantities of cheap wine or liquor are consumed and drinking continues until the participants pass out or the supply is exhausted (1974:75–76). The second is the consumption of alcohol during family and extended-kin-group parties. Levy and Kunitz argue that this pattern of bringing alcohol to the Reservation and the residence group to be consumed by family and kin was found among the wealthy, who often included nonkin who were employed as herders, to bring in the alcohol. Whereas many observers suggested that service in the armed forces led to Indian drinking, Levy and Kunitz see these patterns as well established before World War II. They hypothesize that their spread was related to the stress and demoralization of Stock Reduction and its attendant impoverishment. In their study of male drinkers from the Western Navajo Reservation conducted during the nineteen sixties, most of their interviewees drank before they entered the armed services. During the War, if they drank with Anglos, the Navajos were influenced by whites to drink more slowly, getting high but not grossly drunk or passing out (1974:125–26).

In their more recent study of what they call "Navajo drinking careers" (an individual's long-term trajectory with alcohol consumption), Kunitz and Levy argue that Navajo rates of cirrhosis, homicide, and suicide are similar to the surrounding Anglo-American population and that Navajos have adapted to a regional drinking culture (Kunitz and Levy 1994, chapter 8). Navajo women seem particularly influenced by their husbands and partners in terms of their drinking careers (McCloskey 2000). These topics—the potential impact of army experience, the well-established patterns of residence group parties and male binge drinking, and the impact of husbands on Navajo women's drinking—were subjects for debate during one of our interview sessions.

On July 17, 1994, when we were sitting on a blanket in the mountain area near Eva's second summer home, Eva, Carole, and I had a discussion about why drinking became so important. Carole explained, "I guess, see, the men that got involved together were servicemen. Those days people would constantly get together. I remember, there's always Squaw Dances, and a lot of events that went on. And that's how when they got together, it was more likely an introduction for the ladies to participate. And that was the reason why everybody just started drinking."

I agreed, trying to remember what I had read in Evon Vogt's study of Navajo veterans.[2] "You know other people that have done interviews with servicemen, back in the fifties, when they first came back. A lot of them learned to drink in the war. 'Cause they do that, that sort of binge drinking, when they go on leave. That's when you go out and get drunk for about four days, and then you come back again."

Eva, however, indicated that drinking was important in their kin network at an earlier period. "Probably not. This thing called drinking probably began long ago. We lived down below. We were children at that time when Wally was born. At that time, there was nothing wrong with my older brother. We didn't have any cars. He was very close to Fred Berland. They went everywhere together. His horses [Fred Berland's] were red-brown, beautiful, two of them. My older brother had a horse with spots and a brown horse. Then just as dawn settles, before the rooster crows, the two of them take their horses. Fred Berland would spend the night. And then they say, 'Let's go.' And they set out on down the road on horseback to Navajo Shopping Center [Łigai Yaa'áhí]. And then with each horse packed this high, they rode back pulling the horses behind. They called them 'white tops' [the bottles]. They didn't break easily; they piled them on the two horses and tied some on behind themselves and even loaded them inside their feeding bags. Whenever they got there [to town] they would load up the packs. From evening to twilight to darkness and night [they traveled]. Sometime during the night you would hear the 'ch'ishxiih' sound they [the horses] make with their nostrils, as they were riding the horses back. And a pot of coffee would be waiting for them. This is how those kids were raised, **those Sandman [kids]. They always go to** Łigai Yaa'áhí—**Navajo Shopping Center. They used to get the liquor from there, on horseback. . . . If you want the wine, a pint for eight dollars. . . . This is how the children were raised."**[3]

Carole told me about her family's involvement in bootlegging when she was a young girl, perhaps during the summers when she was home from placement in Utah in the late nineteen fifties. Her aunt Eleanor and other members of the family traveled to Gallup, New Mexico, to buy liquor and then resell it in the Sheep Springs area. By this time, Eleanor and Tom had access to a car or pickup and the fifty-mile journey was not so arduous and time-consuming. "We lived there [in summer, on the mountain at Na'aldzisí]. And then fortunately when it was time for them to go to Gallup, it was a hassle. We had to think about what's going to happen. We were scared at the time when, we were little kids then. Well, everybody else, they got into drinking. And they were drinking most of the time. And there were always fights, to where we end up sleeping in the sheep corral. That's how we were brought up. And Ben Bimá, she was a very good alcoholic, too. Well, at the time as far as I remember, my aunt Eleanor and Tom, they were selling liquor. One time they had me in charge of selling liquor to people that came—me and Ethel at the time, we were teenagers. We ran out [of wine]. I'll never forget that time. They went to town to get some more, but we ran out over here. And Ethel told me to write a sign saying 'No More Wine.' And we did. We put up a sign. You turn off up here. It says 'No More Wine' on that. And when the people came back, my aunt, and Tom—they were really mad at us. Saying, 'Well, you guys shouldn't put up that sign!' in Navajo. And I thought, well, you were telling us to take care of the wine, so we ran out. And there's no choice, just to put up that sign saying 'No More Wine.' And I always think about that, at times. Very funny."[4] Carole laughed a great deal about this incident, which showed how naive she and Ethel had been in drawing attention to the illegal operation.

Carole went on to discuss the price of the cheap, fortified wine called Garden Deluxe or GD, which was about two dollars a pint. They would buy twenty-four bottles of wine at some lower price, "And sell it for two dollars out here. They've been into the wine business for so long, my aunt and Tom. More like I think that's how they raised their kids."

Giving Up Drinking

Sometime in the late nineteen fifties or early sixties Eva stopped drinking thanks to three interconnected influences: (1) her clan sister

Helen Berland; (2) her contact with the Mormon Church and particularly Harrison, her clan relative, and another role model; and (3) her involvement in the Native American Church.

Helen Berland was the daughter of a wealthy family. Since her clan is considered related to the Dziłtł'ahnii clan, Helen was Eva's sister. When I knew Helen, she was married to Fred Berland whose history of bootlegging was just recounted by Eva. She and Fred were sober pillars of the community who had a large sheep herd and lived near a large wash east of the Sheep Springs Trading Post in the winter. In the summer, they moved up on the top of the mountains where they had an extended grazing area and access to a lake known locally as Berland Lake. Helen was Chapter treasurer.

Eva explained that Helen, who was about ten years older than Eva, played the role of a mentor and elder. **"I think about myself—nobody told me to stop drinking. It's up to me, and I just quit. And one time I was going around with my sister, Helen Berland. She taught me a lot. And I'll go around, have a meeting with them, not to do this bad thing.** There is nothing wrong with living good and being a good woman. **I stand for it. I remember my sister. She loves me; she just talked to me. And she brings me food and something. And she dresses clean. And I look at her, and I should do like that. So I start doing it, to the rest of my life over here. And I still remember her name. My sister. I love her with all my heart.** The words that she spoke to me . . . **I still remember it. She talked to me, and nobody talked like that to me. Especially my brother and my sister.**

"I still remember what she said to me. 'You won't be laughed at; live good, and it is good to tell other people,' she said to me. **I still remember what she told me. Yeah, 'when you need a drink** . . . if you keep drinking, **you're not gonna last long.'** And 'it's a dirty thing. Everybody will be talking, criticize you when you drink.' She said this to me and because of that I **just stop. I was sick and I tried my best.** At first it took me four days, then a week, a month, then a year. **I just quit thinking about drinking. I don't want to take it, that stuff in front of me, anymore.** It is good and so far I teach my children. **I talked to my grandkids and my kids."**

About the same time, Eva began attending the local Mormon

Church meetings. She mentioned a Christian Reformed missionary named Mr. Cobbis, but then focused on the important role of Harrison Watchman, a member of her father's clan and thus someone she called "my son."

"He's still Gaamálii [Mormon]. **He used to teach us in Sunday school, Harrison.** So it is **good. They make a living by LDS, too. In the LDS so many white people know me, too. I go to the conference.** I was told to teach. **I go with two sisters and teach the people around Sheep Springs. One time we had so many people attending the church.** Many used to gather. **There were two sisters—an accident; they both got killed. I used to go to houses with them . . . I'm an interpreter. I follow them and teach the people. And I got a blessing to teach."**

Also in this period she began going to Native American Church meetings through the encouragement of Helen and Lee Joe. Helen was the mother of Lena Denetclaw who, in the nineteen sixties, lived less than one quarter-mile behind Eva. Lena, her husband Kevin, and eight children lived in the refurbished and much-expanded house that Helen and Lena's father had built near the neighborhood fields and irrigation project. The Native American Church, or Peyote Church as it was often called in the nineteen sixties, is what David Aberle calls a "revitalization movement." The religion involves an all-night ritual meeting where drumming, songs, prayers, and the eating of the peyote bud are all forms of communion with God. The ritual is conducted by a Road Chief or Roadman who sits along with the Cedar Chief and Drummer Chief in front of a crescent shaped altar that holds the Chief Peyote. The Navajo call peyote "medicine," and the purpose of a peyote meeting is often to cure illness. Meetings are also held to promote future blessings (for a newly married couple, students returning to school, a child or adult having a birthday). They can also avert evil or clear up rifts in human relationships. In addition to singing and drumming, the ritual high points of the meeting include the lighting and passing of ceremonial cigarettes during which prayers are said, the joint eating of peyote at various points, the drinking of water together at midnight and early morning, and the ceremonial breakfast after dawn (Aberle 1991:11).

Eva's Illness

Eva's interest in both of these religions was related to a series of illnesses and difficulties she experienced over a period of at least four years, beginning with the time when she was pregnant with her youngest son, Randy, who was born in 1963. When I was interviewing Carole about her life history in December 1994, Eva entered the room and I told her that we had been discussing her illness. Carole had mentioned that it all started with a car accident. Carole prompted her mother, "Remember you wrecked the car on the way down the mountain when you were with my grandmother [Shoemaker's Wife]?" she said in Navajo to her mother. **"When she was carrying the baby. . . . When Randy was in her tummy,"** Carole turned to me to explain. Again, in Navajo, she asked her mother to recall her experiences, "Remember they told you that something was wrong because of it and Randy?" She had a fractured pelvis bone.

Eva continued to explain the situation in Navajo, "I was injured for only a short time from the car. Then they cut me right here, and it became infected, but I recovered from that right away. Then later on I became ill. . . . And then Randy was still a baby and during that time, I became ill again, but this side was well. . . . **I'm all right on this side when I went in the hospital, and I don't get well, and the medicine man comes to me. I don't get well."**[5]

Carole went on to explain, "After the car accident, after Randy was born, it got infected. I guess they found out that she had an infected pelvic bone. And she went through surgery. And then after the surgery, she got better. She started walking again. And then she ended up in the hospital and that's where she got surgery was in Shiprock at the PHS [Public Health Service Hospital]."

Carole continued, "When Randy was born they told me that they couldn't leave Randy with my mom at the hospital. So, you know, the social service they came looking for me, and I got caught in between taking care of the baby and watching over Randy. And that was another reason why I was pulled out of my high school year. I would have graduated and everything and been in a better position. But, that was the end of it. Then after taking care of my mom for maybe like three years after she was sick, I lost interest in going back to school. But that was when I was in the boarding school. That's when I got pulled out because the social service went up there to Fort Wingate and told me I had to council with them. And they told me that I had to go home due to mother being ill."

When Carole looked after Randy, Shoemaker's Wife was staying with the family.

"I remember when her and I used to take care of Randy. Of course at that time Randy was a little baby, and we didn't have a cradleboard yet for him. And at night I used to sleep on a skinny bed. That was the only bed I had. And I used to have Randy lay inside [against] the wall in the middle of the night; she [Shoemaker's Wife] would get up, and she would build a fire for us. She would constantly keep the fire going because she was always afraid that the baby might be cold, and that was the time when my mom was in the hospital. She would get up and build a fire for us, and Grandma [Sandman] would lie on the other side, too. We all used to stay together. And Joe wasn't with us. And middle of the night, she used to wake up and she used to say, 'Where are you?' I would hear every night, 'Baby,' she used to say, 'Where are you, are you laying on the baby?' It was like for me squishing the baby or something like that, and it was always something it used to wake us up. And Randy was a very good ol' little boy that I remember. I never had any problem with him."

Carole described all of the activities that occupied her time when she was caring for Randy and ultimately kept her out of school. "And at time I used to take him back to the clinic for his appointment and it was always . . . I would always catch rides with Lena [Denetclaw, Eva's neighbor]. And we used to take the baby back to the clinic. People would look at me and say, 'Gol' . . . she's so young, she has a baby.' And here this lady, I was sitting by her, and she look[ed] at me and said, 'Is that your baby?' And I said, 'No, my baby brother.' She looked at me, because they thought Randy was actually my own.

"He'd gotten big, and at the time when he was like a year old, instead of him calling my mom 'Mommy,' he used to cry after me, he used to call me 'Mommy.' I tried to tell him, 'Nope, you're my brother,' but yet still, he used to call me 'Mom.' We had cloth Pampers at that time, cloth diapers, and I was always, constantly busy. We never had running water either, nothing. I had to bring water, fix food for the boys when they came home from school. But, of course, at that time it was always Timothy and Pro [the two oldest sons]. I had to tend them, too. I had to tend Rudy, too. Well, Rudy was more my grandmother's baby, that was my grandma [Sandman]. And he would sleep with my grandmother on the sheepskin. They all did, they used to sleep by Grandma."

Eva's Early Drinking Experiences

When I began living at Eva's house in November 1965, she told me about meeting Joe and revealed that she and Joe used to drink.

> They used to run off to Gallup and she didn't take care of the kids. They had no car, no nice things at that time. They spent all their money on drinking. Eleanor, her sister, had been going to Peyote Church and urged her sister to go. Eva didn't want to go at first; she was scared. One time they finally went, however, and have been going since. Eva explained that peyote wasn't like drinking, like people said. You drank only a little of that stuff (peyote tea) and it didn't make you drunk. It was nice. They prayed for good things at that Peyote Church: for your family, the car, good health. Eva later explained to me that the Peyote Church is held when someone is sick, or when they have bad dreams, or something goes wrong. [Field notes, December 1, 1965][6]

Although by 1965 Eva and Joe were not drinking, there were other relatives that still engaged in the binge drinking pattern that is characteristically Navajo. On one of my first evenings at Sheep Springs,

> there was a knock on the door and Ruda, Eva's third son who was six years old at the time, opened it to let in a very drunk Navajo. He talked in English, which was badly garbled since he could hardly enunciate. Eva shut the door to the back room and just stood in the corner. The *'adláanii* (drunk person) was muttering something about coming for

> the keys. Eva soon suggested that we go over to Pauline's—Frank Sandman's eldest daughter's home. She said I should climb out the back window and get the car started when she went in and picked up the children—Ruda the six-year-old, and Randy the two-year-old. The other two children were already at Pauline's. I made it out the window (with Eva's help) and soon she came with the kids. The drunk stumbled out the front door, so Eva told Shoemaker's Wife to shut the door and then she came to get in the car. [Field notes, December 2, 1965]

We drove over to Pauline's and stayed a half-hour with the kids, Pauline's younger brother, and Eva's mother. Sometime during this period I began to realize that the drunk was Eva's brother, Grant, who lived in a little house about a hundred yards behind Eva's. We laughed as Eva retold the story of Rudy saying stoutly to his uncle, "Go home, go to sleep, or I'll call the police on you." Later Eva told me that Grant was the only drunk around. The incident conformed to the pattern of Navajo drinking I was beginning to see. The Navajo women I lived with protected me from Navajo men (most of them older, but also some nearer to my age) who had been drinking and tended to keep me away from situations where drinking was taking place. Often this was a close relative whose identity I did not always know at first. At the time I did not drink, and I did not want to be associated with either buying wine or liquor for Navajos or dealing with them when they had too much to drink. Navajos seemed not to want to expose Anglos to Navajo drinking behavior given both their sense of Anglo disapproval and their own notions that drinking was not a good thing. The pattern worked well for both sides.

I was sometimes implicated in drinking, anyway. I learned about a week after my first experience with Grant that members of the family I lived with during the fall months had been involved in a drinking binge one Thursday just after I had moved over to Eva's. One of the wives had gotten mad and broken the headlights and taillights on the pickup. Her husband retaliated by kicking her four or five times and hitting her on the head. The father in the residence group had been drinking at a Navajo ceremony around the same time and had spent the night in jail in Shiprock, after being arrested by the Navajo police. This family had been careful not to drink during the periods I stayed in their residence group, but apparently drank when I was away. Around Christmastime, I heard from the trader that there were stories going around that I had been bootlegging for them—taking family members to Gallup so they could purchase wine and resell it on the Reservation at a profit. Given the fact that many of the women, including most who attended Native American Church meetings and those I later came to know as members of the Pentecostal Church, did not approve of drinking, I felt that distancing myself from any drinking whatsoever was essential to the success of my field research.

Eva told me that she started drinking one time at a Squaw Dance (Enemy Way) when one of her boyfriends gave her a drink.

> I asked her what "green gin" was [*tó diłhił dootł'izhí*, blue/green dark water; "dark water" is the word used for whiskey or any kind of hard liquor]. Eva started telling me about the first time she'd ever had any. She said that she was in town with Joe and that she bought a small bottle and drank that in town. Then Joe bought a quart of wine and a larger bottle of gin for Eva, and they rode home on the bus with the bottles in their pockets. She drank the whole second bottle, and she said it really made her sick. The room was spinning around. Eva said that she didn't used to think about her kids, how to make a good living, but would just go into town with Joe and go into the bars and drink. She said she used to use the stuff—all kinds—wine, green gin, etc., but now that she goes to Peyote Church, she doesn't use it any more. [Field notes, December 10, 1965]

Later that day, I was helping Eva finish the top part of her rug, weaving the last inch or so with a long needle rather than slipping the threads through the shed. While we were working, Eva told me that Joe used to "run around" with Eva Tso Bryan (the wife in the family whose winter home I had borrowed the previous summer). "Eva said Joe ran away from her one time, and that while he was gone, he stayed over with Eva Tso, both in a perpetual state of drunkenness. When Joe came back, Eva told him he could go stay with Eva Tso and marry her, but Joe said he didn't want to, so she took him back" (Field notes, December 10, 1965).

Joe was in Omaha during the fall of 1965, working on the railroad. On December 12, Eva and Louise Sandman (Joe's sister and Leonard Sandman's wife) stopped by the trading post. Louise put in a call to her husband in Omaha and then Joe called back on the trading post phone. He had sent $120: $100 to the trader (Evan Lewis) and $20 to Eva, both by money order (Field notes, December 12, 1965). This was a fairly typical arrangement, although sometimes the trader took part of Eva's money to pay the trading post bill, since Eva bought groceries at the store on credit. Joe said he might not be back in Sheep Springs until January 15, especially if it did not snow in Omaha and they could still work on track repair and maintenance. Joe told Eva not to run up the bill and to take care of his mom. Eva reported that he often told her such things, that she should work hard, finish her rug, and not be lazy. Also, she was not supposed to loan their car to anyone (Field notes, December 15, 1965).

With all this information about Joe, I was interested to meet him and got my chance sooner than I had expected. When I returned to Sheep Springs after spending Christmas with my family in Denver, I found Joe had arrived home on December 30. When I first arrived Joe came out the door, but quickly disappeared around the back of the house where he was fixing his car. Eva, Carole, and the four boys welcomed me in for some chicken Eva had purchased at the Two Grey Hills Trading Post.

> Joe stayed conspicuously absent from the house until evening, when he came in and shook hands, and sat and listened while I played the peyote songs (one I had previously recorded over at Eleanor's house) for the family.[7] Eva said that if I was scared of Joe, I could sleep on the bed in the outside room. I said, "Whatever you want," and even though Carole suggested I sleep on her bed after she left (in the same room with Eva, Joe, and the kids), Eva has seen to it that I have stayed in the outside room, each night. [Field notes, January 4, 1966][8]

FIGURE 6.1 The Sheep Springs Trading Post in 1965 where Eva and Joe had an account, and did their shopping and laundry.

PHOTOGRAPH BY AUTHOR.

FIGURE 6.2 Eva weaving a rug during 1965.

PHOTOGRAPH BY AUTHOR.

FIGURE 6.3 Eva cooking on the woodstove inside her two-room home in 1965.
PHOTOGRAPH BY AUTHOR.

FIGURE 6.4 Eva, Grandma Sandman, Timothy, Randa, and Rudy. Randy, the two-year-old, is hiding behind the kitten he is holding, 1965.
PHOTOGRAPH BY AUTHOR.

Joe was a pleasant, round-faced man with dark eyes and a warm smile. He spoke good English and was always willing to joke and tell stories. He had a lot of experience in the white world, both in terms of being in the army and working on the railroad. Joe spoke a little German, a language I spoke, having spent nine months in Germany when I was an undergraduate. We often exchanged phrases like *Danke schön* (thank you) and *Guten Tag* (good day) at the beginning of a conversation. During breakfast the next morning, Joe broke the ice and started telling me how good life on the Reservation was. "In the cities you had to pay for everything, but out here things were free. You could come and go as you pleased." He explained to me that Navajos eat anything for breakfast. He also told me that he had been

FIGURE 6.5 Eva with her children, 2006.
PHOTOGRAPH BY MARGARET RANDALL.

in Italy and Germany during the war—he had been in Sicily, Leipzig, and Berlin. A little later on in the conversation, Joe gave me a list of Navajo swear words, "bear," "coyote," "snake," and "ghost," rather than words like "damn" and "hell," which are used in English.[9] We continued to talk about the various work projects taking place through the Chapter: house construction that employed a crew of men and weaving that employed a number of women. The conversation ended when Joe and Eva had to leave to take Carole back to boarding school at Fort Wingate after her long Christmas holiday.

Joe at the time was not drinking (in my presence at least), but there were a number of occasions where he was with kinsmen or community members who were. The first incident happened one Thursday when Eva and Joe took Randy to Gallup to see a doctor. They also took along Joe's father, Navajo Slim, and Joe's daughter from his first marriage, Emma. My field notes describe Emma, who had been in the state penitentiary for women, as "a hard looking cookie." While Eva was at the Gallup Community Center, Joe and his relatives went shopping and bought some whiskey. Joe thought they should leave town. Emma and Navajo Slim got drunk. "All the way home, Emma kept offering her father some whiskey, but Joe refused. Emma's comment: 'I sure don't like that peyote.' Eva was rather provoked at the whole situation and she was rather mad at Joe because these were his relatives" (Field notes, January 13, 1966).

One Saturday about ten days later, I arrived at Eva's after breakfast so we could attend a ceremony for Ben Watchman's daughter. Joe could not get their green and white station wagon started.

> Eva was mad at him for going to Gallup on Friday. He had taken several men to town, including James Peter, a neighbor who stopped by to ask for a ride. They had brought back a whole case of wine and were drinking. Though Joe did not take part, he was gone for the whole day, and Eva felt that he was aiding and abetting their drinking. This was the reason they were now having trouble with the car, Eva explained. You weren't supposed to have anything to do with drinking if you go to the Peyote Church, and Joe had gone against this proscription. [Field notes, January 22, 1966]

Three Religious Traditions

During January 1966, I moved over to Lena and Kenneth Denetclaw's house, about a hundred yards behind Eva's and Joe's home. Since Lena was the same clan as Joe, they were sister and brother, and since Kenneth (who did not come from Sheep Springs) was born for Eva's clan (i.e., their fathers were both Tł'ááshchí'í), they were also brother and sister. Over the next few months, I often visited Eva and had the opportunity to attend Navajo sings, peyote meetings, and sometimes Mormon Church services with them. During these months, I moved into a world where all three religious traditions were drawn upon to ensure well-being (a state of hózhǫ́ or blessing). It was during this period that I began to see how the three religious traditions were woven together in Eva's life.

One Thursday in January 1966, for example, Eva and I had attended a portion of the five-day ceremony to watch the hataałii prepare a sandpainting and then returned on Saturday during preparations for the fifth and final night.[10] Joe was among those who helped the hataałii, and he arrived late at the Saturday morning portion of the ritual, staying outside the ceremonial hooghan. Later that evening, I attended an all-night Native American Church meeting at Nelson Watchman's house, across the road from Eva's. Nelson had been a Roadman (Nahałáhí) for five years at that time. This was the first meeting that I had attended, and it introduced me to the meaning of the peyote ceremony including the singing, prayers, and curative powers of the ritual.

> By the time we arrived the drum was already strung and the crescent-shaped altar was formed to the west of the fire. The Roadman was trying out the drum when we entered. (Eva had previously gone in and asked if it was all right for me to attend.) Several people were in the [living] room of the house [a two-room structure]. Sheep pelts and blankets were placed around the wall for people to sit on. Soon the Nahałáhí asked me who I was, what I was doing there, etc. Joe interpreted as I got lost in the Navajo almost immediately. Eva had already said a few things about me; that I was learning Navajo, that I came from Denver. I explained that

I was an anthropologist, learning Navajo, and wanted to learn about all parts of Navajo life. I had been to other kinds of ceremonies and wanted to find out about the peyote way, too. The Nahałáhí asked if I belonged to any kind of religion. I said that my folks did, but that I went to lots of kinds of churches. Joe gave me a long explanation of praying, how I should pray in the peyote meeting. He said I should take some of the medicine (the Nahałáhí had said this, too), but not too much. [Field notes, January 22, 1966]

The next morning after I took Joe and Eva home, Joe and I talked about peyote:

He said I shouldn't take too much at first, just a little each time, until it begins to work on you. I asked what happens when it works on somebody. Joe replied that it makes you feel kind of "happy," but that it's not like being drunk, since peyote isn't like alcohol or a drug. It's just a cactus. Joe said you have to stay awake all night, and not go to sleep, but concentrate. Sometimes, you hear a voice and recognize it, so that's why you shouldn't sleep. Joe said that they make the medicine by boiling the peyote, but that some people eat one or two buds. Eva showed me a couple of peyote buds that she had in her purse. Joe indicated that if you carried one or two of these in your purse it would give you good luck. Joe said that one reason peyote wasn't like alcohol is that you always know what you are doing, even when it is working on you, not like drinking, when you don't know what you are doing. Joe said that you should pray for yourself, if you are going to school, pray that you stay in school. [Field notes, January 23, 1966]

When I arrived back over at their house, Kenneth amplified Joe's comments and told me about his own experience. I said I hadn't taken too much peyote since I did not want to get sick (which is a common reaction). "Kenneth said that the first time he took it, he got sick and vomited. 'That was the peyote trying to clean me out,' he said. He said you should pray for things in front of you, like the future, God, and Jesus Christ, and not think about the past and all the bad things in back of you. Then the peyote will work for you, and not against you" (Field notes, January 23, 1966).

The previous Sunday I had been to the Mormon Church service, which was conducted by two young missionaries, or elders, as they were known in the LDS church. They lived in a trailer by the trading post and held Sunday services in the Chapter House.[11] That particular Sunday Eva was not in church (since she and Joe had attended an all-night peyote meeting that Saturday), but I attended with Kenneth Denetclaw and one of his sons.

> We arrived at the Chapter House to find that the elders were not there, but had obviously brought a truckload of people from the sage-covered hills above the Chapter House. By the time the church started, there were probably fifteen adults in the front end of the Chapter House, and an equal number of children. The elders were delayed in starting church since their truck had a flat tire during one of their trips. Once they had arrived the elders asked Kenneth to give the opening prayer, which he did after a hymn, sung in English from Mormon hymn books and led by the blond Elder Round. There was another hymn and then one of the elders took three of the children out to the other part of the Chapter House for Sunday School, while the second elder preached the sermon. The topic of the sermon was "unselfishness," one of a series of sermons on things to practice in order to lead the "good life." I doubt seriously if anyone in the room, except Kenneth, understood the whole sermon. The elder seemed a bit nervous (somewhat due to my presence?), and the delivery was choppy; however, he quoted the bible several times, told stories from the life of Jesus, presented some teachings of Joseph Smith, and even gave an example about the Vietnam war—all stating in one way or another that we should practice unselfishness and charity, even though this may be contrary to our nature. Halfway through, the elder asked Kenneth to translate the sermon, so Kenneth dutifully

took notes. From what I understood and what he told me later, he tried to explain what the words *unselfishness* and *charity* meant since there is no equivalent in Navajo. Kenneth said that they meant "kindness" (*hojooba'* or *'á'áhwiinít'í*) and helping each other (*'áłká'ánijílwo'*). He also mentioned Joseph Smith (though I don't know what he said) and said that the United States was trying to stop the War in Vietnam, but wasn't getting anywhere. After this we sang another song and the elders passed the sacrament—bread and water—with prayers in-between. A few announcements were made: MIA, the youth group, would meet on Wednesday; the Relief Society, the women's group, would meet in Harrison Johnson's trailer on Monday to make shirts; Seminary would be on Friday at Toadlena. A closing prayer was offered in Navajo by one of the elders. Apparently, the elders could pray in Navajo, but didn't have enough fluency to deliver sermons in the language. [Field notes, January 16, 1966]

Anglo Drinking

The differences between Navajo and Anglo drinking were brought home to me during early spring 1966 when my aunt (my mother's sister) died suddenly of a heart attack. She was only fifty-four years old. My stepfather, Walter Johnson, stepped into the breach during funeral preparations and handled many of the details; however, at some point in the ceremony he had been slighted (and treated as an outsider by the family). During the reception afterward, he had gone off in a huff, drinking heavily and pouting, disappearing from the scene and thus creating great disruption. I began to notice that drinking was having a very disturbing effect on our family.

Our family, like many other middle-class families in the United States, participated in the ritual of a cocktail hour. Every weekday morning, my father took the bus downtown from our East Denver neighborhood and returned home about 5:30 or 6:00 p.m. He and my mother would have a "highball," a shot glass of bourbon and some water before dinner. Both my parents and my grandparents had a "bar" in the living room, or in my grandparents' case, in a small room adjoining the living room. This was usually a walnut or mahogany veneer cabinet that, when closed, looked like a small buffet. The top, however, would open out to reveal space for mixing drinks, using the liquor stored in the closed shelves below. There were holders for glasses, a place for cocktail napkins and stir sticks, and room for the metal ice bucket. When company came (such as my grandfather, my aunt or uncle, or family friends), this was where drinks were mixed and served. My grandfather drank scotch and soda, while my father preferred bourbon. My mother originally drank scotch but eventually switched over to bourbon.

The family never drank wine or other liquor during dinner and did not drink after dinner. Middle-class, white drinking patterns contrasted strongly with those of the Navajo. One never drank until drunk and passed out. One was supposed to sip a drink and make it last for a long time, never gulping it down. Conversing and relaxing were very much part of the ambiance that the family tried to create. In my household, however, two "stiff" drinks before dinner must have changed the tone and content of interactions, something I was rarely aware of during my childhood. I can remember that on occasions when we visited my grandparents, we would just sit in the smaller music room, each adult with their drink, while we kids found something to do. On more formal occasions, guests would be seated on the sofa and chairs in the much larger living room (dominated by a large fireplace at one end and a grand piano at the other). In the summer we sat out on the patio by the garage, often while my father and grandfather cooked steaks on the grill.

The unspoken rule was not to acknowledge that drinking had any impact on one's speech or behavior. I remember a Christmas Eve gathering at our house where we were all sitting around the living room with a brightly decorated tree, possibly waiting until it was time to attend the Christmas Eve service at our church. My aunt was perched on a dining room chair placed just in front of our picture window, framed with a flower box and trellis adorned with ivy leaves. She fell off the chair and almost into the green plants. It suddenly occurred to me that she had had too much to drink. Many years later in 1968, after my graduation from Harvard, my mother, my grandparents, my great-aunt, and my sister and I drove out to

Cape Cod for a weekend vacation. We stayed in a motel and were having our cocktail hour in one of the rooms, seated on the bed and several of the chairs. I was drinking a scotch and water in honor of the occasion. As the conversation went on, I realized that everyone's voices were getting louder, that an argument was beginning to take shape, and that I myself was feeling more vehement and at the same time less articulate. It dawned on me that the alcohol was having an impact on how I expressed myself, the tone of my voice, and the growing combativeness of the conversation. I thought to myself, well, all these years, the arguments over dinner, the family tensions surrounding the behavior or values of family members, all were fed by the alcohol. Only when I saw it affecting my own behavior did I understand the power of something that the family never discussed.

In the years after my aunt's death, my uncle's drinking problems became more apparent. He quit coming into work at the law office he used as part of my grandfather's business. He was continually "sick," although there were rumors that it was the drinking and not a physical illness that was keeping him at home. I am not sure that anyone made efforts to get his alcoholism treated or to get him to join Alcoholics Anonymous. I suspect he was not willing to admit that he was an alcoholic. I was not in Denver during those years and was not around to see the visible signs of his deterioration. He died in the nineteen seventies. While my uncle seemed to be a secret drinker, my stepfather's drinking was much more disruptive (partly because I was often around when it happened or heard about it from my mother). Walter was much more uncomfortable with our family and in social situations dominated by those who had more education and sophistication. So on trips or at dinners with the family or my mother's friends, he would drink heavily and then get angry with someone. Then he would leave the room and go off to sulk someplace. If we were at home he would usually slink downstairs to the basement laundry room. His behavior was clearly breaking the cultural rule that one should drink, but not show any outward signs of intoxication.

Alcohol has had a negative impact on both Eva's family and my own. Her brother died in a fire while drunk. My uncle died a slow death from alcoholism. Her second husband Joe eventually died of heart failure, probably brought on by heavy drinking. My stepfather Walter's life may have been shortened by his drinking. Certainly, both Joe's and Walter's drinking had poisoned their relationships with their wives. Yet, alcoholism is a well-kept secret in my family, while the public character of Navajo drinking has only fueled white stereotypes about drunk Indians. Conversion to the Peyote religion and to Mormonism in Eva's case turned her into a nondrinker, while in our family the negative impact of alcohol has gone untreated. The way in which Eva wove together teachings from traditional Navajo religion, the Mormon Church, and the Native American Church gave her a powerful set of beliefs to cope with her own illnesses and difficulties.[12]

A Crisis in Eva's Health and in Her Life

During the year I was in Sheep Springs, Eva was in good health and Joe was home from January 1966 until the summer. After I returned to Boston and remained in the East to write my dissertation and take a job, first at the University of Rochester and later at Brown University, relationships in Eva's family deteriorated.

Eva looked back on her marriage. "And then I spent several years with him. He was drinking and I **got sick**. He never helped me, never. It was just me and my mother. My aunt Ben Bimá, she helped me. He did nothing and always ran off to **Gallup**. There was nothing for the children. There was hunger; there was no food **when I got sick**. Harrison Johnson, my clan father, he helped me . . . to buy groceries for the kids. At that time he worked at the **store** at Sheep Springs. . . . **So he was buying me potatoes**, lard, he bought everything for me. **Couple years**, yes, several years later, I became ill and I went to the **hospital**. **They don't know what, what's going on with me.** I went to the hospital. The **doctors** didn't know what was wrong with me. It will kill you, they told me. And afterward, for that reason I had all those sings and **Navajo traditional medicine men**—they prayed over me. He never helped me. And I . . . **Lee Joe and Helen Joe**, they helped me out. **'Fix the medicine, a whole bunch of it. Not just one thing**. A lot of it. **A whole bunch of it.' And I eat it all. Two**

days went by. **I don't know anything about what happened. I was up there. So the medicine told me**: 'Look at this,' it told me. Mother Earth is cracked open and it was revealed to me. **I saw clear about this much. There was a man, right there. I didn't know it. I didn't recognize** . . . I did not recognize him. Then again he repeated and said, **'I am going to tell you.** I am going to tell you. You have four sons and their father is killing you,' he told me. Go ahead and tell her. **He witchcraft me."**

In translating her mother's account, Carole and I tried to reconstruct when all of this might have happened. It is interesting to observe the differences between Eva's brief and intense version and Carole's much fuller account. First, she added a number of details to Eva's narrative of how Joe treated her. "And he would provide, you know, a little money and things like that, but when he comes back [from working on the railroad] he would talk about how it [the money] was being used. . . . He used to have a bill at the store and he would only get you a small amount. And after that, he started becoming very, very violent toward my mom. He started beating her up, and everything. On top of that, you know, she got really sick. To where she used to go to the hospital, and the doctor used to tell her that, 'just get ready for death, you're not going to live anymore.'"

Second, Carole outlined in more detail what had happened when Helen and Lee Joe had given her more peyote. In Navajo, peyote is called "medicine" (*'azee'*). As Aberle points out in his study conducted during the late nineteen forties and early fifties, most Navajos came to peyote meetings initially in order to be cured. Often the patient had tried other types of cures (e.g., Western medicine or traditional ceremonies), and after these failed, he or she came to the Native American Church to seek a solution. Many times, suspicion of witchcraft or the discovery that witchcraft had played a role in the illness was part of a patient's experience in the process of using peyote (Aberle 1966:183–87).

"I guess Lee Joe felt real sorry for us. And there wasn't anything [to be] done for my mom. And more likely . . . every medicine man that tried to help her wasn't working. So, he gave her all kinds of medicine, told her she needed to eat it all. He came over to the house and asked for her to be taken over there to their house, so that he was gonna help her. So what he did, is he put out all kinds of medicine for her. And, that's what happened." Eva stayed at Lee's and Helen's house for two nights and two days. Eva's family had built a hooghan across the road from their present home at Łitso Dah 'Ask'idí (Yellow Hills), and they took Eva there. She slept for two days.

Third, Carole's narrative included a compelling interpretation of the meaning of Eva's experiences. Carole continued, "We didn't know what was . . . I didn't know what was wrong with her. And, I guess that's the way it works. I guess the Lord was talking to her. Telling her all kinds of things . . . blessing her, a lot of things. And Lee Joe, the only thing he told me to do is put cedar on, for her. Every certain hour . . . and then, that she should be all healed by the next morning. So, we were still sleeping when she got up, early in the morning. She finally came to herself.

"Which is when we all got up. She just eventually started praying. It was amazing how the prayer started helping her. And I guess the Lord told her. That's the only way that she will survive, is with her prayers. And, I guess the Lord told her, 'Do you want to know who's doing this to you? Who's witchcrafting you?' And, the Lord told her, 'I'll show you who's doing it to you. Can you recognize him?' And she said the whole earth was cracked. . . . And way down, where the earth was cracked, that's where you can see the face.

"But she couldn't recognize who the face was. And it kept coming forward to her, and she still couldn't recognize him, who that person was. So finally the Lord told her, 'OK, let me tell you. Did you recognize that person?' And she told him, 'No.' And the Lord told her, 'Let me tell you. It's your four boys' father, that's who is doing this to you. He's trying to kill you.'

"And that's how . . . she felt real bad, and she started crying, and saying 'how could he do that to us.' And, from there on, she quit having feelings for him. And then she told him, he needs to go home—back to his mother and father. And then that one time, we had a real, great big argument with him—before he left—that, he needs to go back to his family, his mother . . . while his mother was still living. And he wanted to know why. And she didn't tell him why. And we had . . . we had a rattle, and we had a fan. And he broke that. He started acting big, 'cause we joined the Native

American Church. And it's not that he didn't understand. And my mother would pray and do a lot of things, the way the Lord told her to do it. And he didn't like it. He would just get mad about it. And that's how, you know, she escaped Joe."

Eva summed up her situation by saying, "After that time because of my power **I could make up my mind.** I wasn't born with it [this ability]. I did not fall out with it. **It's my own doing.** With this you have a mother and a father. **Nobody** can talk about us; it won't do any good. The harm that he did me, **I feel bad about that.** I never thought in my mind that he could do harm like that. . . . There are ugly things within him and he harms people with it, and women are more susceptible. It is called Prostitution Way ('Ajiłee Ba'áádjí). That is what he used against me and wrapped around me. That is why he harmed me. **Therefore I make up my mind.** I started going to what's called the **Native American Church. I never go back** and put my life in danger and be surrounded by it. The only firm step that I put forward, and to this day I am walking around this way. This way of walking around [this way of being] is the very thing I need. By it I will have power [strength], and I will lead my children to what is good. **To this day** my paternal and maternal grandchildren **I stand for it.** And then I talked to them and informed them there are vices that you do not produce."

Eva's words described her own personal feelings and responses, while Carole offered a more external description of how Eva broke off her relationship with Joe. "When Joe left, she said that she had to make up her mind, fortunately, 'cause they were never married. They just got together. And, there was no counseling at the time, when they were getting together to be married. And there was no marriage license involved either. Fortunately she just told him, 'Go back to your mom. You have a mother, and you have a father now.' And I guess, all this time he was being rude and mean, and he tried to do the best he could, in order for him to kill her. After she had her kids, she just decided that the best route for her was to get away from him. And, at the time when she saw him, he was completely dark, black . . . in her vision, when she saw him. And the day he died, that was how he left. He had that heart attack . . . took his life. He was like that; he was really dark. Dark blue.

"And she said now that she has her belief. She has the power of seeing. She doesn't want to continue living with him. So she went ahead and just quit living with him. And now that she has her power and belief that she never realized that he would hurt her the way he's been hurting her . . . by doing some evil things that he knew inside his system. She said that she wasn't his first wife anyway. I think she was his third one, when he passed away. The first wife was in Crownpoint [Smith Lake], and then there's another one in Pinedale. And then she makes it three."

The original diagnosis for this witchcraft had come from Nelson Watchman, who had been the Roadman at a meeting I had attended in January 1966. Carole explained his role. "At that time Nelson Watchman was the only Roadman that we had nearby, and he used to do all kinds of prayers for her. He used to tell her at the time that it was 'somebody else that you live with that is doing this to you.' She thought, oh no . . . it can't be. She kind of didn't believe Nelson. So finally when Nelson told her . . . she found that out herself after she took a lot of peyote, and the peyote told her, 'This is the person that's picking on you and you're not going to live very long.'"

Childhood Experiences that Caused Eva's Illness

There were other causes of Eva's illness as well, ones that needed to be treated through traditional Navajo ceremonies. "Then something was happening to my skin like it was burned. **I was feeling, burning, like my body was some funny."**

The burning and funny feeling was related to the time during her childhood when she had killed the porcupine and helped her older brother butcher it. "And then I butchered a porcupine. I shot the porcupine because he kept going into the garden, eating the corn. So I killed it, into its heart, in here. And then it fell off and I ran back home. Walter's father told me to drag it back.[13] **We built a fire outside and** I threw the porcupine in the fire. Its quills all burned off making a ch'ił, ch'ił, ch'ił sound."

In translating her mother's words, Carole explained, "After she got better, maybe like a year or something like that, she started feeling very funny. Something was burning on her body and she felt absolutely funny to where she couldn't stand going into this old house over here. And they had to build her a new hooghan across the road. And she used to feel better when we stayed over there. For every time she entered this house, something would start bothering her. And she said that up in the mountain when she was young she used live with my uncle Frank Sandman, and Frank Sandman told her to go up to the cornfield. She said that somebody's eating corn, and I guess she found out herself. She had a .22 gun, and she found out that it was a porcupine. So what she did is when the porcupine was sitting on top of a tree, she aimed at it, and she killed him right in the heart. She got him in the heart, and maybe that started effecting her because that's got something to do with the . . . with the Mountain Top Way Chant [Dziłk'ihjí]. . . . And she burned the poor porcupine. And that was what was starting to bother her and started affecting her system to where her heart would feel some way. They had all kinds of medicine men singing on her."

Then Eva told the story of how she had helped her father butcher a bear. "Then during the same time, my father shot a bear, and they butchered it, and I walked in the blood, and I was also holding the bear's hand as he butchered." As Carole said, "She was holding the bear's claws when my great-grandpa was butchering the bear. So now it started affecting her. That's why at times she would think that . . . having her finger crack here . . . like a blister. That's what's bothering her is the blister. I guess the bear's hand did blister. So she had to have a singing done on her, Dziłk'ihjí bik'ihojiitáál [Mountain Top Way]."

Eva then continued, "And so I had a sing. After that I was doing well. I was doing pretty good, and then I joined the peyote way. It is probably true that one gets things accomplished with these sings. And it is probably true that there are so many of these ceremonies going on, but from where I stand the one for me is the **peyote meeting**." As Carole translated, "Fortunately the only one that she relies on right now is peyote meetings and that's how she got better because through them . . . she got her blessings and after she ate a lot of that peyote, that medicine told her that this is what's bothering you."

Divorce and Recovery

The image of her vision stayed with Eva and provided her with a strong sense of what to do. "Well, he was trying to kill me also. **I found out in this peyote told me.** The earth cracked and it was opened up to me. It stood there like a person, but as a small dot. And then it told me to look at it. Recognize it. But I didn't recognize it. So then it told me. It is this person. It told me. 'He is going to kill you, but now you have to overcome his powers,' it told me. **'Nothing is going to happen.'** Then it butchered me; it took out my intestines and held it out to me. 'Look at this, there is nothing wrong with this, what was done to you,' it said to me. **And I don't want to go back to him.**

"After I saw him and I found out, I suddenly hated him so much. I told him to his face, 'Stay away and don't come here any more. I will make a living for my children by myself,' I said. And to this day, I am like this. I have made a living for them. And then he even went to **Shiprock** and filed a complaint against me. . . . A judgment was never made against me."

Eva had two curing ceremonies done for her. One was part of the Mountain Top Way, and another was the entire nine-night version of this same ceremony. The Mountain Top Way is performed for patients who are sick because of improper and dangerous contact with animals who live in the mountains. Disturbing, or in this case, killing the "in-standing-one" or inner spirit of the porcupine and bear was the cause of Eva's heart trouble. Also, Eva explained, "It was doing something to my thinking." Carole elaborated, "To burn [it], it's against our traditional [ways]. You know we can't throw porcupine into the fire, or we can't shoot a porcupine. That's got something to do with the . . . with the medicine man's singing in the Dziłk'ihjí/Mountain Top Way. I guess that actually it really made her sick. It more likely took her mind . . . blocked her mind."

"When it affects you, they say, you run off and you lose your mind," Eva explained. Carole expanded on her mother's thoughts, "I guess it . . . it blocks your mind out to where you just, you've just run up on the mountain. And that's what happened. She kept running out from us. . . . So then she found out through her own hand trembling that the only way she will get better is, there was a Fire

Dance [Mountain Top Way] way up at Twin Lakes in that area, and her hand trembling told her, 'You'll get better at that Twin Lakes [ceremony].' So, we had somebody haul her over there again for us. . . . They did a small ceremony. . . . They did it for her, and after that she got better." Sometime in the fall of 1967 or later, Eva had a full nine-night version of the Mountain Top Way done for her. In about 1993 or 1994, Eva considered doing another Mountain Top Way since the blisters on her hands had reappeared. She paid a portion of the fee to the singer who had conducted the ceremony thirty years before. He was a diabetic then and had to have kidney dialysis every few days, making it difficult for him to perform a ceremony. Yet he and his apprentice were willing to help Eva in this case. It was difficult, however, to raise the rest of the $400 fee and accumulate the cash necessary to purchase several hundred dollars in gifts and several sheep for the dancers who perform on the last night. In addition, support from a wide number of relatives was necessary in order to build a cooking shelter and obtain at least six sheep, potatoes, coffee, pop, and other food needed to feed everyone who attends the ceremony over a nine-day period. Finally, she abandoned the idea. "No I couldn't do it . . . it's too much. Nobody's going to help me out and so then I just gave up." In 1998, the singer died, which put the possibility of a future Mountain Top Way in limbo.

Diagnosing and Curing

After recovery from her illness, Eva began using traditional Navajo hand-trembling techniques, and she also utilized a number of diagnostic practices derived from the Native American Church. She began to pray for those who were sick and administer both peyote and herbal medicines. When I first asked Eva when she had started praying for people, she explained that she did not want to tell me much about her healing practices. "I will not tell you all there is to know about the ceremonies. I will just tell parts of it." Then she went on to give me a sense of how she had waited before beginning her healing practice. "It was about four years. It was me that said I should wait. I was told to help other Navajos with this. I was told that with this [ceremonial power] I was to help people on earth who are afflicted with problems, and that this was the way I was to be.[14] This judgment was made for me. **I said 'Yes.'** Then after I agreed, it took four years before my services were used and then after that it took several years before I began to help Navajos all over . . . from Tuba City, then to Kayenta, and then to Dził Ditł'oi, then to what is it called Montecello and Blanding, then Sweetwater, T'iis Názbąs [Teec Nos Pos], Fort Defiance, Gallup, Bread Springs. From all over, the people know of me and out Huerfano Mountain [Dził Ná'oodiłii] way. Like that I started to live in this way and to this day I continue to do so. It is truly inside me. Not just anyone put it inside me. It was the Holy One who blessed me like this. Accordingly I walk and live."

I traveled out to Sheep Springs with Valerie on the weekend of October 13–15, 1995 during the University of New Mexico fall break. It was a beautiful, sunny New Mexico fall weekend and on Saturday Eva took me up on top of the Chuska Mountains, near the old fire lookout, to gather herbs for her curing practice. The aspens were golden yellow, the Gambel oaks a burnt orange, and both stood out against the green of the ponderosa pines as we drove up the pass. Aaron (Carole's youngest son) and Ryan (Eva's grandson) played with sticks and occasionally helped Eva dig roots or collect the ponderosa pine needles. Following our herb-gathering trip I decided to ask Eva to tell me more about how she came to diagnose people's illnesses. So on this occasion, I said, "I know you may not want to say much about it, but maybe you could talk about that in a general way, just without giving away your sacred knowledge . . . just so I get a sense about helping everybody out."

Eva again explained to me that her curing powers came through her transformation from someone who drank, who did not take care of her children, and who was suffering from several illnesses, to someone who was healed through her participation in meetings, prayers, and ceremonies from three different traditions: Navajo sings, Native American Church meetings, and Mormon Church services. "In the past, well I was not a respectful person as I have told you before, but after I became ill, from then on, that which is sacred blessed me. There from a place that can't be seen, I was told of the kind of person that I should be. And after several months, maybe a year, was when I began to help others and to this day, this is my place in life. . . . And this medicine, I didn't just think about it, I didn't just happen upon it, it came to me in my dreams; I was told that it was all medicine and because of this, I believe my dream too. . . . Every single one of them, each one is medicine. . . . I respect every one of them."

Eva was concerned that medicines and herbs are now just being sold in local flea markets rather than gathered for a specific patient. "And now they are sold at the flea market . . . . From Navajo Community College, it was like that, a girl sat there selling it. She probably just picked it up from somewhere where they dig it up, but as my father used to say, you don't just pick up medicine in passing. It is dangerous to do so because of the person that you are picking it for, it is so that they will get well, this is the purpose for making the medicine. You give the plant hard goods [*nitł'iz*] and corn pollen [you make offerings]. And then you say a prayer for yourself and take corn pollen. You name the person you are collecting for, and then you may collect the plant. But these days you see them packaged and ground. Some of these medicines you cannot grind, nor can they be pounded. All you are to do is tear it into pieces, so that it will bring life back to the person. This is why it is, they say, so that it will fulfill the person back to himself. And one must not use a knife around these plants. This is what my father used to say; you commonly use a sharpened piece of wood. And you're not supposed to handle them very much."

Some of her first experiences with hand trembling dated back to the period when witchcraft was being sent in her direction. She decided not to use her powers of diagnosis, but rather, to wait. "It was just the hand trembling at first, and then it was me that said I wanted to wait. And then this thing that happened to me—what I am telling you about myself—after that was when people began to use my services.

"It was just like that, from the very beginning, when the ceremony was given to me. It was probably at that time, that I was made to help people. According to my way of thinking. . . . I was the one that decided to wait. . . . Well, when it is given to you in that way, then you can begin to use this blessing to help people at a young age, that is how it is."

Carole suggested that, in addition to Joe, several other men had been trying to harm Eva, including Ben Bimá's husband at the time. "And when she was sick, you know, all kinds of traditional doings were going for her and nothing got her better. And she used to get this hand trembling when Ben Watchman's stepdad was doing a prayer for her."

Eva explained that she was having a blackening (*'ant'eesh*) done, and, at that time, she started trembling. Carole continued her description. "And instead of him doing the rest of that, all she did was she just hit him like this, and I guess it was telling her that he's one of the persons that's trying to kill her. . . . The only person . . . the only person that knew that something like this was going on was Nelson Watchman, Grace Watchman's late husband. . . . And he used to tell her that [who's] doing [this] to you is . . . is eventually from the same bed, you know, from the person that you're sleeping with. . . . He's doing that to you. . . . And she didn't quite believe it." It was only after she took the peyote that Lee Joe had given her, and had her vision of the earth cracking open, that she believed Joe's role in trying to harm her. Eva said the hand trembling "just came to her. . . . From a place that cannot be seen, one is given this blessing to live on this earth."

CHAPTER SEVEN

Carole's Adolescence and Motherhood

CAROLE'S CHILDHOOD HAD BEEN DEEPLY AFFECTED BY EVA'S drinking, her illness, and her dramatic conversion. But when I met her in December 1965, she impressed me as a very "American" teenager, immersing herself in the world of new clothes, the latest hairdos, and potential boyfriends. She was also pulling away from her mother, beginning to be an autonomous adult. It was not until the next summer when she became a patient in a Navajo Enemy Way ceremony that I understood the important role that Navajo religion continued to play in her life.

When Carole was seventeen years old she attended the Bureau of Indian Affairs boarding school at Fort Wingate, about fifteen miles east of Gallup and thus more than an hour by car from Eva's house at Yellow Springs.[1] My first impressions of Carole were formed the Friday that Eva asked me to drive her to Fort Wingate to pick up Carole for a weekend at home.

> We arrived at Wingate around 3:30 and had to wait about half an hour for Carole. There was a Navajo Youth Conference going on, and the kids had not had classes Thursday and Friday. Instead they had been attending sessions along with 250 students from other Navajo schools off the reservation,

hearing speeches about education and discussing them. [Field notes, December 10, 1965]

That night there would be a school dance. BIA schools still discouraged the students from speaking Navajo and had no Navajo curriculum, but they had become less like military establishments and encouraged assimilation to American teen culture. Each school had football and basketball teams, and girls—who might become cheerleaders—paid a lot of attention to their clothing, hair, and makeup. Carole curled her hair with large rollers and wore it in a bouffant style. She wore dark-rimmed, black glasses in a more fashionable oblong shape than the dark-rimmed glasses I wore when I was driving. She was only in ninth grade although she was seventeen years of age, since she had missed several years of school taking care of Randy.

Like other American teenagers, Carole was beginning to test her independence and create a life of her own, much to the distress of Eva, who at Carole's age had already been in an arranged marriage for several years. Many of Carole's companions were other female relatives (for example, Eleanor's daughter Ethel) or young male kinsmen (such as Eleanor's son and her "brother" Paul K. Yazzie, with whom she had herded sheep as a girl, or Glenn, the son of Anita and Frank Sandman). The tension between Eva's desire to have Carole stay at home and Carole's wish for autonomy has been a consistent theme for more than forty years. Even as a teenager, Carole was willing to help Eva with household chores while Eva reciprocated by providing Carole with new clothes, food, and a home. Despite this mutual dependence, there has always been conflict over how much Carole should develop relationships, especially with men, on her own and away from her mother's household.

On Saturday of that weekend in 1965, while we were finishing the laundry using the washing machines at the trading post, Carole went outside the building to talk with Paul Yazzie and Glenn Sandman who drove up in Paul's car.

She came back to say that she and Lorraine were going to Gallup with the boys, and she asked her mother for money.

FIGURE 7.1 Portrait of Carole in her high school years.
COURTESY OF CAROLE CADMAN.

Eva was obviously against it and delivered a short lecture in Navajo. According to her summary, she told Carole that she shouldn't be running around, and that when she came home from boarding school, she should stay around and help. The girls didn't return until around 8:00 or 9:00 p.m. Carole brought popcorn and candy, which she passed out to her four younger half brothers. The adults were already in bed. Carole told her mother in Navajo where they had been. She said she had come back with Harrison Johnson [her classificatory "grandfather" and an upstanding Mormon, married to Rose, Eva's brother's daughter]. She had picked him as her escort partly because she was afraid her mother would be mad, and Harrison promised to say something to Eva. [Field notes, December 12, 1965]

Carole stayed home on Sunday. We sat around the house and did some sewing, and around noon we went to the community meeting at the Chapter House, followed by the Sunday afternoon Chapter meeting. It was still going on at 4:00 p.m. when I left to drive Carole, Lorraine, and Ethel back to the dormitory, where they had to check in by 6:00 p.m. In the mid–nineteen sixties, picking up students from boarding schools was especially complicated because a parent was not able to always count on a vehicle being in working order. I was, on this occasion, a welcome taxi driver.

Carole was sometimes late in returning to school from vacations and weekends. In January, she spent an extra day at home in order for Eva and Joe to buy her a winter coat in Gallup. In February, Carole and Eva had an argument about returning to school on Sunday. She wanted to stay until Tuesday so she could get some new shoes. Eva said that if Carole was late to school again, the dorm officials had said they would kick her out (Field notes, February 20, 1966). On June 1, I noted that Carole had not returned to school that week. It was rumored that she had been kicked out of school, because she never went back to school on time (Field notes, June 1, 1966).

That summer brought Carole into greater contact with traditional Navajo religion than had been the case during the winter months when she was in boarding school. In late August 1966, Carole and

Eva decided that Carole should be a patient in an Enemy Way ceremony ('Anaa'jí), popularly known as a "Squaw Dance." Carole and Eva joined with another Sheep Springs family that was already in the process of planning the three-day ceremony for their daughter. The Enemy Way is designed to cure those who are ill because they have had dangerous or improper contact with non-Navajos (or *'ana'í*, often translated as "enemy"). Contact with dead bodies, as often happens in wartime or even at funerals, may make the person especially vulnerable to attacks by the spirits (*ch'į́įdii*) of the deceased non-Navajo. The Enemy Way ceremony itself includes a dramatized ritual attack, which, along with other ritual activities (songs, a blackening ceremony), removes the dangerous elements associated with alien ghosts and cures the patients (Witherspoon 1977:58). Eva had told me when I first moved into her house in December 1965 that Carole had attended the funeral of the Anglo trader's daughter who was killed in an auto accident. Eva said Carole not only looked at the body, but had held the girl's hand (and reported it was "real cold"). Carole had done something similar when a friend died later when she was in Utah. Eva was really angry at Carole and told her after she came back from Shiprock that she "shouldn't do such things" (Field notes, December 7, 1965). At the time, I thought these two contacts were the reasons for Carole's participation in the ceremony.

But in 1997, Carole emphasized only the events in Utah, the second contact, when she explained to me why she had been a patient in two Enemy Way ceremonies—the one in 1966 and another in the summer of 1997. "I had the same spells that I used to have several years back with my head. It was a headache all the time, and I started getting a nosebleed again, and that's why I decided to do the Squaw Dance. Because when I was young I used to have a girlfriend that got killed by a horse, and I ran to her when she was bleeding and tried to pick her up, but—I was holding on to her when she passed away. And every time when I had that headache and that spell it was telling me that I was holding that white girl. I was holding a Bilagáana [white person or American] that was bleeding. That's the only thing that I can remember that I was holding was her. She died not long after. She got killed."

For the three-day ceremony in 1966, Eva and Carole, along with

Eleanor (Eva's sister) and her children, moved some of their belongings, food, and supplies to a shade (chaha'oh) near a new ceremonial hooghan built by the Chapter for such occasions. The Enemy Way ritual involves taking a decorated rattlestick on horseback to a group of nonkin who are the "stick receivers." "In the performance of the Enemyway, a dual organization suddenly arises. One group is formed around the chief patient, and is made up of his [or her] kinsmen. The other group is formed around the stick receiver, and consists of those who are related to him by kinship." (Witherspoon 1975:59).[2]

During the week preceding the ceremony and from Friday evening to Monday morning when the ritual took place, Eva mobilized her entire kin network to help, using her summer home at Na'aldzisí as a base, and then later the tent she pitched in back of the shade near the ceremonial hooghan. Ben Bimá, who used to herd sheep with Eva's mother, offered her jewelry and sash belt for Carole to wear, while Carole's paternal uncle Diné Ts'ósí (or Slim Man) and Shoemaker's Wife (her grandmother who lived at Eva's house) both contributed sheep for the buckets and buckets of stew that would be produced over the weekend. Eva's mother, Mary Sandman, ground white corn with an old-fashioned mano and metate and helped prepare the drum that would be used in the ceremony. Joe made shelves for the cooking shade, ran errands, bought groceries, and chopped wood. Even Grant, Eva's brother, helped with the hauling of water and wood chopping. Eva herself baked more than forty loaves of yeast bread in an oven near the ceremonial hooghan.

Carole spent the days before the ritual making the three-tiered, silk skirt she was to wear with a velveteen blouse, woven red and green sash belt, silver and turquoise necklace, and bracelets and moccasins.

At one point she and Eva had an argument about the skirt and Carole lay on her bed pouting and crying. This phase soon passed, and during the ceremony, Carole was preoccupied with being a patient: entering the ceremonial hooghan when the hataałii needed to perform parts of the ceremony, riding in the lead car when the stick was being transported to the stick receiver's camp, and traveling at the head of the long procession that took food to the stick

FIGURE 7.2 Carole wearing her traditional Navajo silk skirt and velveteen blouse before the Enemy Way, 1966.

PHOTOGRAPH BY AUTHOR.

receiver's group near the end of the ceremony. Carole's symptoms subsided and only surfaced occasionally until 1997 when the headaches and nosebleeds became severe. She then participated as a patient in the Enemy Way for the second time.

It is tempting to think of Carole's life at this stage as split between an Anglo-oriented school environment, where an all-Navajo student body participated in aspects of the broader American English-speaking culture, and a Navajo home environment, where Navajo was the dominant language and where traditional Navajo ceremonies and the Native American Church guided thought and behavior. It is probably more appropriate with Carole's orientation to think of her life, however, as one of weaving together both cultures, becoming thoroughly bilingual, entwining her experience in the white world with her participation in Navajo ritual and Native American Church meetings. The Enemy Way, in particular, healed her from the contaminating effects of the white world.

The Birth of Tina

In the fall of 1966, Carole went back to school, and I returned to Harvard University to write my dissertation. San Juan County began busing students from the Sheep Springs area to the public high school in Shiprock, fifty miles to the north, making it possible for Navajo students to live at home rather than being shipped off to boarding schools as far away as Chilocco, Oklahoma, or Phoenix, Arizona. Those who had been attending the boarding school at nearby Fort Wingate could also remain with their families. Carole attended school at Shiprock and took the bus to school each day. She started seeing Wallace Ben, a student whose family lived in Shiprock.[3] In 1997, Carole told me more about those days. "And then when I was going to Shiprock High, I got involved with Wallace. Him and I, you know, we were going together. I met him when I was in school, in Shiprock, and then that's when, you know, my little girl Tina started arriving. I went to school even though I was carrying her. And I remember he wouldn't let me come home when I was carrying Tina. So more likely we stayed over at his parents' place . . . and I went to school with him every morning from there. . . ."

"So you quit school in the middle of the year?" I asked. "Yes," Carole replied. "After Tina arrived, we had Wallace's mom take care of the baby for us. And she was really good with the baby. Of course, that was her grandchild so, she took care of the baby, and him and I went to school, and we finished that whole year."[4]

During the summer tensions developed in Carole's relationship with Wallace, partly because she was spending time with her mother while he and the baby remained in Shiprock and partly, I suspect, because they were teenagers and inexperienced in managing relationships. For example, at an Enemy Way ceremony, she discovered her sister Mabel (her father's daughter by a second marriage), sitting in a pickup talking to Wallace, who had not even come over to see her and the baby. Since a couple usually does not sit together, especially in a car in a public place unless there is an actual or intended intimate relationship, Carole was angry and assumed that Wallace was intent on leaving her.

It was while the couple was with Carole's mother in the house at Yellow Hills that Tina got sick. The baby's illness was unexpected, according to Carole. "She just started having a fever. She started crying. And I didn't know what was the deal with her. And she was OK 'cause she's a very happy baby. And all of a sudden, you know, I took her back to the clinic. The doctor said, 'We'll keep an eye on her tonight, and we'll test her,' you know, with some of the tests that they usually provide for the babies. So we left her over there. And we came home all the way out here and told her grandmother and Wallace that, you know, the baby was in the hospital. And we came back out here 'cause they gave . . . they grow corn and gave us a whole batch of corn.

"So when we came back, we were sitting out here. We cooked corn outside for the boys, ourselves and Grandma [Sandman]. And that night, you know, I felt lonely for her. I should have stayed in Shiprock, you know, that was the feeling I had."

"Would they let you stay?" I asked, wondering if they would let mothers stay in the hospital with sick children, something I suspected was discouraged in the nineteen sixties.

"I would have stayed, you know, at Wallace's place," Carole replied. "They wouldn't let mothers stay with their infants in the hospital at that time. So about midnight, a policeman pulled up and wanted to know if I had a child in the hospital. And I said yes. And then the policeman told me that 'she's gone, she died.' And that was, you know, a total shock for me. I went back inside and I told my mom, and then about one or two o'clock I ran over to Lena and woke her up.[5] And she drove us all the way into Shiprock that night. And she was still in her little crib where they kept her. All they did is they covered her with a white sheet. And I ran in the minute, you know, we pulled up. I ran in to where she was. She was just lying there like, you know, she was asleep. And I grabbed her, and I held her. And then that's when Wallace arrived, too. And we just both stood there until the nurse took us away from there. And they took her downstairs to where, you know, they usually keep them. So it was tiring, you know, to take care of the funeral business, arrangements."

The doctor told Carole that Tina died of natural causes. They called it crib death on the death certificate. "At the time I really didn't know what that meant, see. She was normal . . . 'cause when I left her, you know, she was so happy. She was standing in the crib; she was smiling. And I went to her, and I kissed her, and I said, 'Bye bye baby, see you,' you know. And she was just normally smiling. She never had diarrhea because I took care of her. And at that time, Randy was like three years old, or four years old. So I took care of Randy, and I knew what to do with a child, you know. And, that [when] they have diarrhea, it's time to discontinue their milk, every time they have diarrhea. But she never had any diarrhea. . . . And after that, you know, I just lost interest in everything. I didn't know what to do. We had the funeral and, of course, Wallace's mom, Wallace, and everybody showed up, his sister. . . . We just put her away. She's buried over here at the cemetery in Sheep Springs.

"And after that I just stayed home and . . . and not really did very much. Until Terry decided to take me in because she knew I was going through a lot—a lot of stress and everything.[6] And at that time Terry lived in Canoga Park, California. And she came out and she told me that she'd take me in, and maybe, I would forget things. And more likely I stayed with her for like maybe six months I think.

"I got to where we started looking for a job for me. We ended up at this Laundromat. A big Laundromat to where you press all kinds of people's shirts . . . you press. I started working at that company. I was working with the presser machines. So I worked there like maybe three months. Then I really had nothing to come home to. I felt that way, you know. I guess my mom felt the same; she missed me quite a bit. And she went to peyote meetings. I would write to her and tell her that I wasn't going to return. So I lived out there. . . . And then I came . . . I guess my mom had a peyote meeting and they ran a peyote meeting for me and all of a sudden, I felt lonely and I wanted to come home. So I told Terry, you know, that I'll go ahead and come back home. And after I came back home I stayed here."

Carole remembered Wallace's parents fondly and particularly emphasized how they encouraged her to go on with her life after Tina died. "They said really good words to hear. I was told by both the father and the mother—for me not to have a terrible life, to carry on. They would always love and respect me, and I was always welcome in their home. And whenever I would see them in Shiprock, they would never ignore me. And I always had their love and respect. I was treated as a woman, as their daughter. I was never a stranger to them. I guess in the same way they had love and respect for all their kids. There were good words that were said to me at times when I lived with them."

A Relationship with George Johnson

Even before she met Wallace, Carole had a relationship with George Johnson. He was Helen Joe's son by an earlier marriage. Helen and her husband Lee had been important members of the Native American Church and had introduced Eva to the healing powers of peyote. I remember George in 1965 as an affable, joking man about my age with a young wife and baby who lived in a small house just in front of his mother's place in the flats—a large residence site with her two married sons and a married daughter.[7] Lena, her oldest daughter, lived a hundred yards to the east of Eva and was one of the women I lived with in 1965–66. Helen and her children were members of the Bit'ahnii clan, the same clan as Joe Price, Eva's husband. So there were kin relationships as well as religious ones that connected Eva's family with Helen's; however, Carole was not a clan relative of George's and hence could have an intimate relationship with him.

A year or so before I came to Sheep Springs, when Carole was about fifteen or sixteen years old, George was living in California and was in the armed services. She met him through Harry Chee, a cross-cousin (*bizeedí*) since Harry is Kiyaa'áanii, Carole's father's clan. At the time Carole was going to school in Ignacio, Colorado. Navajo teenagers usually have close relationships with their clan relatives, their sisters, brothers, and cross-cousins, and often go places in single-sex groups with them. Sexual relations are prohibited with these relatives, although cross-cousins often engage in joking and teasing each other. Relatives of the opposite sex are often instrumental in providing the means for a young man and woman who are not related to get together. By the nineteen sixties much of this courting behavior took place at ceremonies, fairs, and in cars and pickup trucks. In this case, Carole met Harry and George at the Shiprock Fair, when she could not find her mother who was supposed to meet her at the fair and take her home for the weekend. She accepted a ride from Harry and George, which allowed Carole and George to get acquainted in the back seat. The next day Harry's sister persuaded Carole to go with her and Harry to take him and a friend so they could catch a bus in Flagstaff and return to their railroad work. Carole was surprised when George appeared with his car and discovered that he would be driving the group. Later she laughed at how she had been tricked, but was secretly pleased to spend more time with George. He continued to express an interest in Carole, despite the fact that he married and moved to California where he was in the National Guard. When he returned to Sheep Springs, he would drive over to Carole's house, pick her up, and take her out.

"He's about three or four years older than I am. And his wife, oh, his wife came over one time and said, 'I heard you're going around with my husband.'" At that time he was living with Lula and they had a one-year-old son. In the following years they had two more children. Valerie was present when Carole explained this to me, and part of what Carole said was actually addressed to her daughter, who did not know the details of her mother's relationship with her father. She did not realize, for example, that George was married when Carole was pregnant with her.

"And, he moved into Gallup," Carole continued, "and stupid him. Even though he lived in Gallup he used to drive all the way out here just to come and see me. And he used to help me out with funding every . . . every time I used to get my checkup. He used to come around. He used to ask me when I was going for my checkup again. And he used to give me money, for gas money and stuff like that."

Valerie wondered if the checkups were for her, something that Carole confirmed, "For you, when you were in my tummy. And when I had you, I don't remember when I had you. I think I had you in the evening also. And Auntie Rosie was the one that gave him word that you were born.[8] And the next day, I guess he snuck up there to the hospital. He was still livin' in Gallup. Snuck up there, and I remember he was standing right by the door lookin' out to make sure Lula don't come walking in on us." Carole laughed remembering this awkward situation.

"So, I told him he's stupid. I told him, 'Get out of here if you're gonna be so damn scared. I don't want to see you anymore.' I said, 'I can raise this child all by myself.' So, after that, he still used to come around when Jay's dad was livin' with us here." Valerie remembered that George used to come around in a brown pickup truck. At the time Carole was married to MacArthur Cadman, the father of her two middle children, Erica and MacArthur Junior (Jay/JR).[9] "At night he came over and he says, 'I'm gonna beat the shit out of that son-of-bitch that's in there. What the hell is he doing here?' you know, all that shit. Oh, I used to hear a lot of stupid things."

"But he was never interested in leaving Lula?" I asked.

"Well, he was about ready to leave her, and she left him because she found out that he was, you know, doin' that. And she moved, I think to Flagstaff. . . . And she went and moved on to California. . . . And after that, you know, good old George stayed around. We used to fight quite a bit. He used to accuse me of all kinds of things that I never thought of doing. . . . Me messin' around behind his back and stuff like that."

"He should talk," I quipped.

"So, I told him, you know, I didn't want to get involved. One of these days I don't want to end up with a blue eye or a black eye. At the rate, he eventually slapped me across the face just because . . . of Jay's dad.

"So, after that, you know, I figured, 'Nope. This is no more.' So, I told him, 'Don't bother me anymore. Be on your own, I'll be on my own.' But yet still, I think he still has feelings because every time I pass him, or something like that he'd wave. Or when he sees me. . . . He works for the Utah International power plant. . . . Yeah, he's with another woman. And constantly those two fight all the time."

Valerie's Birth

Valerie was born in 1973. I was living in Rhode Island, and I did not come back for a visit until the summer of 1975, when Valerie was already two years old. I still have photographs of Carole holding the two-year-old Valerie and standing next to Eva in the cornfield. I had just accepted a job at the University of New Mexico and would be moving to Albuquerque in January 1976. Over the next three years, I saw Carole and Eva frequently since I drove out from Albuquerque during the semesters when I was teaching there. It was during this period that Carole was married to MacArthur Cadman and had two more children, Erica, born in July 1976, and MacArthur Junior, born in April 1978.[10] I met Carole's husband MacArthur a number of times. He was older than I, a quiet man who knew little English and who was an excellent silversmith. During these years, he and Carole often made trips to Albuquerque, Flagstaff, and Phoenix to sell his jewelry. Carole gave me two rings that he made, and I wore them for many years; however, I never knew the full story of how MacArthur came into her life until I began interviewing her.

The Arranged Marriage with MacArthur

When I asked Carole to tell me about her marriage to MacArthur Cadman, we were sitting in the bedroom of her mother's house at Yellow Hills on a Saturday evening in October 1995. Carole was propped up on the double bed and I was sitting in a chair, the tape recorder placed between the two of us. Carole suggested, "Let my mom tell that story." Eva was sitting next to me at her loom, finishing a rug for me. The "thump, thump" of her weaving comb punctuated her narrative as she pounded the weft thread down tightly after she pulled the thread through the warp strings.

"Well," Eva started, "There was a man buying wool, and that was what he was called—'Wool,' from Mexican Springs, he said.[11] They would come over, him and MacArthur Cadman. Eventually, he asked me. 'Let your daughter live with this man,' he asked me. 'He is a good man,' he said. Instead he was lying. It was because of that, that there was no one to care for her that I agreed. 'He probably is well behaved,' I said to him. So it was because of that, it was."

Carole was more adamant. "It was like a forced marriage. . . . Many years back, I guess, people used to do that . . . give you away like that to somebody else you don't know. And all this time I had no idea. And then one day, they were supposed to come over, and here I was, I ended up in Shiprock. I was in Shiprock . . . at that Shiprock TrueValue store that used to be a café. And all of a sudden about five or four o'clock in the evening, here she was with those two men. They were looking for me. And, she got mad at me over there. 'Why are you over here? You're supposed to be over there [at home at Yellow Springs]. These guys were supposed to come over!' You know, all that crap. So I got mad and I just took off from there—from them. I didn't come back with them. And I used to know a girlfriend in Shiprock, and I stayed there overnight at her place, 'cause I didn't want to get involved with him. So, after the next evening I came back over here, and here they were, they came back over here again."

A little later on in the conversation, still curious about how she might have arranged a marriage that Carole clearly did not want, I asked Eva how she'd gotten to know Elton, "Was he a relative?" Eva explained in English, **"He talked to us really nice, and we know him and he wanted us to help with something, like carrying the woods down for us and bring the water. That's how we know. . . . I thought he was a good man. One time I got mad at Elton, too. Bunch of lying. . . ."**[12]

Carole concluded her description of the arrangement by saying, "So, that's how they put me together with him. . . ."

"So, how come you finally agreed?" I asked.

"Well, she forced me, you know, my mom forced me. 'Aw, he'll take care of you . . . '"

Eva interjected, "See that Elton, he's a slime."

Carole wanted to continue to tell me how they both had been persuaded by Elton that MacArthur would be a good husband, "He [Elton] used to say that he's a very good serviceman and stuff like that, and that he will . . . he'll, you know . . . I'll be wealthy after, you know, after he starts helping me . . . helping me and everything he can. But I found out that, you know, it was totally a different story after maybe like a couple, three months later or something like that. . . . He was an alcoholic. He drinks and after that Erica was born. A year later I think."

Erica's Birth

At the same time that MacArthur's drinking was becoming a disturbing reality, there were difficulties with Carole's pregnancy. In order to overcome these complications, Carole had to rely both on Western medicine and on the help of Helen Joe, a member of the Native American Church.

"When Erica was being . . . when I had her in my tummy at that time, I used to go in for my regular checkup. I was due any day, and when I went up there the doctor said she was totally standing up inside of me. They told me her head was up here, and her legs were down here. She was breeched. And they told me that if she doesn't turn herself around that they're going to do a C-section on me. And they gave me an appointment to go in for the C-section. Like after my regular daily appointment, two days later they told me to go ahead and go in that week, that they're going to do a cesarean for me and take her out instead of me having her breech. 'Cause they were telling me that, you know, it's dangerous to have a breech. . . . So I got really scared, because I didn't want to have a C-section done, so when I came home I was scared about it. Then I told my mom, and then at that time, Helen Joe was the prayer lady. She was very special to us.

"So I went up there and I told her, I said, 'You know, they're telling me that the baby is staying inside of me.' And I told her, 'Do a prayer for me.' And she said, 'Oh, they're lying.' She said, 'By the time you get back over there to Gallup, it's going to turn itself around. Don't worry about it.' She gave me this real tiny small peyote. Yeah. She said, 'This is for the baby and you.' She said, 'Don't worry about it. You're going to have the child normal.' So I went back over there to the hospital.

"And the doctor checked me with the machine that they put on your tummy. What was it called—ultrasound? That machine, you know, they were putting that on my tummy. And I could see the baby's head, that it turned itself around. The baby's head was down here. I guess within the two nights that I'd been here, it turned itself, and I used to feel the great big pain, I guess it was turning itself around.

"The doctor looked at me and he said, 'What did you do?' He said, 'The baby's head is down here. You're very lucky, woman!' I just smiled at him and I said, 'I don't know.' And within that week she came. So actually, I didn't have to go in for a C-section. And after she was born, I had Helen Joe do a blessing."

A Deteriorating Marriage

Although Carole found great pleasure in her new daughter, her relationship with MacArthur continued to decline. "At that time I was employed under the Community Health Representative. And I was with that for about eight years with the Navajo Tribe and while I was working, you know, he used to sit home here, and when I used to come home in the evening he used to get mad at me, and saying that, you know, I was cheating behind his back to where I must've been seeing another man. And it got involved so bad to where he used to abuse me. So after his jealousness, I left my job. . . . I left the CHR job because he used to get mad at me for coming home maybe a little, thirty minutes late or something like that. And then after that, he wanted to move back to his mom's place, and I lived over there with him. He used to abuse me in front of his mom, when he was drunk. He used to drink quite a bit. And then there was that one evening he took off with my daughter, Erica, and we found her in Gallup with some other people. And he was drunk in my car."

Carole first lived with MacArthur in her mom's house at Yellow Hills, and it was during this time she was working as a Community Health Representative, commuting some days to Shiprock where the district office was. Her job was to visit Sheep Springs families and help them deal with health issues, educating mothers, children, and other family members on diseases, maternal care, and common health problems. Later, in the spring of 1980, she was able to get a home in the new housing area near the Sheep Springs store.

She moved over to the new housing when Jay was a baby. "And he [MacArthur] stayed there with us. I figured that he would automatically change his attitude and stuff like that, but it got worse to where he almost ran over me there."

"That's the time he pulled you out of the car, right?" I recalled. I remember hearing this story on one of my visits to Carole when she was living at the housing. "That was when you were in the driveway or something like that?"

"And I used to hide over at Lee Joe's place," Carole continued. "Remember Lee Joe and Helen? They used to live about two houses down.[13] Lee Joe used to hide me in his closet, and he used to try to look for me. And my mom called the cops and told the cops. And they ran him off from there. That was the last time I've seen him, and I never went back to him."

Earlier, when she was pregnant with JR in 1977, Carole, MacArthur, Valerie, and Erica were staying at Eva's house at Yellow Hills. According to Carole, he was "mad and jealous" and he stabbed himself. "And they took him to the hospital and after that I told his mom, you know, 'maybe you guys are going to blame me for it,' but I said, 'I didn't do anything.' He did it himself. So he was a no-good man. And then after that for about eight or ten years I never went to Gallup because he told me, the day we were leaving him, after we hauled all our stuff back over here . . . the day we were leaving him, that he would kill me next time when he saw me in Gallup. And after that I never, you know, really cared to go back to Gallup and shop in Gallup. I always went directly to Farmington." Carole laughed, relieving the tension that the memories of this incident created.

"Oh," I realized, "That's why you never went to Gallup." I vaguely remembered that often when I took Carole on trips to buy groceries and clothing, she always preferred to shop in Farmington rather than Gallup.

"'Cause," she recalled, "he told me once, 'Someday when I see you,' you know, 'I'll kill you. I'm going to shoot you' and stuff like that."

"He must have been pretty drunk when he said that, huh?"

"I don't know, but I know darn well that he . . . he wasn't any good, Louise," Carole responded in a firm tone. "I found that out."

"And now when he sees me, he doesn't bother me. I actually just talked to him, and every time when JR needs some money from his dad, we go over there. And he'd get money from his dad, and then he'll give me like twenty dollars for gas. And I tell him, well, 'I deserve more than that because you used to abuse me,' you know." Carole laughed at the irony of telling her ex-husband, who had become diabetic, blind, and disabled, that he had had such power over her. "And he won't say anything. He won't, you know. So I just lost interest and everything. . . . Why live with a man, when he has to punch bag you all the time and throw you around? Of course, I'm not very big to be pushed around."

"And now he's got a real bad health problem. He totally became disabled, and he can't see very well. His mother used to tell me that all he did was drink, drink, drink after we left him."

When she was pregnant with JR, "He took off with my car. And we had to go looking for my car."

"I remember we looked all over Gallup," I said, recalling a trip we took to Gallup to search the streets and back alleyways during one weekend, sometime in the nineteen eighties, for Carole's blue sedan. "And I can't remember if we found him or not."

"And the next day me and Tim took off over there again to look for him. And sure enough, he had my blue car. . . . And that blue car was just leaving right there by Safeway. Remember where that Safeway grocery store used to be? . . . That car was just turning on to the highway there, onto the street when we were coming. And I remember I was pregnant with JR, and I jumped off and I ran over there to those boys. And there were two men that were driving that car, and I said, 'Park this car over there.' They were all puzzled looking at me, and I said, 'Where is the guy that let you guys have this car?' and they didn't want to tell me. I said, 'You better let me know, before I tell the cops that you guys are in a stolen vehicle.'

"Those guys were just looking at me, and they backed up and they parked the car over there. And I told them, 'Hand me the keys.' I said, 'I'm going to tell the cops if you don't tell me where this guy is.' And then he said, 'He's way over there. He was just totally drunk, and he was with this downgraded woman,' you know." Carole laughed at the image she was presenting.

"And we went over there just to tell him that I was taking the car, and Timothy was just laughing at me. And I went up to him . . . 'cause he used to beat me up when he was drunk. And then I went over there and bopped him on the head and slapped him several times, and. . . . We left him there. Timothy brought the green truck back, and I brought the car back.[14] So about three or four days later he comes back over here, and he wanted that green truck. So I told him, 'Go ahead take the green truck with your stuff.' And of course I had loaded up all of his stuff. But instead of him going home, you know where he ended up? In Farmington. And I guess coming back on Sunday evening he had a head-on accident . . . at Table Mesa. And he totally lost that car, that green truck.

"And when I used to come home from the Thriftway there . . . he used to get mad at me—because you know how talkative I am. He thought I was goofing off, or getting involved with another man or things like that. He used to be a real crazy and jealous-minded person."

At the end of this section of the interview, Carole began to think about her life as a whole. "Now, you know, it makes me wonder. I would have done better if I only had one daughter. I would have gone back to school and things like that."

Coping as a Single Mother

Carole has spent most of her adult life, except for the seven years she was living with MacArthur, as a single mother. As her narrative tells us, she managed this by taking a series of wage jobs and in some periods going on welfare. When Carole was in high school, the only wage jobs in the Sheep Springs area were one or two positions at the trading post and café. A few tribal or federally funded jobs were becoming available such as part-time community development officer and Head Start teacher. Most Sheep Springs residents a few years older than Carole had moved to Denver, Los Angeles, or Phoenix as part of the Relocation Program that provided supplementary funds to move young Navajo couples to cities to find industrial or service jobs.[15] During my fieldwork, fully one-third of the community (mostly younger couples and some single men) was living either in far-away cities or in the border towns surrounding the Reservation, particularly Gallup. Men of Joe's generation and even some of the younger males worked for the railroad during the summer and fall months, while women like Eva and some men were employed on ten-day work projects financed by the Navajo Tribe.

Carole's own job history reflects the fact that most wage employment was located in Gallup until federal and tribal positions (many seasonal and part-time) increased in the nineteen seventies. Carole's first experience with wage work had been her job as a presser in a dry cleaning business in California. After she returned from California, she lived with Paul K. Yazzie, Eleanor's oldest son and Carole's herding companion from when she was a young girl. He and his wife lived in an apartment in Gallup near the central post office. Carole was employed at the Trademart Discount Center just south of Gallup. There she met Bessie, who became her close friend, and later she shared living quarters with her.[16]

During her marriage, Carole was fortunate to hold two jobs close to Sheep Springs that did not entail a long commute; she could get to work even if her car broke down. The first was a position as a Community Health Representative. These jobs, funded by the Indian Health Service, were given to women (and some men) in local Chapter areas. They are good examples of the new federal and tribal jobs that were created during the nineteen seventies to employ Navajos in the rural sectors of the Reservation, rather than in Agency towns like Shiprock, Window Rock, or Tuba City. Carole visited families in the Sheep Springs area, discussed health issues with them, disseminated information to new mothers, and helped residents take care of their health needs.

The second was a job at the Thriftway Convenience Store, which was located in the Sheep Springs Café and owned by a chain that had bought out the owner of the old Sheep Springs Trading Post. During these years in the early nineteen eighties, she lived with MacArthur and her three children in one of the new, federally funded houses in the neighborhood constructed near the trading post, often referred to as "the Housing." Work was within walking distance and Carole's steady job provided the family with enough money to afford the expensive electric bills (which included heat), as well as a telephone and a car. Eva and Randy, who had just graduated from high school, often lived at the housing with Carole rather than in Eva's house at Yellow Springs. Even one of Carole's other brothers (Rudy) stayed in the three-bedroom house part of the time. When Carole lost her job at the Thriftway, she was no longer able to keep up with the bills and moved back over to her mother's house. After she split up with MacArthur she went on welfare. Her experience with Aid for Families with Dependent Children (AFDC) was sometimes a negative one.

Carole was always in search of a job, but most in the Sheep Springs area lasted only a few months or even weeks. In some years, Carole worked during the summer months on a road crew building and repairing highways in the Gallup area. Her job was to hold up "Stop" and "Slow" signs and direct highway traffic around the construction crew. She was employed by a company that was building the interstate near Jamestown, east of Gallup, and later worked on the interchange between Highway 666 and the road to Window Rock, the Navajo capital. She usually commuted a distance of one hundred miles every day, driving to Gallup or J. B. Tanner's at the Interchange and back to Sheep Springs. The children were in the care of her mother.

During other summers she worked as a supervisor for a tribal program that employed Navajo youth from the local Chapter. During the school year, Carole was sometimes able to work on a twenty-day project at the Chapter House, as her mother had done in the nineteen sixties. Each job removed her from the AFDC rolls, but after the job ended, it would take her several weeks to reenroll. I remember once she had a short, three-day job directing traffic at the Northern Navajo State Fair in Shiprock the first week in October. Someone saw her working and reported her to the local welfare office. After her payments and food stamps were cut off, it took her weeks to get "back on Aid." Then, she was sometimes penalized for sharing a house with her mother, a very common situation on the Navajo Reservation beginning in the nineteen seventies when many Navajos started living in multi-room houses rather than one-room hooghans or cabins. Nuclear families or mother-child units that would have been independent (eating and sleeping in a different structure) during the previous generation were now under the same roof sharing a butane stove, a refrigerator, and bathroom facilities.

There was one caseworker that was particularly difficult to deal with. "She was a bitch," Carole recalled. "Excuse my language, but, you know, I had the hardest time with her. . . . Remember she kept closing my case because, me living with my mom . . . living under my mom's roof and stuff like that. . . . And I couldn't be my kids' payee, remember? My mom had to be the payee."

"Why was that?" I wondered. Carole tried to explain. "Because I kept looking out for a job, remember? Or it's because that we were living under her roof, you know. I had . . . she had to be the payee. She was actually the head of the household. That's what they consider . . ."

Carole was able to continue getting welfare during the nineteen eighties because MacArthur became disabled.[17] In 1985–86 she began to study accounting at the Crownpoint Institute of Technology. During the nineteen seventies and early eighties educational programs on the Reservation had increased both with the founding and expansion of Navajo Community College (later Diné College) and the Crownpoint Vocational School. Carole completed her GED (equivalent to a high school diploma) and received a certificate in accounting. She lived in the dormitory at Crownpoint (about fifty miles from Sheep Springs) and returned home for the weekend. At the time, Valerie was twelve, Erica was nine, and JR was seven years of age. After she completed her coursework, she applied for jobs, including a position at a new shopping center in Shiprock. She was disappointed when she could not find anything and resigned herself to the fact that Navajos in the Shiprock area were probably given preferential treatment in shopping center hiring. When we talked in 1995, her hope was to take more courses in business accounting, so she might become a store manager. She had discussed this possibility with the current store owner (a local Navajo) who was exploring the possibility of taking over another convenience store, especially if the Thriftway chain was thrown off the Reservation.

Eva's Experience as a Single Mother

Eva, like Carole, was a single mother during the nineteen seventies, but she had a very different relationship to the local economy. Carole supported herself with sporadic wage work, some jobs lasting three or four years, but each followed by a period of unemployment and dependence on welfare. This is a different experience from that of Eva's generation. Like her mother, Mary Sandman, and her aunt, Ben Bimá, Eva had long been part of a credit-based trading economy, bringing her lambs, wool, and woven rugs to one of the local trading posts for credit. In the nineteen fifties and sixties, women of Eva's generation began taking their rugs to traders in Gallup where they received cash rather than credit. At the same time, they were being drawn into the wage labor market, which also paid cash. In the nineteen fifties, Eva, for example, worked in the sugar beet fields and was employed at the local trading post. But families were still using the trading posts for credit in order to buy some groceries, cloth, and household items. When they were together, Joe's railroad income often went to pay off their credit account at the Sheep Springs Trading Post. Sometimes, Joe's check also generated some cash. After Eva and Joe split up, Eva had some claim on his income for the support of her four boys. Eva continued to get short-term employment once or twice a year on the ten-day work programs available at the Chapter House. A similar program that provided a work crew to build houses at the scattered residence group sites in the Sheep Springs area afforded Eva the opportunity to work in construction.

"I liked working on the land and doing men's work. . . . I thought about this and put in an application there and went over there. At that time Charlie Manuelito and Lee Benally were the bosses there, and they said that I could probably do it." We discussed when this might have happened, and Eva and Carole remembered an equal opportunity policy stating that a woman could do a man's job. I thought they were referring to Title VII of the Civil Rights Act, which was signed into law during President Johnson's administration.

"Then after that I went there, and an application was filed for me. And then I was accepted. I was told to go to work. I don't remember what day that was. And then I went to work, even though it was very cold—the snow was blowing. I worked under those conditions. I bought all my own tools. 'This is what you must have,' I was told. And so it was kept there at the worksite in a box: the shovel, the pick, and things like that. And as for the lighter things such as the level and the measuring tape . . . **the measuring tape I carried in my bag. I used pants.**

"I know how to paper the roofs and the walls, mix cement and floor tile. And those that come together, the wood **roofing**." Eva worked a year on an all-male crew, and then the second year, Helen Matches, another Sheep Springs woman about her age, joined the group. "The rock slabs from the east side, the thick ones that are in there from here to that doorway and over there, I did those to here and halfway." Carole explained that her mother was describing the flat rocks that are used to decorate the front of a house and that are cemented in between. Sometimes when they were pouring a cement floor, they had difficulty with the cement mixer. "The floor in Benjamin Sherman's house is not made of wood. That was very complicated and hard to do. That cement was always the same. Sometimes the cement mixer would break down, and we would have to use the hoe like this. **We used a backhoe like this.** Sometimes we would put it all in the mixer and mix it, and it would make a 'dooig, dooig' sound. And then over at Toadlena, I would carry my things over there, very cold before the sun came up."

Carole explained that they didn't have a car at that time, but Eva would catch a ride with one of the male crew members. Eva said that she got along with the men, "I worked well with them." Sometimes after they got paid, they drove to Shiprock or Farmington to buy steak. **"And we pitched in the gas and filled up the gas for John McBrown or Andy. We took turns to use their car**, so I worked well with them. And now when I think about it, I did something good." Eva explained how she felt about constructing houses, **"You think about what you want to make it, and you think about what you are going to put in it and fit it. That's how it is. Put your mind in that house."** Not all her coworkers felt that way. **"Some of them**, they don't appreciate it. **They don't care. They just work."** Sometimes Eva would cook for the men. "We had our own lunch. **Sometimes in like this weather, Jonas tells me**, 'Build a fire, **make fry bread**,' Navajo tortillas cooked over hot coals, **'and go to the store and get meat and cook it outside for them.'"**

Some of the women members of the Sheep Springs Chapter complained about Eva's working. Their complaints seem based on the fact that they were only assigned to teams that worked on projects that lasted ten days, while the house construction crew was employed on a yearly basis. **"Those ladies were at the Chapter, I know how they are. And they talk about me, and Jonas told me to go to the meeting and tell them. So I did and I stepped in front of them, in front of all the people. 'Now I'm right here. You have to complain right here. I'm standing in front of you guys.'** And so, **I tell them, 'Who's the one that's talking about me? It's not your job. It's not your money.' I told them just not to bother me. They quit complaining."**

I wondered why the men hadn't complained, just women. **"Not the men. I know the men are good when you work with them . . . teach you. I love my brother the way he teaches me, and . . . I worked well with them over there."** Eva earned $398 every two weeks during the two years she worked on the housing crew.

Eva also had several opportunities where she was paid to help teach the summer students. She was on the summer student committee, and later in 1990–91 she was part of the Foster Grandparent program and helped at the Sheep Springs Chapter preschool. She helped students learn their clan relations and talked to them about the traditional Navajo behaviors of getting up early in the morning and running to the east. "They didn't know about it. **When I worked with summer students, I talked to them, and they told me. I talked to the kids and they don't know their clan. I asked them.**

Nothing. . . . They don't know what they are. **And their dad's side,** nothing also. **They don't know. I don't know what kind of mom did they have, and what kind of dad.** Who is their father, and who is their grandmother, and who is their paternal grandfather? **You have to teach them, how you raise your kids. I was like that, so my kids know now."**

"So did they go back and ask their parents what their clans were? Did they learn them?" I wondered.

"Yes," Eva replied, **"The next day we met together, and I know. I told them, 'Did you know your clan now?' They say, 'Yeah.' 'So, you have to put it in your mind. Like your Social Security, or your census number. You have to put it in your mind and remember what's your clan. Don't look at your dad all the time, and your mom. Your mom's not going to last forever. Any day any time, they have to leave you behind. And you start by yourself from there on.' That's what I told them.** So this is how I talked to them. 'I will not live for you forever,' your parents will say to you. 'This is what my mother said to me, and so I also use the same teachings as my own now.' **I talk to them what all my dad and my mom told me. 'See, for the rest of my life I'm not gonna take of all the time from you. So sometime I have to leave you behind, you have to do it your own way. You do it yourself.' I talked to the summer students, the kids. Some of them . . . there's only a couple, three or four, I think they went into college."**

Many of Eva's community activities were not performed for wages or a stipend. Rather, they were part of her participation in the local Chapter and in Navajo ritual and family life. In the late nineteen sixties and early seventies she was a member of the Sheep Springs Community Action Committee that included Helen and Fred Berland, her sister-in-law Anita Sandman, and Nora Watchman.[18] The Community Action Committee, started under the Office of Navajo Economic Opportunity (ONEO), a part of the Johnson War on Poverty program, became a community planning committee that worked with Chapter officials to initiate and plan community activities. They also handled some of the Chapter funds, for example, depositing the cash generated from the Sheep Springs Chapter laundry into the Chapter bank account in Gallup.

Eva was also a member of the Road Committee, which discussed the dirt roads that connect the paved highway and scattered residence groups. They discussed which roads should be graded (by the county and the school system), where stop signs were needed, and where the school buses should be routed. She often opened Chapter meetings with a prayer, and when someone in the community died, it was often Eva who got a ride to Farmington to announce the death, tell people about the meeting of relatives to raise funds for the funeral, and to let relatives know when and where the services would be held. She also made announcements of upcoming Navajo ceremonies like the Fire Dance (Mountain Top Way) or Night Chant (Yé'ii Bicheii Dance) held during the fall months. **"If they need help, they come and ask me for it and I go over there. They don't buy me gas and they don't pay me. . . . I help them out."**

Over the years, Eva was also associated with a number of initiatives fostered by the Indian Health Service. She has a certificate that recognizes her training as a parent counselor with the Baby Bottle Tooth Decay program sponsored by Navajo Child Development. Here, parents were counseled not to fill baby bottles with sugar-fortified juices or popular soda pop, which caused severe tooth decay in many Navajo toddlers. In 1992 she participated in the Sheep Springs Community Health Fair.

Finally, she was a member of the Sheep Springs Farm Board for many years, a group in the Yellow Hills area that worked with two Bureau of Indian Affairs (BIA) employees to develop a better irrigation system for the fields that Eva and other families used during the summers.

As indicated in chapter 6, Eva is also called upon to diagnose illnesses and the source of difficulties for a wide network of Navajos, including many who are members of the Native American Church. Patients, or those for whom she prays, will pay her often with cash or sometimes with several boxes of recently harvested melons or squash, a sheep or young calf, or a load of wood.

Like others in her generation, Eva has been dependent on the cash economy for her entire adult life, but this has not always meant formal wage work. "Work" for her has included a number of so-called traditional activities, primarily weaving and curing, which have provided either credit or cash so that she could buy food, clothing, and other consumer goods and obtain transportation for herself and her growing children. She has had to piece these activities together with short periods of wage work, which she has found through programs offered at the local Chapter level, funded by tribal or federal dollars. Finally, she has received some payments from the Railroad Retirement Board after Joe's death and Social Security payments after she turned sixty-two in 1990.

CHAPTER EIGHT

"It Was Really My Grandmother Who Raised Me"

Valerie's Childhood

AS EVA'S CHILDREN BECAME ADULTS, SHE BEGAN TO ASSUME the central role in an extended family. When her son Timothy married Ida, he went to live matrilocally at Ida's mother's residence group, a very typical pattern for most Navajo men, but Eva saw her son and his growing family regularly. Randa and his wife, Ellen, sometimes lived with her mother and sometimes with Eva, often occupying a small bedroom in the expanded house where an extra bedroom and a bathroom had been added, complete with plumbing and hot water. Carole's daughter Valerie was Eva's first grandchild, born when Carole was living with her mother. When Carole married MacArthur and went to live in Mexican Springs near MacArthur's mother's sister, Valerie's world revolved more around her grandmother, her great-grandmother, and her uncles, Rudy and Randy, who were still living at home.

Valerie remembers that her mother never told her much about her birth. "Well, I was born on June 15th in 1973. My mom said that when I was born, I'm not sure if this is right, but she said I was born in the evening, late in the evening. And I was born in Gallup Indian Medical Center. . . . And I never saw . . . I don't think there ever was any . . . I've never seen any pictures of myself when I was young. I don't know if my mom ever had any. I don't really remember a lot of stuff myself when I was small. But the stuff that I do recall is what my grandma [Eva] told me. She used to tell me that I was spoiled. And that she used to give me a bath twice a day, in the morning and the evening. Back then we didn't have any water at the house or electricity, so she had to carry buckets over across the way, across the road, by Grandma Eleanor's. You know where that water is? She used to carry buckets from over there and bring water back just so I could take a bath. And she said if I didn't take a bath, I would cry and I would get really fussy. And that is one thing I always remember, my grandma says. She always used to tell me, too, that 'Your uncles took care of you.'"

"But do you remember that?" I asked. It was something Valerie often said when she was making a presentation in my class. "Do you remember your uncles taking care of you?" In past generations, a Navajo's mother's brother (*hadá'í*) was an important source of advice and discipline, since he is the older male in one's own clan. Usually, the mother's brother would live matrilocally with his wife and children in a distant residence group (as Carole's oldest brother Timothy was doing during Valerie's childhood). In Valerie's experience, however, her uncles were co-residents in the same households, sometimes as teenagers who would tease her and make her cry and in other cases as elder guides who taught her to clean house and take care of herself.

"I remember briefly . . . like Randy and my uncle Rudy. I remember them holding my hands, pulling me somewhere. I don't remember what we were doing, but I remember them holding on to me."

Valerie had vivid memories of her great-grandmother, Grandma Sandman. "I remember some small things about her at the Housing. . . . She used to sit outside in the front porch area; she never used to do anything. She just used to sit there with like an apple or an orange, and she just used to eat it; she just sat there. I always wondered what she thought about, but I never really asked her."

Valerie, her mother, sister, and brother moved over to Eva's when Valerie was eight or nine years old. "I remember Great-grandma, she never stayed at my grandma Eva's house during the day. She always stayed at her house. . . . In the mornings, she'd roll up her little goat skin or sheep skin and take it back to the house and then in the evening she'll be bringing it back. . . . She liked this perfect little spot right by the sink and the stove near the door. My mom and my grandma Eva used to tell her, 'Put your bedroll over here; you'll sleep over here by this side.' And she used to say, 'No, I don't want to,' and I remember her saying *nahjí* 'over there.' She said, 'No, there're spiders on that side.' And I always remember, I would lay by her. I'd lay down by her, and she would either scratch me, or she'll run her hands through my hair like this. And to this day, the only way I would sleep really good is if somebody was petting me like that, or running their hands through my hair. This relaxes me completely. That was something my grandma Eva did to me, too, when I was little. . . . I remember one time, too, we were over home by ourselves—me, and my great-grandma, and I think it was Randy or Rudy. I can't remember which one it was, but my great-grandmother gave me things I wasn't supposed to have. For example, my mom and my grandma Eva always reminded me, I always used to want to taste coffee, and they wouldn't let me. They told me that it would stunt my growth. But when I went to Great-grandma's house, she poured me a cup of coffee, and we sat there and had coffee. . . . She put three lumps of sugar and cream in her cup and also gave me three lumps. And we'd sit there and drink coffee. I always remember she always had something like little treats. . . . She always had a whole bag of cinnamon rolls or cookies. . . . We always had something sweet to eat every time I was over there. Sometimes I would fall asleep at her house. There used to be a lot of magazines and newspapers in my great-grandmother's house. We used to sit and look through magazines. . . . I remember the times when she had trouble with Grant, too. I remember one time she was crying. She came to the house and said that Grant was drunk. And she said, 'I'm scared of him.' And I think that's when she started staying at the house a lot more."

When Carole was first married to MacArthur in the late nineteen seventies, she spent some time living at Mexican Springs with MacArthur's mother. "Yeah," Valerie remembered, "We went over there. Once in a while I'd go back with my mom over there. But most of the time I think I stayed with my grandma. . . . But I would go back to Mexican Springs and I remember . . . I think I used to live in a hooghan. That's when my mom had that old station wagon, that brown and yellow station wagon, a long time ago. . . . To me she [MacArthur's mother] was really mean to me, and they used to have a mean rooster. That's all I remember."

I recalled driving Carole and the children to Mexican Springs once, and we stopped to see MacArthur's cousin/sister who lived in some federally funded housing near the trading post.[1] We never drove all the way to MacArthur's mother's residence group because it had recently rained, and the roads were too muddy and treacherous. Valerie recalled that she hardly ever stayed with her mother during this period. "Even when my mom came home, I never went anywhere with her. I stayed with my grandma all the time. 'Cause I remember my uncles used to say, I used to call my grandma 'Mom.' . . . And my uncles used to say, 'That's not your mom, that's your grandma, that's *our* mom.' They used to say that to me. They used to make me cry, I know that."

"Your uncles?" I asked, not remembering any of them as particularly aggressive. "How'd they do that?"

"They used to . . . they used to like, I don't know. They used to hit me on the hand like that and just play with me. Just hit me on the hands. . . . But I would go run to Grandma and Grandma used to get mad at them, 'Leave her alone, she's my baby.'"

I wondered what language Valerie had learned as a child. I only remembered her mother speaking to her children in English. Now I thought that perhaps since she was around Eva a great deal that Eva might have spoken to Valerie in Navajo.

"I think, she spoke to me in Navajo. A little English here and there when I started school. I think I knew both the same . . . at the same time, yeah, 'cause my uncles talked to me in English, too."

When JR was about two years old, in 1980, Carole and MacArthur moved into the new housing complex that had been built about three hundred yards from the old trading post and café. The trading post itself had been abandoned, and the café became a Thriftway, a chain convenience store managed by a series of Anglos (Bilagáanas). I remembered attending the official dedication of the housing when my son Peter Bret was about four months old. Carole had made the girls red velveteen traditional blouses and very pretty red and white–patterned silk, three-tiered skirts. Her own blouse and skirt matched those of the girls.

We watched from the big picture window in the living room as Peter McDonald, then President of the Navajo Nation, delivered a speech at a small viewing stand that had been built across the street. Valerie instead remembered a time when it was cold outside and she was wearing a jacket. She had a little scooter bike and was playing with her sister Erica, her brother JR, and her two cousins (Timothy's daughters), Lolinda and Rolinda.

"Because I remember going to school from there—one whole year. And I remember summer, too, 'cause it used to always rain, and water used to just pour down the street. And we used to run in the rain, and my grandma and my mom would get after us 'cause that evening our legs would start to hurt. We used to get in the mud, too.

"I remember, too, as a little kid . . . well, my mom hardly ever bought me anything, like toys and stuff. I'd go to town with Grandma, and my grandma would buy me dolls, and doll clothes, and doll accessories, like shoes and purses, and hats and clothes. I had tons of [doll] clothes. I had like a whole shoe box of clothes, full of clothes. And I remember my cousin, Linda Sandman.[2] She lived up the street from us at the Housing. . . . I'd go over there like every evening after school and on weekends. She had dolls, too, and we had like a big ol' Barbie bus and Barbie house. And we used to go over there, and play and trade like clothes and stuff and fight about whose stuff was better. I always remember that my mom always used to say, 'Why don't you just move over there? You spend so much time over there, why don't you just move over there?'

"And I remember my uncle David, David Nelson, my grandma Rena's son. . . . [3] They used to live right next door to us, too. . . . Me and Yvonne are about the same age. Maybe she's like a year older than I am, but we were in the same grade. And she used to call us. We used to have a phone back then. She used to call us and tell us, 'Now go get your dog.' . . . It was a big white dog. . . . And if it didn't know you, it would bark at you and growl at you. And they used to be scared of the dog. They would want to come over, but they would be scared of the dog. Rena would cry from the door, 'Get your dog!'

FIGURE 8.1 Carole with her daughters Erica (left) and Valerie (right) when their house in the Sheep Springs housing area was dedicated in 1980.
PHOTOGRAPH BY AUTHOR.

FIGURE 8.2 Carole with her children, 2006.

PHOTOGRAPH BY MARGARET RANDALL.

And that dog used to like to ride with us, too. We'd take it to the mountains. My mom will put it on top of the car, and we'll drive through the mountains like that."

As she was growing up, Valerie was often left to mediate between her brother and sister. "I used to always watch them. My mom would go somewhere. She used to tell us, 'You guys stay home. And Valerie, you watch your brother and your sister.' And I used to hate to watch them, because they always used to fight. Me and Erica always used to fight, because I think I would always get toys and stuff from my grandma, and I think Erica used to be jealous. She used to yell at me, throw stuff at me, and I used to throw stuff back at her. And her and Jay, they always used to fight. I remember one time, we were at the Housing and we were fighting about something. I don't remember what we were fighting about, but Jay threw a fork at Erica, and it cut her lip. No, it cut her right here on the cheek. And then one time at Grandma's house, we fought. We were bad, me and Erica. I threw the bag [the size of a backpack] at her and it cut her lip. . . . 'Cause I remember one time, just recently, Ditto told her, 'God, Erica, you have all these scars on your face.'[4] And she said, 'Well, thanks to my brother and my sister.' But she was mean; she was a brat when she was growing up. She got away with lots of stuff. I kind of thought that was unfair sometimes."

Valerie went on to tell me about Erica's relationship with her mother. "I think it was because my mom had difficulty with her when she was little. . . . She had health problems when she was little. . . . I don't know if my mom ever told you, but she used to like have seizures and stuff. . . . Erica used to have lots of seizures. And I remember one time it happened at the Housing. I don't remember how it happened or what caused it, but all of a sudden, my mom had her on the table, and she put a spoon in her mouth. And we were crying, that's all I remember. And my mom to this day . . . if Erica ever says something to her . . . my mom, she never gets mad at Erica for that reason. She always says, 'I'll never say anything to hurt her or disown her because I almost lost her when she was young.' That's what my mom kept saying. Because we had this whole deal about the car, when my mom bought me the car." Valerie was referring to a family argument that erupted in the spring of 1996, when

Carole used her tax rebate to help Valerie buy a car so she would have transportation in Albuquerque. Erica felt that Valerie was the spoiled daughter who always "got everything."

Valerie, for her part, felt she had always depended on her grandmother and uncles, rather than her mother, for financial assistance. She felt critical of Erica's behavior. "My sister said a lot of things to my mom. . . . I mean I would never say stuff like that to my mom. . . . She was really mad about the car. And I just think that she got away with it. If I were to say that to my mom, either my uncle Beam would get down my neck about it, or my grandma would."

Valerie explained that she depended on her grandmother for money. "Every time I needed money when I was in high school my grandma was there. My uncle Rudy was there, you know. Of course, I understood that my mom didn't really . . . she never really had a steady job. And you know I never looked to her for stuff. I never did. It was always my grandma. My grandma always gave me money. My uncle Rudy always gave me money, you know. And for my mom to not say anything to defend herself about what Erica said to her just . . . just pissed me off."

I commented that Erica must feel like Valerie is the favorite child. "Yeah," Valerie replied. "And she also told me, too, that every time my mom gets money, she asks my mom for money. And my mom says, 'I gave it to your sister.' And she told me one time, 'You're spoiled. And you have everything you could ever want.' And I said, 'Well, I've always been close to Grandma.' And I said, 'You don't have the kind of relationship I have with my grandma and with my uncle, too.' She didn't talk to them, you know. . . . I just think that I have a better relationship overall with my uncle and my grandma than she does. And I think she resents me for it.

"And one thing, too, that I always remember is that every time my grandma and my mom used to fight, I was always like the mediator. . . . Like my mom would say, 'Go tell your grandma this' or 'Your grandma's like this, you know.' And my grandma would be on the other side. 'Your mom is like this. Go tell your mom she's this.' I was always stuck in the middle, and I hated it so much. And I was always the one my mom would tell me, 'Go see what your grandma wants. Go see if your grandma's hungry,' you know, when they were fighting. 'Go see if your grandma's hungry. Go take this to your grandma.' It was always like that, I used to hate it. . . . Sometimes my mom, too, when I was young, I kind of felt tension. Because I used to talk to my grandma, when they were mad at each other. I used to talk to my grandma, spend time with my grandma. And then I'll go and spend time with my mom. And my mom would always say, 'Let's go.' She would ask me, 'What are you gonna do? Are you gonna stay? Are you gonna go?' And it always depended on where they were going . . . if they were going to like stay at somebody's house or to go in town, spend the night in town . . . I'd make the decision to go. Most of the time it was spending the night in town. . . . We would stay at Gallup at the truck stop."

"And why were they fighting so much in that period?" I asked. "Did your mom want to go out with guys?"

"I don't know," Valerie answered uncertainly. "I think that has something to do with it, because . . . she would leave with either Marilyn or somebody.[5] And my grandma just hated it, you know, because my grandma's the traditional kind of person who believes that the mother should stay home with her kids every day no matter what. It would be OK to work and stuff, but that was the role of the woman, from my grandma's point of view. But my mom went and did whatever she wanted with her friends and came home the next day."

I remembered Eva telling me at various times (perhaps during phone calls) that Carole was "running around." It must have been difficult for her to establish a relationship with a male, since someone would always see her with the new person, and gossip would get back to Eva or other family members. I remembered one summer during the early nineteen eighties when Carole visited me in Albuquerque with a boyfriend on a trip that lasted several days. They had clearly left the Reservation in order to have some time together.

"See, she used to do that," Valerie commented. "She just used to take off and not tell us where she was going or when she'd be back, you know, she'd just leave. And for a while there I used to hate it. . . . I think that's why I never got along with my mom . . . I didn't respect her, because she did that. I think I spent a lot of time with my grandma and my uncles. . . . I really hated it. We would need her. I just didn't like it. . . . I spent a lot of time with my grandma. My grandma used to tell me, 'This is wrong; this is right. You grow up this way. You [should] be outspoken; you do whatever you want to do. Don't listen to what other people say; you do what you need to do.' She taught me with this thing that she grew up with. I think that's why my mom did kind of bug me. I never said anything about it. I never . . . when she would come home . . . I would ignore her. I'd say, 'Where'd you go?' But I never got as far as . . . where I would like yell at her or tell her I hate her. . . . I never got that far. I never really, really got mad at her. I just would ask, 'Where'd you go? How come you didn't come home?' Or, 'Who were you with?'"

I noted how difficult it must have been to form a relationship right under the eye of a watchful mother. Among middle-class women of my generation, going away to college basically removed personal relationships from the purview of the older generation. I remember in my high school days in the late nineteen fifties that I pushed to be independent, something that was probably made easier because my father had died and my mother was somewhat "at sea" trying to rebuild her life. I got my own car, a red Ford convertible, at sixteen, which I used to drive to basketball games with all of my girlfriends in the pep club. I had my own telephone by the time I was a senior and editor of the school newspaper so that I could communicate with others on the newspaper staff (and of course, chat with my girlfriends). My mother did try to keep track of me and make sure I got home at a reasonable time, and she was often upset when I would stay up all night to finish an assignment. But since I was not dating or drinking (and no one was doing drugs in those days), she did not put limits on my activities. Going out of state for college meant that I could become even more independent, coming home only for Christmas, spring break, and short visits over the summer. I drove from Colorado to California, usually with a friend, often driving twenty-four hours straight in order to get home for Christmas after finals or so I could spend some of my spring break on the ski slopes. Although my mother lamented that I was never home enough, she must have felt there was little she could do about it. Even for a family that had been centered in Denver and Golden,

Colorado for seventy years, in my generation it was becoming accepted to go away to college and move to another state. Working class and ethnic women continued to live with their parents. They were under much greater scrutiny and had to live with their parents' approval and disapproval of their activities.

This was also true in Navajo families, even though many children spent months away from home at BIA boarding schools or with Mormon Placement families. When they were home, parents tried to keep an eye on their children. Since kin networks were so large and extensive, it was easy for a parent to find out where their child was through gossip. In Carole's generation, the car and pickup truck afforded the possibility of seeing males outside of kin contexts, but Eva worried that this also led to drinking and promiscuous behavior. Thus Eva was always concerned if one of her sons or her daughter went off to town—or worse—stayed overnight in Farmington or Santa Fe. Eva's watchfulness did not cease when Carole became an adult and mother, so Carole always had to deal with her mother's criticism and concern, especially when it came to relationships with men.

We agreed that because Eva was managing on her own, she probably thought that Carole could get along without a husband. Valerie said, "But my mom probably thought otherwise. You know, my mom probably needed a companion. She needed somebody to help her." But it was also true that, "My grandma always disapproved of all the guys my mom had."

Grade School

Valerie had sketchy memories of her early school years. She attended the Head Start program at the Chapter House. Head Start in Sheep Springs dated back to my 1965–66 fieldwork period when a Vista Worker began kindergarten classes for four year olds in the Chapter House. Soon a Chapter member and neighbor of Carole and Eva took over the teaching. By the time Valerie attended in 1977, the students graduated in the spring with a certificate and a ceremony where each student wore a cap and gown. "Yeah, I went to Head Start. I don't remember too much about it but I remember graduation. I think we had to do this dance or something, I don't really remember. I remember Dad was the bus driver, and I remember this trip in preschool we took to here to Albuquerque. . . . We stayed in a motel on Central somewhere."[6] I recall going over to the motel to visit with Carole, who was one of the parent chaperones, and also seeing Valerie. "The only thing I remember about that trip is that we were waiting in line to get on the bus, and my cousin Linda [Sandman] was there, my cousin Yvonne [Nelson] was there, Elsie Gould's son—we'd just call him Johnny. And my auntie Elsie always teased me about this.[7] She said, when we were on our way to Albuquerque, 'You told your mom. You said, "Mom, I don't like my name Valerie. Call me Josephine now. My name is Josephine. My name is not Valerie."' And from then on, Elsie Gould called me Josephine. And she said, she used to tell her mom—her name was Rebecca Charley, 'How come she doesn't like her name, Valerie? That's a pretty name?' She [Rebecca] said, 'Josephine sounds awful.' So they always tease me about that, to this day when I see them. Especially Elsie Gould. Every single time I see her, she says, 'So you still want your name to be Josephine? Or do you want us to call you Valerie?' I always remember that. But that trip to Albuquerque was really the only thing I remember about preschool, and then getting my diploma for Head Start, 'cause I wore a dress. I remember I wore like a traditional dress."

Valerie attended grade school at Newcomb, the same school that Carole attended. "I went to grade school. I don't remember kindergarten. I remember first grade because Mrs. Williams was my first grade teacher, and she's still there to this day. . . . She was a sweet old lady, she's not old but she's maybe like. . . . She's a little older than my mom, maybe. She's a real sweet lady. She's assistant principal there now, and she still teaches, too. Erica was in her class, Jay was in her class, and Aaron was in her class . . . all four of us."

I remembered that I, too, had a first grade teacher named Williams, though she was Miss instead of Mrs. She was an older lady, with white hair, but I remember her being stern and strict, not a "sweet old lady." She was the one who started to teach us to read, getting us to recognize the letters printed in black that were posted above the blackboards at the front of the room. A largely white and middle-class group, we were primarily Protestant with a half-Jewish or Catholic child melded in. Miss Williams made sure we filed out the school door to the playground in an orderly fashion and sat correctly in our seats. But like Valerie's, my memories of grade school are now vague and shadowy.

"I don't really remember a whole lot about grade school. I don't remember too much about it. . . . I do remember my fourth grade teacher. Her name was Mrs. Brimhall. She was a tall lady. She was real tall and had glasses, and she was really nice. And then my sixth grade teacher or maybe seventh . . . his name was Mr. Aber. He was a black guy. And he was kind of feminine in a way, 'cause they used to make fun of him. A lot of my classmates used to make fun of him, and I really didn't like it. . . . I think he was the first black person that I ever encountered. He was strict, but when you talked to him. . . . I tried to carry a conversation with him one time. 'Cause he would appoint somebody when he would leave; we wouldn't have like a teacher's aid. And just that day he would appoint somebody to kind of like look out when he left, and several times I was appointed that person. And he would come back . . . he'd call me Miss Valerie . . . and he'd say, 'Now Miss Valerie, how's everybody doing?' Or he'd say, 'Now who acted up?' and he'd name out some boys 'cause they were always in trouble. And he was mean, too, 'cause when the boys would tease him, or when he was angry at them, he'd go right to their face and tell them, 'You sit still,' or 'You listen,' or 'I'm taking you to the principal's office.' He'd get right in their face.

"And I remember another lady, too. I think she was my third or fourth grade teacher, her name was Miss Bash. . . . She smoked a lot 'cause you could smell her. And she was old. She was dingy, kind of. I remember her teaching reading. She was a nice lady, I think, but she was kind of weird. . . . All my classmates used to make fun of her. And they used to put like lizards or stuff in her desk. And she'd totally like freak out. And those kids would get pulled by the arm to the office. And we would just laugh 'cause seeing her jump or something—it used to be really funny. But we used to be real mean to her. And that's all the teachers I remember."

"So who'd you hang around with? What other kids did you hang around with when you were in grade school?" I asked.

"I hung around with my cousins Linda and Yvonne, basically the people who lived around me [at the Housing]. Not till junior high did I make different friends. I met some girls from Sanostee and one other girl from Little Water and others from Burnham. This was like seventh grade, 'cause I think I still have pictures of us when we were younger. When we were in seventh grade, that was when Yvonne and Linda both went to the Placement Program. . . . They left, and they went to the Placement Program, and I stayed home. That's when I met my other friends. There was Barbara, there was Shonda, there was Lucille, there was Harriet; there were those four. Harriet was from Tocito [Tó Sidó], Barbara was from Little Water, Lucille was from Newcomb, and Shonda was from Burnham.[8] We hung out together. We played basketball together. I think that's when I first started playing basketball, in seventh grade. That's what we always did, we just got a ball and went out there and played basketball during the whole free period we had at lunch. That's what we did, play basketball."

I asked Valerie if she had played on a team at that time. "I just played with my uncles and those girls all during lunch. And I remember in seventh grade—I'll never forget this—there was this girl. Her name was Alinda; she was from Sanostee. She was mean. She used to hate us. I don't know why. . . . I think she was kind of envious of us, because we used to play basketball with the guys. . . . I remember one time I was going back in to Mr. Aber's class. Right from around the corner she grabbed me. She grabbed my hair and pulled me. And she started to hit me, and I started to fight back. I hit her back and Joanne—you know, Benny Joe's sister—she caught us. So she lifted us both by the arms and took us to the office. I was crying, and I said, 'I didn't do nothing to her. She just jumped at me. She started hitting me.' And we were lucky the principal wasn't there that day. It was the assistant principal, Mr. Brimhall. That was [my teacher] Mrs. Brimhall's husband. . . . Mr. Brimhall just told us that we need to not fight again. If we fight again, we are gonna get taken home. They told her to go back to class first. So she went back to class, and when I went back to class, she was crying in the hall. I didn't bother her or nothing. I just went back to class, and I guess all my friends and everybody saw what happened. They came, and they were saying, 'You hit her good.' But I never bothered her again. . . . She never bothered me again and I still graduated with her. She talked to me in high school. She came around."

Seventh grade was also a time when Valerie worked in the cafeteria. "One thing I used to hate about that grade was that we had to volunteer in the cafeteria to serve the students. They had a shortage of cooks or something. The only good thing about it was that if you're hungry by 10:30, 11:00, you get to eat early."

"What was so bad about it?" I wondered, since this was Valerie's first experience at service work, even though it was not paid.

"It was just not what you would do. I don't know, I just didn't like it. The cooks were kind of mean and . . . if your classmates were going by, they teased you, and I think that is why I didn't really like it, because they teased us a lot. But after a while we never really cared. [We never would] bother with it. And in eighth grade we did it, too, at the high school. We had to go down to the cafeteria and help serve down there."

Thus early adolescence was a period of transition for Valerie with new friends and uncomfortable work experiences at school. But it was also a period when she experienced the transition to womanhood, which is especially marked in Navajo culture through the Kinaaldá.

Kinaaldá

When she was twelve years old and in the seventh grade, Valerie entered menarche, which is celebrated in Navajo culture with the Kinaaldá ceremony. Although it had been a part of her mother's and grandmother's experiences (see chapters 4 and 5), by Valerie's generation, fewer and fewer Navajo girls were taking part. In some cases this was because parents were affiliated with Christian denominations that rejected participation in Navajo traditional ceremonies. In other cases, the girl's female relatives were not interested or could not marshal the financial resources to put on the ceremony. And finally, in a number of cases, the embarrassed girl did not want to participate and female relatives acceded to her wishes. Valerie herself had mixed feelings.

"Back then, you know, I was scared. I didn't know how to deal with this as far as my grandma putting this stuff on, you know presenting this ceremony to me. I didn't have a choice. I wasn't asked. No one asked me if I wanted to have it. Just one day, 'You're going to have this.' 'What?' you know, I cried. I remember I cried, 'No, I don't want to have this. Nobody needs to know.' My mom and grandma sat me down and said, 'It's not for anybody; it's for you as an individual. You'll learn stuff from this, and it's important to preserve your culture.' I remember them talking to me and telling me this. Not my mom, but my grandma did. She said, 'It'll make up who you are.' I'll always remember that. In Navajo she [Eva] said, 'It'll make up who you are. We're doing this for you because we care about you.' That's what she said, and I didn't argue. Even if I had said, 'No,' it would have been done anyway. Back then you know, like I said, it was something you don't really talk about, you don't really let anyone know."

I played an important role in the ceremony. At the time, the fall of 1985, I had just moved back to New Mexico to finish writing up my *Sunbelt Working Mothers* study. Carole was in Crownpoint during the weeks studying accounting. So I picked up Carole on Thursday evening and drove her and my son to her house at Yellow Springs. Eva's sons, particularly Ruda, had built a four-sided structure to be used as the ceremonial hooghan. We slept in Carole and Eva's house, but the hooghan was where all of the important activities took place, including the mixing of the batter for the ceremonial corn cake or 'alkąąd. Eva and Carole had chosen me to represent Salt Woman, much as the kinaaldá becomes Changing Woman, the Diyin Diné (Holy Person) for whom the first Kinaaldá was performed. Salt Woman is the woman who guided Changing Woman. In Anglo terms, she is an "ideal" woman, one who has "physical strength, perfect health, beauty, energy and ambition." She should be personable and friendly (Frisbie 1967:359, Schwarz 1997:176). This person ties the kinaaldá's hair with a buckskin thong the first day and also molds her on the last day of the ceremony. Molding echoes the creation of the Nihookáá' Dine'é by Changing Woman and the molding of infants. "At puberty, every Navajo returns to the soft, malleable condition characteristic of newborns. At this time, a young woman's body is considered 'very sensitive and fragile' (N. Tso, 8/8/92). She is molded to reap as many lifelong benefits as possible from this temporary condition" (Schwarz 1997:191; see also Frisbie 1967:359). As Elizabeth Yazzie explained to Wesley Thomas, "If that is not done the kinaaldá will not grow properly. When you are older your body will be in a proper form, not all lumpy and awkward. During the kinaaldá, she is stretched, she is pulled and massaged. She seems to be strengthened and all her limbs are pulled in all directions" (Schwarz 1997:191). Sunny Dooley explains the philosophical and religious ideas behind molding in relation to the Kinaaldá: "She is molded to be in the image of Changing Woman, meaning that the four aspects of her life are balanced. Her spiritual, her emotional, her intellectual, and her physical. Those four entities have to be in balance and congruent to grow with one another" (Schwarz 1997:192).

During the three days of the ceremony, I took photographs, especially of the making of the 'alkąąd or corn cake, which was made on the last day and baked in the ground overnight. It is round to represent the shape of Mother Earth (Frisbie 1967:12). The cake is cut on the last morning and removed from the ground. A small piece of the cake is buried in a depression in the middle of the hole as an offering to Mother Earth.

During the mid–nineteen nineties, I usually invited Valerie to one of my anthropology classes to show these slides and tell the class about the meaning of the Kinaaldá for her. On February 12, 1998, I tape recorded her commentary. The excerpts from her narratives are similar to other descriptions of the Kinaaldá by anthropological observers (Frisbie 1967, Schwarz 1997:190–229), which also include Navajo commentary. In addition, Valerie's comments give her own view of what was happening, often interspersed with her feelings.

First, Valerie described the clothing that she wore during the ceremony. "So at the beginning of the ceremony, my mom and my grandmother helped to dress me in this velveteen clothing you see here, which is like traditional stuff people wear when they have these kinds of ceremonies. And you will notice that I have a lot of jewelry on. The jewelry there is not all mine. Different pieces of the jewelry all belong to different members of my family and my extended family. And the reason why they gave them to me to wear at this time was because I was considered to be a holy individual during that time. . . . The ceremony itself lasted four days. During the first day of the ceremony my mother woke me. I had to be up in the morning—I think this was around 4:30 or 5:00 in the morning. I had to be up and ready and dressed. After I was all dressed and ready to go they made me run.

"Part of the ceremony included that I would run. And running signified strength. Every time I ran, I ran a little further. And that helped me to become stronger and more motivated later on in life. I guess that was the idea behind the running. I ran three times a day, in the morning, the afternoon, and the evening. You always go off to the east."

The kinaaldá also grinds the corn for the cake. Traditionally, this was done with the help of several female relatives and took several days, since a stone mano and metate were used. In 1985, Valerie ground some corn using a modern corn grinder and the rest was ground at a commercial mill in Farmington.

"During the ceremony, there's a lot of people that come to help and also during the ceremony, it is my responsibility to try to help people who come, to feed them or clean up after them. During these four days I did various tasks. I was on my feet constantly every day. I didn't cook. That was one of the things that was considered a taboo, to not touch fire or work with fire during that time. I cleaned, washed dishes; I ran around with bowls here and there, because we had one house over here where all the dishes were and the kitchen was. And we had the Kinaaldá house over here and then we had some people cooking outside like this. So I was back and forth constantly all day long. . . . I didn't get to rest at all. And my grandma pointed that out to me almost every second of the day. Every time I would have time to stop and breath, she would say, 'What are you doing standing there? You are supposed to be doing something. Go do something.' She would chase me off and I had to go do something."

Valerie described the preparation of the 'alkąąd, the large Navajo cake made from ground corn mixed with hot water and wheat germ. "The Navajo cake is cooked outside in a hole maybe three and a half or four feet in diameter, and maybe about a foot deep, in the ground,

FIGURE 8.3 Valerie stirs the corn batter for the 'alkąąd (cornmeal cake) with the 'ádístsiin (stirring sticks) blending the cornmeal with hot water until it becomes smooth.

PHOTOGRAPH BY AUTHOR.

that was dug out in the morning. The Navajo cake is supposed to go in it. During all of this time, there is a huge fire going in that hole. As they begin to prepare for making that Navajo cake, they boil outside buckets of hot water, and they add cornmeal and a little bit of wheat germ, not too much, and they boil that outside. . . . As they bring those buckets inside [into the ceremonial hooghan], they pour them down into these big old tubs and inside you have women stirring them, mixing them like you do a cake. . . . The sticks that they use to mix this Navajo cake are called 'ádístsiin. . . .

In order to protect the cake from getting dirty, because you are cooking it right out on the ground, here you see my two grandmothers showing me how to sew corn husks together to protect the bottom and the top of the Navajo cake. They were instructing me on how to do it. The corn husk sheets are supposed to protect the cake,

FIGURE 8.4 Valerie places corn husks in the right position before sewing them together. She listens to the instructions from Eva while they are making the bottom lining of the pit where the corn batter will be poured for the 'alką́ąd.

PHOTOGRAPH BY AUTHOR.

just like the regular corn; the husks hug the corn itself. There is a top sheet and a bottom sheet.

"Here you see my grandpa and my mom and grandmother and one of my relatives cleaning out the hole. And here you see them taking the logs out to the hole. Of course the bottom layer of the corn husks go in first. They just use the additional pieces of corn husk and everybody holds them. There are a lot of people around the circle, like you see here. They will . . . in order to protect the batter, they hold the corn husks up around the sides of the ground so no dirt gets in it. The majority of people that come to this traditional Navajo Kinaaldá ceremony are the women, the older women. It is customary for the people who have these ceremonies for them to bless the cake, to pray that it gets done first of all. That's what I prayed for.

"Here we are putting a thin layer of dirt on top just to keep the hot coals from burning through the paper sack. . . . [9] Then you put the fire back on top. . . . You have to get it in before the sun goes down. During the night they have the Blessing Way, the Hózhǫ́ǫjí, ceremony on the kinaaldá. . . . And that goes on all night. I had to participate in the singing and the praying. . . . We stayed up all night doing the singing and the praying. Here you see me running out in the morning, around four or five that morning. Before they let me run out, they washed my hair in yucca plants, just to cleanse it for the day."

Then Valerie described how the cake was cut and distributed. "The four middle pieces were the biggest pieces, and those four pieces went to the people in the community who helped out the most. So in my case, one of the biggest pieces went to one of those people who sang all night, the medicine man. The others went to the three people who helped out the most. They were helping and helped cook and were just there the whole time. I did have to cut some of the stuff out myself. Before the cake was passed out, my mom and my grandmother put out a table, and they put all the cake on there just to cool down. Also they were doing that—it was my job to mold people, still keeping in mind that I have spiritual powers during those four days. And this is just to assist in healing people's aches and pains.

FIGURE 8.5 Valerie blesses the 'alkąąd with cornmeal.

PHOTOGRAPH BY AUTHOR.

"Before I did this Louise molded me. The reason my mom and grandmother chose Louise was because she was a successful person, the way that my mom and my grandmother wanted me to be. Before the whole ceremony starts, they pick this one person that they want the kinaaldá to role model after. Being that she was a new member of our family, they wanted her to be a role model for me. Before the ceremony started, she tied my hair with a buckskin strap. Of course, she molded me and at the end of the ceremony I mold everybody else."

In addition to these specific ritual activities, I helped to sew the two circles of corn husks that provided the bottom liner for the cake and the protective top layer. I also helped stir some of the batter and did various chores like washing the dishes, cutting up vegetables for the stew, and running errands for Carole and Eva.

As Valerie grew older she began to appreciate the impact of the ceremony on her later life. "I look at it today, for example, if I were to have kids, if I were to have a daughter, I would very much like for her to have this only because it would help her to establish her identity and to preserve the culture. It's like April, Rudy's daughter. She had a choice. . . . People asked her, 'What do you think? Do you want to have it?' She was, 'No' all the way, and I just wish that whether or not—I just wish that it wasn't—I don't know. It's kind of controversial, because you impose something on someone that they don't want to do. It's like you're invading their space, you're hurting them kind of. You know what I mean? But I don't—when you look at it today that's how it is, but when it was placed upon me it was like, 'We're doing it for your own good, we're doing it because we love you. We're doing it because we care about you. We want to shape your future for you.' That's what it was back then, but now today it's like, 'OK, what do you want to do?' 'No? Alright.' That's it."

"Why do you think April didn't want to do it?" I wondered. "She'd never been to one? Or what?"

"No," Valerie replied. "She's been to many. Her grandma used to participate in these things, her mom's mom. She said her *bináli* [paternal grandparent] and her aunty wanted her do it; her mom and her grandma wanted her to do it.[10] I just think it's just . . . she just didn't want to because she was embarrassed. I think that's it. I wish that she would have had it. You never know how she'd be now. I haven't talked to her. I haven't really seen her for a long time so I don't know what she's like now. But I think it would have really helped her. I think she's really—I don't know, she's just hard to deal with. But, I don't know, that's a whole other thing. I was limited to a lot of things. My grandma and my mom were very strict with me. They made sure that I got stuff done. They made sure that I got home at a certain time. They made sure that I went to school every day. They were strict about everything. My uncles were strict with me. I remember one time—I'll always remember this. Uncle Randy said, 'Clean the kitchen. It's your turn to clean the kitchen. You make sure you wash those dishes.' He was going outside to chop wood or something. I said, 'No, I don't want to do it. You do it, you never wash dishes.' He turned right around and he looked at me and he said, 'Don't you ever talk back to me. I cleaned your shit when you were little, so don't you ever talk back to me.' He made that really clear to me, and thereafter I never talked back to him, because he took care of me when I was little. I'm grateful for that, but it's like I disrespected him. I realized that. It's like, 'God, why did I do that?'"

Grandma Sandman's Death

A few months after Valerie's Kinaaldá, Grandma Sandman passed away. I was near Tucson, Arizona, at a conference and rented a car to drive up to Flagstaff and then on to Sheep Springs so that I could attend the funeral. Eva and Carole had taken care of Grandma Sandman even as she became increasingly frail. Valerie remembered the incident that precipitated their decision to put her in a nursing home near Gallup, New Mexico. "She slipped, I think. She stepped on something. And she hurt her hip. And they took her to the hospital at Gallup, and they told us that it was going to be a while before she healed. That's when my mom and my grandma made the decision that they wanted to put her in a nursing home. . . . And I remember that being really hard for my mom, because . . . Great-grandma played a major part in my mom's life, too. . . . And it was real hard for her to do, but she couldn't take care of my great-grandma by herself—you know that would mean like bathing her and carrying her—because she was still really active."

Valerie had very vivid memories of the day her grandmother died. "That day that my grandma passed away, my mom had gotten a message. And the message was that for you to call the nursing home. . . . And all I remember is that everybody was at the house. . . . My uncle Beam [Timothy, Eva's oldest son] took it really hard. I know there was a truck that was parked, and everybody was standing around the truck, talking about going to Gallup. And we all left for Gallup, and we went to the nursing home. They had moved my grandma from the south wing. . . . Before she died she used to talk about her sheep. She used to say, 'I need to go home; there is nobody watching my sheep.'

"And that used to just break everybody's heart, I always remember because when we were leaving, my mom and my grandma, they would be crying. As a little kid, I think I didn't know how to express my feelings. . . . You're a little kid in town, you know you're excited to be in town, but at the same time you know you're visiting somebody who wants to go home, and they can't go home."

"Yeah, the place was pretty sad," I commented. I visited Grandma Sandman in the nursing home one time with Carole, Eva, Valerie, and the other kids on one of my trips to Sheep Springs with my son Peter Bret. The nursing home reminded me very much of the one where my mother and grandmother had put my great-aunt Eva when she no longer could take care of herself in her tiny apartment in Golden, Colorado. It was somewhat like a hospital, long curving corridors with tiny rooms on each side of the hallway, each housing (even "warehousing") an older woman or two. Most of the residents in the Gallup home were women, and a number were Navajo. Most of the attendants as I remember were non-Navajos, though there were two or three staff members who were Navajo and who could speak to the patients who, like Mary Sandman, were monolingual in Navajo. The care was custodial at best. Patients were rolled out in their wheelchairs to the dining room at regular mealtimes and were fed American-style meals on trays with plastic plates and glasses. Like my great-aunt's nursing home, the rooms had only enough storage space for a few clothes and a small number of personal items. The one time my mother and I went to visit Aunt Eva, she cried when we left, not wanting to be left alone again. I sent her a bouquet of flowers for Christmas that year, but they arrived just after she died and were given to her doctor.

If the estrangement of my Aunt Eva was great (and we always suspected that it hastened her death), the cultural chasm between the Gallup nursing home and Mary Sandman's life was even greater. There was no Navajo food, no way of being outdoors, and no way to communicate with most of those who washed her body, gave her medicine, and helped her with her bodily functions.

I said to Valerie, "I remember one time when we visited there were a whole bunch of cards there. You know, they put the cards up, the birthday cards on the wall or something like that." This had been for Grandma Sandman's one-hundredth birthday, I recalled. "She turned, I think she was like a hundred and one when she died," Valerie said. "And they also had this picture of my grandma with lambs. . . . I remember that, too. We used to go like in the afternoon like around twelve or something. She would be having lunch. She'll be in the cafeteria and we'd go in and sit there. She'd say, 'Here eat this,' And we'd say, 'No, it's for you. You eat it.' She would always offer us something. My mom would always bring her stuff, even two like little pieces of cake or like cinnamon rolls. She used to like to drink pop. Shasta Orange I think she used to like.

"I always remember that every time we would leave, my mom and my grandma would be crying. And the day that my great-grandma passed away—I remember they moved her to the to the north wing. . . . And my auntie Rosie, I think she's the only one [of our other relatives] that I remember that was there. My auntie Rosie, my mom, my grandma, my uncle Beam [Timothy] . . . I don't know who else was there. They let us in, and there was just this curtain that was just wrapped around where her bed was. And she just laid there like she was sleeping. And my mom went over there, and my mom picked up her hand. She was holding her hand and she was crying. And my grandma was on the other side. I didn't touch my grandma or anything. I just stood there and watched her."

My great-aunt's stay in the nursing home dated back to the mid–nineteen seventies, at a period when there were no "independent living" or "assisted living" retirement centers. Our family could have afforded in-home care for my great-aunt, but she was often treated as a "poor relation" by my grandmother, someone who was supported, but never at the same level of affluence that my grandparents enjoyed. My grandmother was able to remain in her own home during the last fifteen years of her life because we were able to find a live-in Japanese caregiver, first part-time while she continued working, and then full-time after she retired, when my grandmother needed more attention and care. These options are not open to many Navajos who now face a difficult set of choices. In the mid–nineteen eighties, Eva and Carole were having a difficult time taking care of Grandma Sandman in a house without running water and electricity. In addition, she was increasingly incontinent, and after she fell, was bedridden for many months. Modern Navajo housing with narrow doors, front steps, and internal steps between rooms makes it impossible to use a wheelchair. Faced with what seemed to be an impossible burden with potential danger from bedsores, difficulties in lifting a disabled person, and problems of managing medication, Eva and Carole chose the nursing home, but not without regrets. Even Valerie felt the impact of the choice.

"And after she died we always wanted to go back and get those pictures of her with the lambs. We never got them back. And I think for the reason that I saw my grandma when she died, to this day it's really hard for me to go to a nursing home, because Duane's mom's grandmother is in a nursing home in Farmington. And it just breaks my heart every time I go. And my -nálí, my dad's mom Helen, she's in a nursing home and I just can't . . . I don't want to go for that reason."

CHAPTER NINE

Valerie's High School

THE TRANSITION BETWEEN GRADE SCHOOL AND HIGH school was somewhat blurred for Valerie because the new Newcomb junior high, which houses the seventh and eighth grades, was just being built. So eighth and ninth graders were in the high school building, while sixth and seventh graders were in the grade school.

Two teachers, one who taught science and the other who taught social studies, were the instructors she remembered from this two-year transition period. "I remember I had this science teacher, his name was Mr. Williams. He was probably the best . . . the very first science teacher that I ever had liked. He was funny. . . . I think he was my science teacher in both eighth and ninth grade. And he made the class interesting. He made it fun. And I always remember Mr. Williams because, first of all, he was my first-grade teacher's husband, Mrs. Williams, and we always would see them if we went to an open house or we went to a Halloween party or carnival. They would always be there together, and they were just really nice people. And what I remember most about Mr. Williams was in my freshman year, I asked him to sign my yearbook. And he wrote, 'I always wondered where you learned to whisper.' I always remember that. I never figured out why he wrote that—I don't remember whispering in this class. . . ."

"So what was that about?" I wondered.

"I don't know!" Valerie said emphatically. "I remember having lots of friends. I knew a lot of people in junior high. When I was a freshman, most of those kids that I grew up with in grade school stayed there, too. So you really knew each other. I always had friends in almost all my classes."

"So you were whispering to them in class? Is that what he was saying?" I said, figuring that was the most logical explanation for his comment.

"I think so," Valerie acknowledged, pointing to the underlying teasing nature of the inscription, pointing to misbehavior in class, but in a gentle way as if it might be an asset as well as a liability. "Yeah, 'cause he was funny and good, but he was strict. He let you get away with so many things, but you knew there would be consequences.

"And I remember one other teacher. His name was Mr. McGraf. He was a short, little guy and had a bald spot in the middle of the head and hair on both sides of the head. And he taught social studies. I had him I think in eighth grade, and then I had him as a freshman, too. He was really funny. He would crack jokes in the middle of class and . . . and if he caught you eating or drinking or chewing gum, you know he'd embarrass you. 'Cause I remember some kids, they'd chew gum in class, and it really bothered him. If he caught somebody chewing gum, he'd make them put it on their nose. And it would be sitting on their nose, throughout the entire period. I always remember that. And Mr. McGraf and Mr. Williams, they were really good friends."

Basketball

The biggest marker of the beginning of high school for Valerie was her acceptance into the girls' basketball program, which became the defining activity of her high school years. "I played junior varsity basketball. It was hard. It was really hard. I remember when we played in seventh and eighth grade. We played a lot." But Valerie was not part of a team until she was a freshman in high school. "I remember the very first day of practice. There was over like eighty or ninety kids who tried out. And that year we had a bunch of new freshmen that were transferring from different schools. We had a lot of new people. I remember some people who lived in the Sheep Springs area—they tried out, too. There was this boy from Sheep Springs, his name is Wilbert Yazzie; his twin sister joined. We were both in the same grade at one time but I think she was retained [held back a grade].

"These practices were so hard. We ran and ran and ran. I bet our coach just wanted to see who could survive physical activity. And we did, at least some of us did. We kept running and running every day of practice. After practice I was so exhausted I'd go home and was too tired to do homework. My mom and grandma didn't have electricity. I went home and sat at a table that had a little oil lamp—kerosene lamp. You know, eat your dinner, wash up, and go to bed. And I remember the first, the very first week of basketball practice I was sooo sore. I woke up one morning sick; I felt so awful. Like my body was just so tired.

"My mom and grandma noticed that I wasn't feeling good. My mom said, 'You know, get up and get out of bed. We are taking you to the hospital' 'cause I was just so weak and in so much pain. I had been eating and taking care of myself physically, but I never had been through this much physical activity before. I could barely walk because my body was so sore. I was really sore. . . . My mom took me to the hospital and all they gave me was just aspirin and Ben-Gay. That's all they gave me, and I had to stick it out. But that's it. We returned home late afternoon about three o'clock, and I remember I had to go to practice. If I didn't go to practice my coach would be upset, 'cause she was always yelling at us, 'Make sure I see your face tomorrow.' You know, she'll say stuff like that to us."

The coach was Janet Simms, and her assistant was Amelia Joe. Valerie did get to practice that day. "I made sure I walked around, you know. I made sure I got my blood flowing. I got there to practice, and I was kind of lagging behind. And Simms pulled me out and she asked me, 'What's wrong with you?' you know, 'what is it?' She said something about, 'You were working so hard the last few days, and you're lagging behind, what's wrong? Are you sick?' And I said, 'No,' I said, 'I'm sore.' She laughed. And then I knew she just had this way of making you want to work harder, just little words that she said. It's hard to explain. She was harsh, but sensitive in her own way. And she would say, like, 'What? Can't deal with it? You can't take this running?' She'd say little stuff like that, and it would just make you mad. I would want to just prove her wrong. And that's what I did. I worked hard the rest of the practice thereafter. Of us freshmen—there were maybe about five of us—and we told each other, no matter how hard it was, we would make it. We'd try to make the team. There weren't many freshmen in high school that could play ball and also have a chance to play varsity basketball."

Most of the students dropped out by themselves. "And when it came down to picking eleven junior varsity and eleven varsity kids, she chose nine. No wait, I think she chose only about seven varsity people from the seniors and juniors. She chose seven of those people, and she chose five of us from the junior varsity to fill her team. So there was me, Harriet, Kimmy, and Frieda. We played junior varsity, but we would sit out one quarter so we could have that quarter for the varsity if she needed us.

"I was on the varsity team but I didn't get to play much when I was a freshman. But we did play a lot when we played with junior varsity. And I never had so much fun in my life. I think the best part of high school was playing basketball, because we went on road trips. We had fun, you know; we built our team up from a bad team to a very good team.

"And during my sophomore year she got married. She married Scott Holst. He was the boys' basketball coach. . . . They got married. She was a really tough lady. We never thought she'd get married. You know, like, 'Oh man, you'll probably beat him up.' We used to tease each other like that. And she said, 'We're getting married, and you guys are all invited to my wedding, if you can make it.' She sent us invitations, and she flew back to Iowa. That's where she got married. I think the only person that got to go was Shannon."

Shannon was one of the varsity players who became a close friend of Valerie's. The older girls were tough on the freshmen. "Yeah, they would really intimidate us. I kind of think that maybe

Ms. Holst told them to be rough with us, be mean with us, make sure that we did things right, 'cause they kind of taught us stuff, too. I learned a lot from playing Shannon. She was two years older than I am. She was a senior when I was a freshman. We got to know each other real well. We played against each other during lunch or early in the morning. That was another thing, too. In the morning when you got there—you got up like at six o'clock, six fifteen—you got up to get ready 'cause you had to be at the bus stop at seven o'clock. Sometimes you'd stand out there in the freezing cold. When you got to school that morning our coach wanted people to be in the gym shooting around, making twenty free throws every morning. And that's what we did. We shot free throws for twenty minutes in the morning. We were late to our first class, but that was OK, 'cause she'd write us a pass. For some people who had a low free-throw percentage, she'd make them go at lunch, too. I remember a couple games I didn't do too well, and she made me come in for a whole two weeks.

"And then after school all the basketball players had to get down to the gym at 3:30 p.m. Practice started at 3:30. School was out at three o'clock. So that gave you thirty minutes to get out of class, run to your locker, pack up your homework, get to the gym, undress, get on the floor, and jog around the floor by 3:30. Anybody who was late, after 3:30, had to run a few extra laps. 'Get on the line.' We hated these little runs called suicides. I don't know if you've ever heard about them. There's the whole court; you start at one end. You know the court is divided into quarters. Here's the half line and the quarter line right there and you run from that line there back to this one back to there back to there back to there back over here, back over there . . . just back and forth. And toward midseason she knew that everyone was in shape—we had to do it under a certain time. And she pushed us. If we didn't make it under a certain time, we did it again. We did it until we made that time. She was real hard on us, but I think that discipline kind of made our team a better team, 'cause we worked together and we did a lot of things outside of school, too, together, as a team."

The basketball team provided Valerie with her network of friends and a group that she socialized with outside of school. When

I asked what they did together Valerie replied, "Birthday parties . . . just little get-togethers on weekends. Like Friday nights she'd say, 'a few of the basketball players will get together and socialize.' We'd go over to their homes and hang out. Sometimes, we'd go to Farmington, watch a movie, or have a sort of slumber party. Sometimes we hung out with our coach; she invited us to her cute apartment, two-bedroom apartment at Newcomb. We'd all go over there and kick back and laugh and mess around, just tease each other and just kind of let go. . . . During my tenth grade year I played basketball, too. I don't really remember too much about tenth grade. But I did go to the school dances, basketball games, and volleyball games; however, I wasn't really too interested in volleyball. I volunteered as a team manager, but never played. I practiced with the team but never played."

The Newcomb women's basketball team played in the state tournament, which is held every year in Albuquerque in the first part of March. Teams, parents, and other students come from all over the state for the finals. For some reason, I never went to the games when Valerie played, but I did put up Carole and Eva and other family members who came for the weekend. "We went to the state tournament during my sophomore year, I think. We started moving up. We started winning. We made it to the state tournament. No, that wasn't my sophomore year; that was my junior year. It was the first time we ever went to the state tournament. We got bumped down by Crownpoint, I think it was that year. And the following year we got bumped down by Navajo Academy. Then, another year, we played at Navajo Prep. And we played there; it wasn't Navajo Academy, it was Santa Fe Indian School. We played at Navajo Academy. That was our senior year. We were playing really well. And then just all of a sudden, we just lost. It slipped right through our hands. It was like we slacked off and physically gave up, although we were almost eight points ahead. It was so disappointing. We all felt real bad, 'cause I remember when we got to the locker room, our coach was mad. She was really mad. She said, 'Well, for you juniors, you have another year, but for you seniors, you blew it. . . . ' And afterward, we were going home on the bus, she said, 'You guys just made small mistakes. If you guys would pay attention to those mistakes and you could fix them, you would have won.' This event was one of the few moments I won't forget.

"Another memorable aspect of my high school basketball period was when my teammates gave me a nickname. Everybody had a nickname. It was like we had our own little family, and it was kind of nice. Everyone respected each other. We did a lot of jumping exercises, you know, like jump roping and jumping over lines. Our coach called it footwork. Like just continuously jumping two minutes at a time, sometimes even longer. I don't know why they started, but my team called me Roo . . . like kangaroo. And everybody called me that. It was kind of funny. I'm not quite sure why they called me that, maybe because I could jump . . . I don't know. And that's all I really remember about tenth grade. That was like the best thing—tenth grade was basketball, that's all it was—basketball and studying. That's it.

"I didn't have too much of a social life when I was in tenth grade. Not when I was a freshman, either. But when I got to my junior year, I gained trust from my mom and my grandma, but only for like short periods of time. They'd let me go like on a Saturday with my friends, but we'd have to have a parent around. Well, this involved like going to my friend's house, and my friend driving us. . . . Well, not my friend, but the parents, driving us to Farmington and then getting back late, you know. And we started having sleepovers. We stayed a few times at my friend Harriet's house. . . . We'd all meet up there and hang out there and tell stories and play video games. I remember one year—I think it was my junior year—we went trick-or-treating. It was Halloween, and we went trick-or-treating. . . . Harriet borrowed her parents' truck. We all got dressed up, and we went trick-or-treating. That was fun. It wasn't just the girls, you know, we had a bunch of guy friends, too, that we all hung out with. It was the boys' varsity basketball and the girls' varsity basketball team. We all hung out together. We all had had classes together. We all knew each other from grade school. We knew each other real well. We just had a lot of fun together. We'd eat lunch together. We'd sit down and laugh and joke around during lunch period and also kept each other company after a hard practice for both the boys' and girls' basketball teams."

High School Social Life and Graduation

Valerie's group of friends included Harriet Dale from Tocito, Frieda Lewis from Sanostee, Barbara Yazzie from Little Water, and Kimberly Lee from Naschitti. The boys were Wayland Joel from Newcomb, Daniel Stephens from Tocito, Andrew Curley, originally from Sheep Springs, but who then lived in the Two Grey Hills area, and Wilbert Yazzie, who is a clan relative. The final one was Calvin John from Little Water. Valerie became quite close to Andrew Curley, who was her cousin, first in high school and then later when she went to the University of New Mexico. "He was like the big brother I never had, always a kind of look-out-for-me kind of person. He always looked after me. And I used to always tell my mom, I used to say, 'God, I wish I had someone who was older than I was, just to look out for me the way I look out for my brother and sisters,' you know. . . . And I found that person. I finally got reacquainted with him in high school, and our friendship still continues [at UNM]. And from then on we just got closer and closer and closer, with each other. He's like an older brother."

This group of male and female basketball players spent a great deal of time together outside school. "We used to hang out together. On weekends, we'd all go to the movies or hang out or like park on top of—it was a big old hill by our high school. That big old hill, we'd go up there and just park and laugh, and those guys, my friends, used to smoke. They used to smoke cigarettes and used to get a hold of beer and stuff. They would always just sit there and drink and laugh and be stupid."

Valerie's first serious boyfriend was Calvin, one of the varsity basketball players whom she got to know better in chemistry class during her junior year. He took her to the junior prom, but many times they would just spend an evening together after practice. "You know, sit out at the picnic table, play basketball for a little while and just sit out at the picnic tables and talk. He told me a lot of stuff about himself, his family, the kind of background he came from. We went out throughout our entire junior year." They broke up over the summer when he started seeing another classmate.

Valerie's boyfriend during most of college was Duane whom she met when she was about to graduate from high school. "I never knew Duane when I was a junior. I never knew him during my entire senior year. . . . He was there; I had him in my English class during my senior year. I remember we were all sitting in the hall. It was senior ditch day. I had my yearbook, and I was passing my yearbook around. He wrote something like, 'Good Luck to your future' or something like that." A few days later they spent time together at a pregraduation party in the mountains. Valerie forgot to invite him to graduation, but then asked him to attend her friend Kim's after-graduation reception when they ran into each other after the ceremony at the high school.

My family attended Valerie's graduation, but I was unaware of Valerie's new interest in Duane. Graduations are an interesting blend of obligations to family and a time for teens to celebrate among themselves. Navajos on the Reservation, as well as their urban Anglo and Hispano counterparts, are engaged in a range of strategies to balance family time and time with peers. My partner, my son, and I drove out from Albuquerque that morning and, according to Valerie, returned that evening. When we arrived, we met Eva and Carole at their house in Yellow Hills. We drove to the high school in Newcomb and found a place to park in the crowded lot. Then we entered the high school where the corridors outside the gym were jammed with families and clusters of younger students. We found our way to a set of bleachers on the side of the gym.

The graduation ritual at Newcomb High in 1991 gave no indication that this was a Navajo high school, but instead, one that included Anglo, Hispano, and African-American students as well. Ironically, the valedictorian and salutatorian, both Anglo students, were the only ones to use any Navajo words when they addressed the crowd: "*Yá'át'ééh*," the common Navajo greeting meaning "It is good." Bill Richardson, then Congressman from the Second District in New Mexico, which included San Juan County and Newcomb, delivered the same speech he had given at the high school in Gallup a few days before (probably to a more diverse crowd of Navajo, Hispano, and Anglo students).[1] Richardson, whose mother is from Mexico, and who had been head of the Mexican-American coalition in Congress, delivered a speech devoid of any reference to the ethnic or class background of the students. He stressed the ideas of democracy and government service (with references to Robert Kennedy and JFK), urging students to look to their futures. A few years later, when Erica graduated from the same high school, one of the teachers gave a speech entirely in Navajo, and at least one of the school board members present was Navajo, addressing the crowd in Navajo and giving his clan affiliations before switching into English. He talked about the problems facing Navajo youth, including the increasing number of teen pregnancies and problems with drinking and drugs.

For Valerie and her classmates, many of whom were the first in their families to graduate from high school, the day was one of celebration and relief. In Eva's family, Randy, her youngest son, had been the first to get a high school diploma, and Valerie was the second. Randy, in particular, hugged his niece and congratulated her for being the second child in the family to progress this far in the U.S. educational system. Students are primarily concerned with spending time with their friends during the days just preceding and following graduation. On the other hand, most extended families hold a reception for the graduate. If there are two graduates in one extended family (e.g., children of two siblings or even cousin/sisters or cousins), two receptions might be combined into one. It may be held at the residence group of the graduate the afternoon of graduation or the next day.[2] The menu usually includes mutton stew, fried bread, and if a sheep or lamb has been butchered, grilled ribs, liver, and *'ach'íí'*—delicacies that are served immediately after the animal has been butchered.[3] In addition, there will usually be some sort of green salad, Jell-O, carrot and raisin salad, or fruit salad with whipping cream, as well as a large graduation cake (purchased from a Gallup or Shiprock supermarket) and ice cream. Families also give graduation gifts, sometimes inexpensive personal items or larger gifts like the radio and cassette player we gave Valerie.[4]

Valerie recalled what happened after we returned to Albuquerque following the ceremony. "I came home and I changed my clothes. I don't remember where everybody else went, 'cause when I got home nobody was home. We just went to this big ol' party, I didn't get home until the next morning about eight o'clock. And everybody was all getting ready, serving food. They were putting all the food out. All the relatives were there. My mom was interrogating me. 'Where have you been? What did you do? Who were you with?' And Randy came out, and he said, 'God, don't lecture her, she just graduated.' And everybody was laughing at me cause I had a really bad hangover. People were laughing about me. All I remember eating that day was steak and blue cheese. I dipped my steak in blue cheese."

Valerie mentioned that she continued to see Duane that summer and prepared for college in the fall. "You came down for that week in the middle of the summer, right?" I recalled that Valerie had participated in the Summer Enrichment Program at the University of New Mexico for first-generation, minority college students who might need extra counseling and orientation in order to succeed in a large university environment.

Valerie and I then talked about how Duane became a student at UNM the next year (fall 1992). "I don't know, this whole debate of whether or not he was going to come down here. . . . And I helped him through his whole application process. Mr. Revis over at the high school helped him to get into UNM. . . . He had already established a folder full of art stuff that he had been doing. He had a bunch of art, you know, posters up in his room. He was pretty much interested in art. . . . He did like a whole course load of stuff like art stuff. He had art classes. Toward the end he invited me to his senior prom. I remember we went all out for this. He rented a tux. I bought a white dress. The morning of the day of the prom we left from Farmington 'cause we needed to pick up our corsages. We got home late and we had to rush to get ready. Bo took pictures of us when were getting ready to take off. It was a nice time."

"That's the picture that your mom's got, isn't it? Isn't it on the dresser or the wall?" I recalled the photo above Carole's bed in her house. When I was staying in that room, where we often conducted interviews, I often stared at the photo for minutes on end, thinking how Valerie and Duane looked like such a perfect prom couple, decked out in their evening clothes. It was typical of the kind of high school mementos that end up in living rooms and bedrooms across the country.

CHAPTER TEN

Valerie's College Years

IN THE FALL OF 1991, VALERIE ENROLLED AT THE UNIVERSITY of New Mexico. I was on sabbatical at the University of California, Berkeley, so I was not around to help Valerie make the transition from high school to college, something that is particularly difficult for students who come from small towns and Indian reservations. During our interviews I particularly wanted to get Valerie's view of how she managed during that year. I began by asking how she decided to come to UNM and what her first year was like.

"I really didn't have any intentions to come to college when I was a sophomore at senior high school. I didn't. By then I was tired of school. I wanted to do something else and that was to go into the military. I brought the idea up to my family, maybe like mid–senior year, and it clearly wasn't what my family wanted me to do. My mom didn't think it was a good idea only because, I think maybe, because I was her oldest. And she didn't want me to leave right away. And then Grandma, I was really close to Grandma, too, so I think maybe that's another reason I didn't go—because of Grandma. She and I were really close, and she didn't want me to go. But my uncles, they were different. They really wanted me to go. They encouraged me to decide for myself what I wanted to do. They more or less said, 'If you want to do it that's what you should do.'"

"They did not particularly like the military?" I wondered.

"Yeah," Valerie emphasized. "They said, 'If you want to do it, you do it.' My uncle Beam [Timothy, Eva's oldest son], I remember him in particular saying that it's a good opportunity for me to get off the Reservation by making this choice of joining the military. And I really wanted to do it. When I was growing up, I think I struggled a lot. I mean as far as being in high school, I had a lot of limitations. I went to school with kids who wore really nice clothes; they wore really nice shoes. Some of them had cars. I'd look at that, and I'd think, God, one of these days! I don't want my kids to ever grow up the way I did. I didn't want them to have to be limited to things. That's one thing that I decided. And also with Aaron, too. I wanted him to grow up with people taking care of him. Knowing that he has . . . I wanted him to know that he had older brothers and sisters that can take care of him. And I think that's one of the main reasons why I wanted to do it: because of Aaron. At one time Erica and I talked about it. We always said that we're not going to let Aaron grow up the way we did. So my uncles were really encouraging me. They really wanted me to go, especially my uncle Beam. He really wanted me to go to the military. I didn't really hear too much from my uncle Rudy [Eva's third son] or my uncle Pro [Randa, Eva's second son]; they never said too much about it. But my uncle Beam, he did ask me one time why I didn't want to go to college. I told him I'd been through twelve years of school, and I didn't want to go anymore. He laughed, but I remember him telling me that if I wanted a good life that I had to make that decision, not to listen to anybody else."

"And your mom's reasons and your grandma's reasons were mostly because you'd be too far away? That was the main reason?" I asked, wanting to understand their role in Valerie's decision.

"Yes, and somehow, I remember my mom getting in contact with you. I don't know what she told you, but I remember you and I had this talk about why I wanted to go to the military, why that was my choice. And I think that one of the reasons why I didn't want to go to school, too, was because I didn't have any money to do it. I didn't know of the resources that were available to come to school. And when you kind of placed that in front of me, I was like, hey, you know, I could do that. And I remember saying that I would go to college for one year, and if I liked it, I would stay. If I didn't like it by the time the year was over I would still go into the military. And I liked it, so I stayed."

I remember arguing against Valerie joining the army. Valerie had gone on the Mormon Placement Program some time during her junior high years. She stayed with a family in St. George, Utah. The experiment lasted only two days, before Valerie, crying and saying how lonely she was, called and asked her mother to bring her home. I felt the army would offer only another form of loneliness and isolation, and that the rigid military structure would only stifle her potential for growth and development.

Valerie agreed, "It's kind of like a vocational route. From then on I understood. At first I thought that I wasn't smart enough to go to college. I mean I was ranked twenty in my class when I graduated, but that wasn't good because my class had only like fifty people. I had about fifty-four people in my class when I graduated, so I looked at those figures and I thought, well, you know—college—we'll see what happens. And I went and, out of all the people that I've ever known in my high school, there's only like five or six of us that are still in college or are near graduation. I look at all the people that had really good grades and were really smart kids in high school, and they're not in college. They are home taking care of their kids, or they're working at a fast food place. I've gotta look at that and think, whoa, I made a good choice to stay in school."

"I always thought you were smart enough," I said. "Remember one time when you were about seven I gave you this computer—it wasn't really a computer. It was just a little game, a little plastic thing. I remember you really liked that." I recalled the square, yellow, plastic, battery-powered toy. When Valerie pushed the buttons she could add and subtract on the screen.

"I don't remember that," Valerie said, which did disappoint me, since I'd seen it as such a significant indication of her potential. "I remember thinking that, Valerie is college material here," I went on, "even back when you were about seven or eight."

"Really? I never even thought about it. I was fed up with school. I didn't want to go any more, and I thought that I wanted to get away from it. I thought the military would be a good thing, but there's also a lot of reasons behind why I wanted to go to the military. But, I remember when I first came to college it was like going in blind to something that I'd never experienced. First of all, I'd never been off the Navajo Reservation. I was faced with culture shock. There are so many different ethnicities around me and that kind of scared me. I've always been this really conservative person. I'm not open. I don't know, I keep to myself, and that kind of made it difficult for me in classes. I'd see these kids coming out and expressing their opinions, and I'm sitting there like, I don't know what to say. I was scared. In high school I took classes that would prepare me for college, but I don't think they were good enough. I found that out because when I came here my study habits needed huge improvement. I learned different ways to study, different ways to take notes. There was just a whole new experience for me that I had to adapt to. I never lived away from home, too. That was one thing. When I stayed in the dorms I had a roommate, but sometimes I'd get really lonely. My mom would call, and I'd tell her, 'Come down this weekend,' and she'd come down. She came down almost every other weekend. And she would bring me something homemade, something cooked, you know, like meat, or like kneel down bread, or corn, or something.[1] She'd bring me that, because I used to hate eating at La Posada. It was the most awful . . . They had really awful food. . . . It was a step up from food in high school, but if you had it every single day, three times a day, the same thing. After a while you noticed a pattern, you know. And my friends would call and say, 'Let's go to get a pizza,' or 'Let's go to Teriyaki Chicken Bowl,' or 'We'll go over there.' And Shannon really helped me a lot during my first year in college. She was there for me; when I was lonely she'd call and say, 'Hey, let's go do this; let's go play basketball.'

"She lived off campus with her brother. I hung around with her a lot. She was kind of like my big sister. . . . I think she was a junior, because she used to tell me she had a paper due, or she'd have to go to class. She had late classes; I remember that. But on weekends, you know, she'd call me up and say, 'Let's go do this; go watch a movie.' I think she graduated in '89 from high school. She kind of helped to make the loneliness go away, because we played basketball together in high school. She was on our varsity team when I was in junior varsity. A lot of kids looked up to her in high school. She was really well-known by little kids. She hung around a lot of younger people. She was just a really outgoing, friendly, helpful person. I kind of looked up to her, and from there our friendship grew. But like I said, I would spend weekends with her, and sometimes we would take a road trip down to El Paso, or to Mexico. One time we went there and it was pretty fun."

I then asked Valerie what she remembered about her classes. "My classes the first year were . . . I don't remember exactly what I took, but they were kind of medium. I understood everything that was going on, but just because I had poor study habits, that made it difficult for me. I was new to reading fifty pages to one hundred pages in one day. I had to read all this information, and I had to absorb it all. Sometimes I'd find myself getting behind." I recalled that during her second year, when I was back in Albuquerque, she had dropped several classes, especially during the spring semester.

"I think it was my sophomore year that I started to drop stuff, as I got into like my sciences. . . . I was just really scared of the fact that I couldn't handle it. It was just too much at one time, and I never had been faced with that before in high school. I used to think that if I had gone to like Navajo Prep—or Navajo Academy, they called it back then—I would have been OK. But my high school never really prepared me for college. I think only because it's one of those rural high schools where you don't really get good teachers. I'm not saying I had bad teachers, but it's just, they were limited to a lot of things because they were located way out."

"Yes," I agreed. "I think that's true with a lot of high schools in the state probably. And it's apparently because the whole system is not geared to getting kids in [to college]."

"I sometimes wonder if I would have went to a college prep school, I would have been prepared to go to college. During my freshman year I struggled, but it was only my first year and I experienced so many different things at that time that I grew to like it. I liked it. I met a variety of different people. I discovered different things about myself. I discovered that I could do things if I really wanted to. Once I really put my mind to something, I could do it if I really focused. If I was motivated to do it, I could get it done. I'd never written a six- or seven-page paper before and I did them. . . . I learned to adapt to my environment as far as my dorm was concerned, and adapting to this Anglo society, I learned as I went. I think I became more mature after like my second semester in college, because I had different views of growing up, I guess you could say."

"So many kids get discouraged in their freshman year and drop out," I said, expressing an interest in why Valerie hadn't given up and dropped out of college.

"I saw that some of the people that I met or went to the College Enrichment Program with, they dropped out.[2] I saw familiar faces from that group and today, I still see those people on campus, very few. I often wonder if they were discouraged and they dropped out. But, I was afraid that I would be one of those people, because you know I remember, I would work with Lucille, and I would work with you.[3] And you guys would stress that the Native American college dropout rates were real high when I first came to college, and I was afraid. I didn't want to be a part of that statistic. And I think just being the individual that I was, the person that I grew into, I didn't want to fail. If I got a low grade on a paper or a test, I worked really hard the next time to make sure I didn't get that. I think it just all depended on myself as an individual. I've always been really motivated to do stuff, once I get started, you know. A good example is basketball. You know my freshman and my sophomore year I really didn't care too much about it. But it became the only thing that I was attracted to when I went to high school. It was the main thing that I wanted to do so bad. As time went by, I worked harder and harder. I got a chance to play on the varsity team, and that's what I wanted. I wanted a chance to letter in high school, and I did. So, you know, I think . . . I mean that has a lot to do with how I was raised."

"So maybe it's that experience that you can transfer to this new setting?" I suggested.

"Yeah, it's this new setting, I can learn to handle it the way I did basketball. But I was scared. I was really scared of failing, but I had reinforcements. I had people telling me that, 'There's this available for you,' and I took advantage of those services. I took advantage of the CAPS, I took advantage of Lucille's academic advice, and yours.[4] I think that's what's really helped me."

"I think you had more trouble your second year." I remembered Valerie's grade point average dropping below the acceptable level and my efforts to keep her from being dropped from the student loan program or being put on academic probation.

"First of all, I was fresh into these science classes. I knew I could handle them, but I had a real big problem with procrastination. I think I had an easy semester my freshman year—the second semester my freshman year. I had it easy, I thought, because I had an English class that I got a B in. I had an academics class that I got a B-, A- I think.[5] But I think I kind of slacked off in my second semester, my second year.

"I think I became a little discouraged because I wasn't doing so well in the science courses. And, now that I think about it, I really don't think that I tried hard enough. I mean, I could have. . . . I probably could have put a little more extra time into it as far as CAPS and studying a lot. Because a lot of the things that I picked up later, with the upper-class curriculum, I think involved a lot of critical thinking, analytical thinking, and I think that if I was able to put more time into the science, I probably would have been able to do it."

Valerie explained that she had always wanted to go into nursing. "I thought that that was always what I wanted to do since I was little. I tried to play nurse, and of course it really interested me as far as seeing television shows or seeing any kind of trauma—blood. That always seemed to really catch my attention. And when I graduated from high school I thought, well, cool that'll be something that I can try. When I would get sick or make my way to the hospital with my mom or my grandma, I always admired the nurses and their responsibility. It seemed like it was a big responsibility. And so I tried it. I went into that field with that interest, however, I was not prepared educationally. I wasn't prepared for the math, and that was what became really difficult for me. And I struggled with that major for maybe four years."

"I remember some of the nursing classes that you didn't do really well in. I remember you took Joan Bradley's class [Introduction to Nursing]." Valerie got a D in this class, something that I learned when I talked to Joan, whom I had known for a long time. Once I found out that Valerie was doing so badly, I began helping her study and prepare for exams.

"That was one part that I had to blame myself for, procrastination on that. I know that I could have done really good if I had applied myself. But I didn't apply myself to my full extent. That's one thing that I really wanted to do. I wanted to become a nurse. I still do want to become a nurse, but I've almost exceeded my college career. I want to get done. I want to get into a related field that would be easier for me to take another step into nursing. So I chose health education. That's when I started going the health education route. I took first aid classes, consumer health, community health, human sexuality, personal health. I took a variety of classes, and I found that those classes I did better in. They were lecture classes, but I did better in those than the nursing courses. And I thought, hey look, this is an alternative to going around and getting a nursing degree if I still wanted to."

"Is that probably because the nursing classes had more science in them?" I asked.

"Well, yeah, I think that one of the reasons is that they were more science classes, and I've never been fond of math, and it could be hard. It's really hard to study math and science in college. I'm finding that out now. I think during my sophomore year I was more familiar or more comfortable with college life because I had learned a variety of skills and I met different people."

Adjusting to Life at the University

When Valerie was a sophomore, she continued to have a relationship with Duane and they lived in separate dormitories. During her third year, they moved into a rented house about one-half mile off campus that they shared with two Anglo men, both of whom Duane had met as a freshman. Valerie talked about how her life was different during this year and the impact that Anglo leisure activities had on both of them. "There were just so many other things that I found. I was new to the city. I didn't know anything about the city. By that year, we were going to play golf, we were going to play pool, we were going to Cliff's [a local amusement park], we were going to parties. There were so many things that I had never experienced when I lived on the Reservation. I think that played a part of my not doing so well in my sophomore year. But I learned from that because I had to take some classes over. I think my third year in college I learned that I can't have all this fun and still be in college the same time. I can, but I've gotta work my butt off to do it. I learned a balance a little bit. But as far as classes and my studying is concerned, I think I've improved a lot. My study habits have been much better. I can read a lot in one night. My reading rate has gone higher. My vocabulary is wider. I have a wide variety of words that I use now."

"What about your personality? Do you think your personality has changed at all?" I asked.

"I think so. . . . I used to be a reserved, keep-to-yourself kind of person. Now in class I'm the first to raise my hand and speak whatever I feel. I'm at ease. I'm not as afraid as I was before, as far as speaking out in class discussions. I've always been a really friendly person, but I think I've exceeded my friendliness here. I have a lot of different friends, and they've told me that I was cool."

"Do you think all that shyness or reticence is cultural?" I asked. "Because Indian kids in classes often don't say much."

"I think so, because like I said, when I first came to college, I was afraid. I was scared to say something, and I think just changing from one culture to another was a large factor. As I got comfortable with this culture I adapted. I learned the Anglo way of surviving in this culture."

"So how would you characterize the Anglo way?" I wondered.

"Everything, like being outspoken, the way people dress, the way people take time to dress up, the way people carry each other in a conversation. I remember one time I went to class. I think it was Alan.[6] I think it was him. We had a Navajo class, and he was really. . . . I don't know what the word is—he was really close. He kind of invaded my space. And I'd never, never had experienced anybody like that. I've always kept like this little box here. When people come to you and talk to you real close, they say, 'Hey, how you doin'? or, they are really interested in you as an individual. Whereas when I grew up on the Reservation, I'd never experienced anything like that. You know I had Anglo teachers, but they weren't too personal. But when I came here I experienced that. I learned that people were really personable."[7]

I introduced something that textbooks often talk about as a Native American/Anglo difference. "There is also this thing about eye contact. Anglo people look you right in the eye."

"YEAH," Valerie emphatically answered. "Yeah, I remember that being a big deal that I had to deal with. Because I remember when somebody would look you in the eye, you'd feel threatened. On the Reservation people look at you straight in the face and you're like, 'What did I do?' you know, you feel threatened, whereas here it's normal. And now when people aren't looking at me when I'm talking to them, I feel like they are not giving me their attention. There are just so many different things that became apparent to me when I moved from one culture to another. Like on the Reservation you're not supposed to be too open-minded, you're not supposed to speak out too much. Your elders are the people who are the ones who got their points across. And over here in Anglo society it's like anybody had an opinion, anybody can say whatever they wanted to say.

"And I noticed that when I went home, I easily was attracted to the older adult conversation, like with my uncle Beam, my mom, and everybody. It was comfortable for me to join the conversation. Whereas when I was younger, or when I first left, it was like, sshhh—you know. Don't say anything; just sit back. I never really have engaged in a conversation with my uncles. I faced a lot of different changes. Just a way of living. I had money, and I had to learn how to budget my money. I'd never done that before. It was kinda new. I was open to a lot of different resources, like clinics. Back on the Reservation, there's a lot of women out there who are limited to . . . I mean their public health is readily available to them but they don't go to get a physical or get a mammogram or it's not consistent. They don't do it every year. Whereas when I came here, that was available to me, and I took advantage of all these services that would help me physically."

"Do you sometimes learn about those through your friends or contacts at class?" I asked, not really anticipating Valerie's answer.

"No, you know what, I think I learned the majority of those

from you. Because you would ask. . . . Remember that time we had that talk about birth control? I think we kept incorporating different things like my eyes, my ears, or my annual physical—pap smears—stuff like that. I kinda got all those from you. My friends say, 'Where's your mom?' 'She's at home. I have two moms; one's over at the Reservation and one's over here in Albuquerque.' 'Oh, you have two moms?' 'Yup.' But, I think the majority of that is what I learned from you."

A Break from School

After five years at UNM, Valerie was beginning to accumulate enough credits to take care of her general education requirements, and she was finding her way into a Health Education major. She and Duane continued to live off campus. During the summers, they returned to Sheep Springs where they lived with Carole and Eva and worked for various Navajo Nation programs for college students. For much of this time they did not have a car, making getting to and from school difficult. Valerie sometimes rode her bike, took the bus, or borrowed a car. In 1996, they moved into an apartment on Comanche Street about four miles from campus. When JR, Valerie's younger brother, graduated from Newcomb High School, he came to Albuquerque to live with them.

These were difficult months, and several times I was called on to intervene and help them pay late rental fees or bail JR out of jail after he and a friend drank too much beer and threatened to have a fight with the neighbors downstairs. Valerie did not tell me until our last interview that she and Duane were having difficulties as well. "I think that Duane and I decided that we wanted to get out of Albuquerque." They had financial difficulties and several times I had to help pay the rent. They decided to go to Salt Lake where Carole's brother Randy and family were living. Erica, Valerie's sister, was working there, too, and jobs were plentiful, according to Valerie's relatives. Leaving Albuquerque would give them a chance to start over and to remove themselves from their current situation.

"We both agreed, 'This is our opportunity to make our relationship better,' and we left. We had no plan. Nothing. And that turned out to be a bad decision because not only did our relationship not get better, it got worse. I discovered more things about him. His alcohol habits increased. I turned out to be the bad person all the time. And I think that was kind of when I said I want to go home. 'Cause this was all I knew, and Albuquerque was home to me. . . . I didn't have a support system up there—as far as friends were concerned—as I did down here. And I was miserable. I really was miserable."

Duane, Val, and JR left Albuquerque in December. In Salt Lake, Duane and Jay were able to get jobs in the warehouse where Randy was employed, and Valerie worked for a temporary agency. January came, and they didn't return to reenroll in school, which worried me, since I felt that dropping out would place Valerie in a long stream of low-level clerical or warehouse jobs. The warehouse job that Erica had paid much better than fast food jobs in Albuquerque, but for someone who had completed two years worth of college credits, it seemed like a "dead end." Valerie remembered, "I really missed school, and I didn't think that if I stayed up there that I would have [finished]. First of all, I'd have to pay out-of-state tuition. I remember going to the community college and trying to get into a class there, and it was so difficult to do. I guess you could think about it as a learning process. You know, to pick up and take off and not have any plan and everything and turn around . . . not so much backfire . . . but it just wasn't comfortable. That wasn't familiar to me. So that's when I turned around, packed up my stuff, and came home."

In March 1997, Valerie and Duane returned to Albuquerque. They couldn't enroll in classes until the summer session, so Valerie began to look for a job. They lived at my house in my den, which had a foldout couch, sharing the downstairs bathroom with my teenage son and storing their clothes in a dresser in the downstairs coat closet. "I mean everything started to look really positive from that point 'cause I got a job. And pretty much I was looking forward to going back to school, and that's exactly how it happened. I mean everything kind of just fell into place. But as far as our relationship was concerned, it didn't get any better. I mean I tried . . . I think I tried to hold off a long time, and I just wasn't happy."

Entering the Workplace

During her first three years in college, Valerie found it difficult to work and take classes at the same time. She did try work-study jobs at the university and a number of retail and fast food jobs around Albuquerque, but none lasted very long. Finally, after she and Duane came back from Salt Lake, Valerie found a job with St. Joseph 60 Plus Services, a health and wellness program for older adults.

"I got that job when I got back from Salt Lake. I really was interested in that job because it was along the lines of my field. It was health education. It was a wellness program for the geriatric population. And they did a variety of different things: health education as far as teaching them about different diseases, heart attacks, diabetes, as well as prevention like exercise, diet, nutrition. We hosted programs or seminars that were related to that, and I thought that was a really good place for me to start. That job really tested my ability to organize and plan things because as a health educator, I know some independent health educators. . . . They did a lot of open seminars where they had to prepare their presentation, not only the information in the presentation but also they had to worry about other things as far as being able to establish the location, whether or not we're going to have sponsors, literature, pamphlets."

Valerie was the assistant to the director of the program and made most of the arrangements. "And I also arranged a lot of the speakers. I interacted with a lot of educators who specialized in cardiology or physical therapists. My boss was an older lady, and she was a really good teacher. She would give me a list of things we needed to cover within the next three months, and it was my responsibility to look into our resources. We had a bunch of resources: previous speakers, the St. Jo's newspaper, anybody that I knew right off hand from school, or speakers, or my professors, if they knew anybody. She would give me this entire list and say, 'OK, we need people for these subjects. We need to find people.' So what I would do is I would research and find people who were available or who specialized in certain areas."

There was a membership fee each year, and about ten to fifteen people participated in each program. Valerie discovered that many of the participants really wanted something to do with their time. "We did a survey at one time and asked questions like, 'What attracts you to our program?' I remember one question specifically asked why people came, and when we tallied up those results, we found that the majority of the people did it because it was something to do outside the house; they weren't locked up in their homes, and they wanted to get out. So, we worked with a lot of volunteers, too."

Valerie felt very good about the services the program provided. "We hosted a lot of programs for like woodcarving and like hiking. We did a lot of that stuff, and the men participated. The men participated in the cooking classes that we had. And every month we'd have some kind of festivity, either like a birthday party where all the members who had birthdays in that month . . . we'd celebrate their birthday. And it was nice because we all went out to eat, or we all would have breakfast somewhere, and we celebrated their birthdays. They really, really liked it. And to see them interact with each other was really, really . . . it was comforting. It was. Just to see them. I mean, we are talking seventy-five, sometimes eighty years . . . they're interacting with others. That is just something that they enjoyed as opposed to being home."

Valerie enjoyed this job and was hoping to be able to direct the program when her boss retired. Unfortunately, the hospital closed the program, and Valerie was forced to get another position within the hospital, this time in the radiology laboratory in the film library. This involved a lot of attention to detail, since she filed x-rays, and the individual films had to be in the correct order. "That's one thing I really found interesting was that I was able to learn a lot of the different parts of the body . . . what happens to some of the parts of the body. . . . I got to know the radiology doctors really well. It came to a point where I could ask them a question about a certain film, and they will explain to me what was going on. . . . That was real interesting to me. . . . Because of my interests in what they did, they really came to trust what I did. They would give me extra things to do. I would be able to relay the results to the floor or to a different doctor, if the doctor was on the phone."

Valerie was enthusiastic about what she learned. "I liked that job. It was a good job. It kept me busy and I learned a lot about the human anatomy. I learned a lot about patient preparation for different exams. I learned a lot of medical terminology." The doctors engaged Valerie in humorous banter when she mispronounced some of the medical terms they were using. "And they would tease me. They would say, 'Say that again,' and I would say it again and they would laugh. 'You know, I'm not the one with a medical degree.' They would say it real slow for me, and then I would be able to say it after that." Some months later she moved from the film library up to the front desk where she took phone calls, coordinated the patient visits to the radiology lab, and supervised the patient escorts.

"The only reason that I moved to the front was because of my schedule at school. I really needed some study time, and I thought that job would be good for me. So I requested a transfer. And I transferred from the back position to the front position, and that worked really well because I came in at two thirty and left at eleven o'clock, and I was able to get some study time in. That was the reason why I switched to the front desk, because it allowed me to study."

But the front desk job carried important responsibilities. "I supervised the patient escort people, too. They were my responsibility. I needed to know exactly where they were at all times because they were our transportation. And if one day we had twelve exams we needed to do in one night, those people needed be on top of things and it was my responsibility to make sure they did it."

Student Teaching

Before Valerie could graduate with her BS in Health Education she had to take two important steps: pass the first part of the New Mexico Teacher Assessment Exam and complete a semester of student teaching in her subject. Valerie had put off the exam for several semesters, partly because it was difficult to find time to study and partly because actually getting one of the allotted spaces for the exam was difficult. Several times she applied to take the exam and found that there were no available spaces left. The exam tests the prospective teacher's general knowledge, vocabulary, social studies, math, and analytical skills. Valerie had heard "through the grapevine" that the exam was hard and that students had to take it twice. "I thought, oh my God, what if I don't pass it the first time around? I was really nervous about it." She went to her academic advisor and he gave her the registration packet, advised her to purchase a study guide, and suggested that she attend a review class. "I went to that class, and we went through every section, and we talked about math, we talked about general sciences, about vocabulary, language, and we did everything. The instructor then provided us with examples and test taking strategies. Basically, he just told us this is what the exam was like; this is what you need to do. And I was afraid I was going to have a really hard time with the math section. So, I did a lot of the math problems that were in the study guide."

Despite her preparation, the day of the test, Valerie was nervous. "It was an all-day Saturday test. I went in at seven o'clock and took this test. I had to write an essay. I did a math section, an English section, a social science section. Then we had to write an essay. And that was it. I was really freaked out. As I said, I was really scared because I wasn't quite sure if I was going to pass it. And I was really nervous." Valerie found it hard to concentrate since each section was timed, and it took about ten minutes to gather her thoughts for the essay. So she ran out of time in terms of completing the essay. "But I did the best I could, and I passed it. So, it wasn't so bad." She found out that she passed several months later and was much relieved. The good news came a few months before graduation and in the middle of her student teaching.

During the spring of 2000, her last semester at UNM, Valerie did her student teaching at West Mesa High School in the Health Education Program. She worked with two different Health Ed teachers with freshmen students enrolled in the required health education class. She found it challenging to deal with teenagers, especially when she had to be at school by 7:20 a.m. and meet her first class at 7:45 a.m. "Let's say maybe twenty-five to thirty people are staring at you every morning at a quarter to eight. They're not the happiest people on the face of this earth. And they expect you to be prepared. And that was hard. . . . I don't want to say tiresome, but it was tiring, but at the same time it the kept me on my toes . . . because these kids were so analytical. They were so ready to jump at you, if you said something wrong, or if you gave them some kind of misinformation or . . . they were easily ready to attack you." These students were "straight out of junior high. I needed to be really, really careful with what I said in front of these kids. I needed to be prepared. I needed to be able to keep their attention. I needed to be able to keep them interested in what we were learning. And I had to have the appropriate material available to make sure they learned something."

Although there was a set curriculum she was supposed to cover, it was Valerie's responsibility to come up with concrete lesson plans with specific examples and exercises for the students to do. "So while this stuff was there, it was just my responsibility [to make] a curriculum, being able to have a teaching strategy, what my objectives were, what I wanted the kids to learn. . . . The activities, any kind of homework assignments or whatever, I needed to have all that prepared every day. Notes, lectures—I needed to have that all ready the night before or the morning of [the class]. It was a lot of work. But I learned to plan ahead. I planned a week ahead every week because if the last minute I did something. . . . It was crazy because not only do you have to be prepared, [but you have to know how] the presentation relates to what we talked about yesterday. [You have to know] whether or not we should have a homework assignment. You know, it was really a lot of work."

Valerie also recognized this was a crucial time in the lives of her students, and a health class could give them important, accurate information about a healthy diet, sexuality, drugs, alcohol, and relationships, and it could help orient their behavior. "They need to be able to deal with this stuff, especially at that age, because they're learning their identity and that brings on a whole, you know, another basket of fruit. I mean they're dealing with relationships. They're dealing with drugs and alcohol. They're dealing with sex. They're dealing with parental guidance or some kind of parental guidance. Gang activity. No, they don't care about what they eat. They don't care about their exercise. Maybe there are some kids who do care about their exercise. We talked about nutrition." Valerie commented that very few of her students had breakfast and they often ate fast food or pizza, only eating a "real meal" with their parents in the evening.

"We talked about how much water you need to drink, what percentage of your body is composed of water, what kind of vitamins you need for your teeth to be strong. We talked all about all this stuff. And we actually did a project where they kept track of what they ate. These people's diet involved a chimichanga in the morning, a bag of chips, a soda, ice cream, candy. Every day. Maybe one kid out of . . . well no, about three or four out of the hundred I taught actually got up and ate a breakfast: an orange, an apple, probably some cereal of some sort." Valerie discussed exercise and obesity with the students and they, in turn, asked a lot of tough questions about the kinds of unhealthful food available in the school soft drink machines and the cafeteria.

One of the most important topics covered in the course was sexuality. "There was an actual curriculum that was already set that I had to follow. It was my responsibility to obtain the information appropriate for the curriculum and be able to teach that. And it tested a lot of my . . . I don't want to say my intellect, but it tested me. It really did because as far as, let's say teaching sex education, OK, we talked about pregnancy. We talked about fertilization, what happens. I HAD to know exactly how a certain birth control worked in order to give these people the information. I could not make one mistake . . . or they'll be lost. They'll ask, 'Well, I heard this doesn't work like that; it works like this.' What I found really disturbing was that a lot of the information these kids have is just totally false." So Valerie obtained pamphlets from Planned Parenthood and the Center for Disease Control and printed out information from the Internet.

"I really enjoyed that activity that I did because I had a lot of feedback. We spent almost a week on STDs. And we learned the most common sexually transmitted diseases, and then we went right into birth control. But I found that subject to be really, really rewarding because of the results. And we analyzed each individual fact, and we explained why it was wrong. And these kids were walking out of my classroom thinking, whoa! . . . I overheard conversations. I've overheard comments and I even had one kid come up after class and ask me, 'Is that really true, Ms. Johnson?' I said, 'Yes, it is.' . . . I sat there and I explained to him. I had one of my old biology books with me. I used that as a reference and also the health education book that we had there . . . that it was right there clear, in black and white. 'This is how it works. This is what happens, and, yes, you can get pregnant.'"

Valerie felt she was a successful teacher. "I had almost one hundred kids, and they listened to me. They learned to respect me. They looked at me and they thought, whoa, here's this college graduate or the senior in college who knows all this information. . . . I felt really good."

The first few weeks, however, were very difficult. Valerie had to learn how to handle students who tested her authority and talked back to her in class. "At first I was a little discouraged. . . . It was hard because when I went to my very first week, they might as well have butchered me and hanged me off the chalkboard. I was so discouraged. They were mean; they were rude; they were just totally disrespectful. I think I went in there thinking, these kids are gonna listen to me, and we are going to hit it off real quick. But I went in there, and I had to earn their attention. And their respect. I remember talking to my mentor, and I told him, 'I'm so discouraged. I'm afraid of these kids.' And he's like, 'No, don't feel that way. You need to go in there and, although you're scared to death inside, act like you are in control.' Half these kids probably belong to gangs, and I was really, really scared. So that next week I just changed my attitude, and I said, 'You know what, these people, they're younger than I am.' . . . I went in there, and I stood tall. I said, 'OK. This is what we are going to do.' And it took maybe another week, and at that point I was able to put my foot down and say, 'OK, you need to not talk.'"

One young woman was particularly hostile. "I don't wanna say she was a bad apple because she was smart. She was a little slow, but I think she had this reputation to uphold. She came into class with this attitude every day, and she talked while I talked—totally disrespectful toward everybody around her, calling people names in class. And I came out, and I told her, 'Don't say that in class.' And she turned around, and she called me a bitch. I got really upset." Valerie ordered her out of the room, gave the class some instructions to take notes, and went out into the corridor to confront her. "I went out there, and I told her, 'I warned you numerous times, and you're just continuing to be disrespectful. I'm leaving it up to you right now. What do you want to do? Do you want to be in my classroom or not?'"

The girl explained that she was having a bad time in her personal life, but Valerie replied that she should not bring these troubles into the classroom, even though Valerie would be willing to talk to her outside of class time. "She got choked up. I saw tears in her eyes, and I gave her an ultimatum. I said, 'You know what, this is. . . . It's either black or white; you're in or out. . . . I can turn you into the office and you can stay in ISS [the detention center] for the rest of the semester or you can sit in my classroom and learn.' She just looked at me and she goes, 'Well, all right, I'll stay in your classroom.'" She walked back into the classroom, and Valerie had no further problems with her, although, unfortunately, she was suspended from school three weeks later because she had gotten into a fight.

In another incident, a male student continued talking during class, and Valerie finally insisted that he teach the class himself. Valerie gave him a set of notes, sat in his seat, and then played the same role as he had: the boisterous student who does not pay attention. Other students had been told of her plan, so they made it difficult for him to even take roll. In frustration, he gave up saying, "I can't do this." "He was a real smart kid. But I just wanted to teach him this little lesson, to let him know how it felt when you're up there and you have all these people looking at you, and you have some other person trying to make all this noise and get all this attention. And this interrupts the entire class. He knew he was put on the spot. And from that point on he would talk every now and then, but I would look at him. He goes, 'OK, all right, I'll stop talking.'"

In many ways Valerie felt she was very successful with teenage students. "It was interesting and fun. It taught me lots of things. And I know those kids learned a lot of things. So, I think if I were to choose between geriatric and high school, I might lean more toward the younger generation because they will probably keep me busy. They probably will. That is one thing that I had thought about when I went into health education. I knew if I decided to go with teaching in high school or grade school, that if I change just one person out of an entire population of students, then I would have done my job. I had this teacher who taught me this, and I listened to what she said and she was right. But, you know, I talk about going back to teaching now, but I'm not really sure exactly at this point. I'm not real sure what I want to do."

Breaking Up with Duane

During March 2000, a few weeks before her graduation from UNM, Valerie ended her relationship with Duane, one that had lasted nine years. "I wasn't really happy. I think that most of it had to do with just the fact that there was one lifestyle that I wanted to live, and I just didn't see . . . any kind of opportunity for advancement in that relationship. I really did care about him a lot, but I wasn't going anywhere. I felt like I was being held back to a certain extent. . . . I'm not blaming him or anything, but it just was my time to move on, I think. Basically, I had matured and I wanted a really steady job where I devoted a majority of my time to that.

"But I just felt that I needed to go on, and get out of the lifestyle we were both living in. And being that I was graduating from college, I think it was a big step that I needed to take. I remember it being really difficult to make that transition but I had some . . . I had some really good friends who kind of helped me out with a lot.

"I remember at one point I told him I would be there for him until he graduated from college. And I helped him. I think I really, really helped him out a lot." I responded that, "I think he probably couldn't have gotten through without you." Valerie agreed, but went on to say that the relationship had positive aspects for both of them. "He's probably matured just as much as I have from this relationship as far as being responsible and knowing that he needs to take care of himself and be able to hold a job—a steady job—and be able to pay his bills, you know. I think it was also beneficial for him as well as me—as well as myself."

Graduation and a New Job

Graduation was a joyful occasion for Valerie and her family. She wore a traditional Navajo outfit of a red velveteen blouse, white three-tiered silk skirt, concho belt, and moccasins. Her hair was tied

FIGURE 10.1 Valerie in her silver cap and gown right after the University of New Mexico graduation, May 2000.
PHOTOGRAPH BY AUTHOR.

in a traditional Navajo bun, but like all the other BA and BS graduates, she wore a silver cap and gown over her other clothes.

The main UNM graduation ceremony was in the Pit (the basketball arena) on the second Saturday in May 2000. I rented a cap and gown and marched down the steps of the Pit to sit with other faculty, all the time keeping my eye out for Valerie and her family seated in the bleachers. She proudly walked up the ramp to receive her degree, and then received it a second time at the College of Education's graduation ceremony held in Johnson Gymnasium in the early afternoon. I hosted a family reception at my home in the North Valley. Eva, Carole, Valerie's brothers, her uncles, and a number of her cousins joined the group of well-wishers who shared our food and the graduation cake. Everyone got a chance to pose with the graduate in a series of family portraits.

After Valerie graduated she began thinking about getting a job that had more to do with her degree in health education. She took a position at St. Joseph's Hospital with the physicians' group where she started making $9.46 an hour, a healthy raise from the $8.00 an hour she was making at the radiology lab. Valerie at first thought that she would be able to have an opportunity to use this new position as a patient services representative to develop a health education program for the geriatric patients. At least this was the promise made to her in the interview. But when she began the job, she discovered that it was primarily a clerical one.

As she explained, "Since a lot of cutbacks were made at St. Jo's, that's one of the things they cut . . . just the idea that we needed a health educator within this program. So that's where that stood. And I picked up the responsibility somewhat as a receptionist, kind of clerical person. . . . My title is Patient Services Representative, but I do a variety of different things. I do referrals. I assist in training the front desk people. I assist in the phone answering. I also assist with some of the doctors . . . more clinical stuff as far as relaying results, getting back to the patient, taking doctor to doctor calls, calling in medication, which I'm not supposed to do, but I do."

One of Valerie's main responsibilities was to complete the referrals to specialists. First the doctor had to recommend the referral, and then Valerie contacted the insurance company. "I guess you

FIGURE 10.2 Valerie at her desk, working as a patient services representative.
PHOTOGRAPH BY MARGARET RANDALL.

could say that is my sole responsibility: making sure the insurance company gets the stuff. The insurance company is contacted, given the physician name, the diagnosis. They go by codes, so you have to give them an appropriate code; a certain skin pigmentation, skin cancer, urinary tract infection . . . all of these have codes. And it has to be accurate, in order for them to do appropriate billing. . . . If there's no approval from the insurance company, there is nothing in the computer system, they refuse to see that patient. Let me give you an example. The patient says, 'I need to go see Dr. B for a cardiology consult, because I had a heart attack.' I fill out the paperwork . . . the patient has St. Jo's Medicare Plus insurance. I choose the appropriate paperwork, fill out the patient's name, SSN [Social Security Number], DOB [Date of Birth], the plan that they are on, the diagnosis, the ICD9 [International Classification of Diseases, ninth edition] code, and the ordering physician's name. It is faxed to the insurance company. OK. That's done.

"I also have the responsibility of keeping track of medical records releases to lawyers, doctors, Department of Veteran Affairs, Social Security, disability, the patients themselves. We designed a spreadsheet where we keep track of all the information that leaves our office: the patient's name, DOB, where it is going, whether or not we were paid for it, why the patient is leaving. I mean there are a lot of rules and regulations and policies and procedures you need to follow as far as that's concerned. We can't fax medical records. We need to have an authorization of medical records release from the patient or the power of attorney for that patient. There is a lot of little things involved in that."

Valerie described how busy the office was, and how she often picked up the slack when a coworker was fired or on vacation and tried to help the doctors, especially if they were handling their own patients and filling in for a colleague on vacation. For example, rather than calling the doctor to the phone to deal with a patient who has a problem, Valerie would pull the patient's chart, bring to the doctor's attention what medication the patient used, and get his OK to call the pharmacy with the authorization. At one point during the day of our interview she reminded one of the doctors, "You are just lucky you have me."

She felt supported and appreciated by the doctors and her coworkers for the extra help she gave. "I think that is really appreciated in our office because the MAs [Medical Assistants] thank me for it. The doctors thank me for it. I have an e-mail from Dr. G. that says, 'I'm really thankful that you are helping out.' Dr. M., he'll come out and say, 'I'm really grateful, thank you.' I mean it's not a genuine gesture where they take you out for lunch or anything, you know, it's just knowing that they appreciate your help is kind of satisfying."

Valerie felt that through this job she learned a lot of medical terminology and also how the insurance system works. "I'm learning a lot about what drugs are used for what patients' diagnoses. I've also picked up a few ICD9 codes. For insurance I picked up a lot of this stuff. I'm learning to understand how these insurance people work, patients' benefits. I'm not quite clear on some of them still but . . . what kind of specialists they are able to see and . . . I've learned a lot of that stuff."

A Relationship with Donovan

Valerie first met Donovan during her second year at UNM (1992–93). She used to play intramural basketball with his sister, Carm, whom she met at the university gym, and was invited to play with a group of women that played regularly. She met Donovan when she attended a party with her friend, Shannon. Then she would see him on campus occasionally and hang out with him at Donovan's cousin's house or a local sports bar where they would watch football games. After graduating with an engineering degree, Donovan got a job in Albuquerque. "We had similar interests and similar traditions and teachings that I noticed. And he just instantly became like a really good friend that I could talk to. And it got to a point where we pretty much . . . maybe every other weekend or every weekend we hung out. . . . I found it so easy to talk to him and express my feelings and concerns and that is just how it started. Everything started out that way.

"I got to know him really well. He shared a lot of personal stories with me, as I did he. We gave each other support, encouraging each other that it would be OK; everything would work out. And it always did. Everything kind of turned out for the better sometimes. Sometimes, in my case, it didn't [in terms of her relationship with Duane]. You know, it kind of just was getting worse and worse, and I wasn't real happy. And he was always just so supportive. I mean, you know, very generous and very kind—unlike anybody I've ever known, you know, as far as a guy's concerned."

Donovan took a job for two years in Redding, California. When he left, Valerie felt the loss. "When he left I felt sooo miserable. I don't know why I felt that, but it was like somebody ran over my cat. I felt really, really just sad. I was so sad. And I think it was at that time that I knew I really liked him. . . . Of course, he called me on the road from like Arizona and Las Vegas—just south of Las Vegas. And then when he got there, he got established—got an apartment and everything. He would call me, and from that point on we talked probably maybe three or four times a week via e-mail or at work and slowly Duane and my relationship just withered away."

Donovan returned to New Mexico and got a job with the Indian Health Service as an environmental engineer in the Santa Fe office.

"He was always just really supportive of what was going on with me, helping me move on with my life. He also understood my need to fulfill my personal goals. He's really responsible. He was a really good friend of mine first before I got to know him real well. Just listening to him . . . to our conversations and what we talked about, I think that's what attracted me to him because he knew what he wanted. He was responsible. He had goals. He wants to further his education. He wants to be able to live comfortably. One of these things was to have a house and be established financially before deciding he wanted to get married and have children. And that's kind of ironic how . . . I don't want to say I fell into that lifestyle. Since the first time I met him I knew somehow that he was going to be a part of my life."

Valerie went on to describe how their relationship was evolving. "He's a hard worker, you know, he's very helpful, not only, you know, like, financially or as far as, like things around the house. . . . But I can't help to notice that he's just much more cooperative and much more helping. He's always lending me a hand. And I can be a quiet person sometimes. I like to be alone sometimes, to just be by myself and think about things, and not always [about things that are] bad or worrisome—things that are going on in my life. I think that is one thing that he doesn't . . . isn't really adjusted to." Valerie explained that Donovan would sometimes think she was upset or mad, but really she just wanted to be by herself for a while. "We're still learning things . . . about ourselves . . . being with each other. Our life is different now as far as when we used to know each other before. For one thing we didn't live together. And we see each other every day and every evening, and we both leave for work at the same time, and we sit and have dinner together."

Valerie and Donovan have worked out a division of labor that was not what Valerie had expected. "It's like a routine. He gets home sometimes before I do, and he starts dinner. When I get home before he does, I start dinner—kind of like a mutual thing. We do laundry together, and it's kind of like a fifty-fifty thing. You know, it's kind of nice. I had a really hard time with it at the beginning, because I was always doing everything. I gotta do laundry, I gotta cook dinner, I gotta wash dishes. I always did everything. And now I've got somebody who's stepped in and said, 'You don't have to do anything.

You don't have to do everything by yourself.' I kind of was offended by that because I felt like he was invading my space."

At this point in our interview I interjected, "I think women sometimes feel that way, a sort of possessiveness about the kitchen or something," thinking back to interviews I had conducted in the early nineteen eighties with working women who had young children, some of whom continued to do most of the cooking and cleaning. "Yes, right—a woman's role to bear children and work in the kitchen, you know, and it's different. He's just . . . he's different. He just freaks me out sometimes in a fun kind of way. And he really takes care of things, too. He values what he has. He takes really good care of his vehicle and the house. And that just shows me again, his responsibility. And his obligation now to me and the baby. He talks about our plans and retirement and what we're going to do. He wants to get his PE certification, which is his professional engineering license. And right now he's just field engineering."

Having a Baby, Getting Married, and Planning for the Future

In November 2000, Valerie learned she was pregnant. "I kind of was freaked out at first because I wasn't quite sure what was going on. I was not feeling really good and had some problems. I was really afraid because I was making this huge transition and then I was . . . then I was pregnant. And I wasn't quite sure if I could handle it. I mean as far as keeping somebody to help me raise this child. I had second thoughts. And I don't know, I think I kind of looked at it at a different angle. I made decisions in my life for certain reasons and I believe as a Native American sometimes . . . things happen to you beyond your control that you have to accept. Whether good or bad, you have to deal with it to make it work. When I found out I was pregnant, I had no symptoms. None whatsoever. They had to take a pregnancy test at least three times."

Valerie and Donovan had long discussions about the implications of having a child. "He made a commitment to me, and at that point, we would talk about getting married and stuff like this. He always told me that he really, really wanted to be with me. I was kind of at this point where I was quite sure I wanted to believe him.

I've known him for a long time but we were just starting off in this relationship and boom, you know. . . . And he said, if I remember correctly, he said, 'Well, I think we can do this.' So, I said, 'Are you sure?' and he said, 'Yes.' 'Are you positive?' and he said, 'Yes.' Later that night I asked him again and he said, 'Yes.' And then he started talking a lot. God, we were only six or seven weeks pregnant, and we were talking about day care and all this stuff, you know, 'What are we gonna do? And when are we gonna tell our parents?'

"I said that if I was to be married, I would be married one time, and I would not be divorced. And I'm afraid that if we rushed into this marriage and got married just because I was pregnant, it wouldn't make sense. I mean, we've known each other for a long time, and we've both cared about each other for a long time, and we were each other's support system . . . but that doesn't mean that we need to get married. You know, 'I care about you and, I don't think we need to rush into this.' I said, 'Let's take things one step at a time. And after the baby is born we'll plan to get married.' Lots, lots of things could happen in that time period. And, so I know he's not . . . he still wants to be married. But we've made an agreement that it will happen after the baby is born."

Valerie and I discussed what kind of wedding she might have. On a recent trip to California for the wedding of a friend of Donovan's, she recalled that they discussed what kind of ceremony they might have. "We were talking about what our wedding is gonna be like, and what are we gonna do, and are we going to have a traditional wedding or your average Anglo-American wedding. I always wanted an Anglo-American wedding. Nothing fancy shmancy, just something nice, something nice and simple. But, you know, we were considering our options and our financial situation. If we planned it and everything we could probably be able to have two weddings but I think it would be too much." I recalled that two Anglo friends of mine, both scholars who had studied the Navajo, had had two weddings, one an Anglo one and the other a traditional Navajo wedding. Valerie then suggested that she and Donovan would probably have a Navajo ceremony. "I know we both want a traditional wedding. That's probably the main thing that we want to do is have a traditional wedding. His concern was the fact he wanted to know where I wanted to be married. We don't really belong to a church, the both of us, although I was baptized as Mormon. We haven't really decided on that. But I think our tentative plan so far is that we have a Navajo wedding—have like a small gathering, a small dinner and then, maybe the next day or that same evening, have a different kind of reception. Maybe like in Gallup or somewhere."

I asked Valerie what her plans for the future were. "I want to go back to school. I really want to go back to school. I've been exploring some options. I wasn't quite sure on exactly what I want to do as far as my health education degree. I know that I had a taste of teaching, and I'm not quite sure if I still want to do that; however, I've considered possibly getting in with the public health service and possibly being able to [get into] health education that way . . . you know, environmental health or community health, somewhere along those lines, and still have a pretty good job as far as with the government. I think as a Native American I may have precedence as far as getting a job here or on the Reservation somewhere. I think that's what I want to do. I'm looking into environmental health, but my options are still open. I have plenty of time to prepare. Not only that, I looked into graduate school, and I talked to my advisor about it, and he suggested that I get a little bit of experience first, before I go back to graduate school, and find a focus . . . what I want to do. So, right now I really haven't had the opportunity to do that because I'm preparing for my baby. . . . That is going to take a lot of time for a while. And, in the meantime, although I'm not happy with what I am doing in my job, it's a job and it pays me money. And Donovan is also [encouraging about] that job. He knows I don't like it. He just encourages me every time. He did the same thing for a year. I've only been out of college for about eight, nine months. It's almost about a year. And he said, you know, he had a crummy job for about a year after he graduated. So, he's reminded me that we're going to come up. I just need to be patient, wait and hold on to this job."

Valerie looked back on her college years and her graduation and felt that she accomplished a lot. "It's really, really hard, but I'm glad I did it. I'm glad. I worked really hard, and it just kind of puts me a little step further than most people. I don't want to compare myself to others who have children and maybe have taken the vocational route and have chosen to become parents. I look at it at a different level now. A good example is my friends from high school. They all chose their lives right now. And, I don't look down at them for any reason, because I considered myself to be not one of the smartest people in my class. And all the people who I thought were going to succeed didn't. And that kind of just proves to me that if you work hard enough, you can graduate."

Valerie's thoughts came together just before she actually went through the graduation ceremony at the University of New Mexico in May 2000. "I think it was the night before. When everybody was here [at Louise's house in Albuquerque] and we're trying to figure out where everybody was going to sleep, you know, and we were here until about eleven o'clock at night and got home and laid there and I thought, oh my God, I'm graduating. It was a good feeling. And I thought that I did explore a variety of different classes, and it helped me to improve my academic ability. At the end I was just able to take a deep breath and say I did it. And you know, it felt good. It felt really good. And I know my family was really proud of me."

Epilogue

2006

ON SATURDAY, AUGUST 26, 2006, I GATHERED WITH EVA, Carole, Valerie, and other members of their extended family at their home in Yellow Hills. We were celebrating the August birthdays of several family members including Carole's, whose fifty-eighth birthday was that very day. Several of us had come from regional cities and towns outside the Reservation. Erica had traveled from Salt Lake with her husband, Oscar, and her two-year-old son. Since she rarely visited, this made the weekend a special occasion. Valerie and Donovan had come from Farmington where they had been living for two years. I arrived with Margaret Randall, who would take photographs for this book as well as revisit the family she had met five years before on our first picture-taking trip. Others had come from nearby. Timothy, Eva's oldest son and Valerie's uncle Beam, his wife, and two daughters drove from their home in Sanostee, thirty minutes away, while Pauline and Roslyn, daughters of Eva's oldest brother Frank and his wife Anita, came with their spouses from their separate homes about three miles away.

As we drove to Sheep Springs, Margaret and I talked about the landscape, less familiar to her, but driving along the highway north toward Tohatchi, Naschitti, and then Sheep Springs always brought back memories of driving this road several times a week in all seasons during the nineteen sixties. The expanse of the landscape is often breathtaking. That day, the wide-open sky was a bright blue, with cumulus clouds already beginning to gather. The broad plain below the deep blue/green Chuska Mountains that loom to the west of the highway seemed almost lush and green from the heavy August rains, with orange mallow and yellow rabbitbrush blooming by the side of the road. When Margaret and I arrived around 9:30, we joined Eva sitting in her yard and discussed our trip, the day's events, and the book contract I had brought out for Eva to sign. Carole had left in the pickup truck with her friend Bessie to purchase a sheep for us to butcher for the occasion. By the time Carole finally arrived with the sheep around noon it was beginning to sprinkle, so Haley brought out an umbrella to keep the rain off of us. Carole organized the butchering, with help from Ida (who had come with Carole's brother, Timothy). She chose a knife from the fancy knife set Erica had given her for Christmas and sharpened it. After the three of us lifted the sheep from the truck to the ground, Carole slit its throat while Ida held the sheep and I caught the blood in a pan. I was out of practice, not having helped butcher a sheep for several years, so I was not much help in removing the pelt or the head. Jay and Rudy helped us carry the heavy sheep over to a hook so we could hang the carcass upside down. Carole took expert control of the butchering, slitting the breastbone and pulling out the innards so that Ida and I could catch them in a pan. We carried these over to the shade where Eva, Ida, and I began cleaning the stomach and intestines. The small intestines were thoroughly washed and then later made into 'ach'íí' (the small intestines wrapped around pieces of the lining that holds internal organs together). The ribs, liver, and 'ach'íí' are grilled on an open fire and are the delicacies that are often eaten first, with Navajo tortillas (náneeskaadí) and roasted green chilies. I had not had 'ach'íí' for at least a year and was looking forward to it.

Using a cleaver, Carole finished the butchering, cutting off the two front legs, then separating the left hind leg and ribs from the backbone. These she hung over a wire stretched between the trees and covered the meat with cloth. She then severed the backbone from the right hind legs and ribs. The meat was soon taken into

FIGURE 11.1 Haley protects the sheep from the rain.

PHOTOGRAPH BY MARGARET RANDALL.

FIGURE 11.2
Carole kills the sheep while Ida holds it down and Louise catches the blood in a pan.

PHOTOGRAPH BY MARGARET RANDALL.

FIGURE 11.3
After the head and pelt are removed, the carcass is hung up and the front is slit open. Carole pulls out the stomach, intestines, and internal organs while Ida and Louise catch them in a pan.
PHOTOGRAPH BY MARGARET RANDALL.

FIGURE 11.4
After the forelegs have been removed, Carole uses a cleaver to take off the left hindquarters as the carcass hangs from the right.
PHOTOGRAPH BY MARGARET RANDALL.

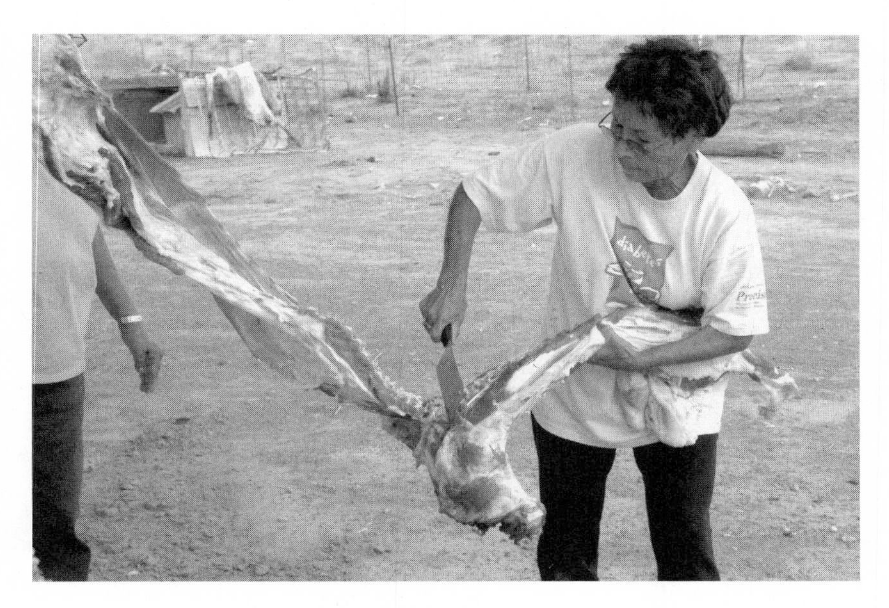

FIGURE 11.5 Carole removes the backbone from the right leg and ribs.
PHOTOGRAPH BY MARGARET RANDALL.

FIGURE 11.6
Eva cleans the small intestines. They will be wrapped around pieces of the inner lining to make 'ach'íí', which is braised over a fire with the ribs and liver, some of the delicacies eaten first after a sheep is butchered.
PHOTOGRAPH BY MARGARET RANDALL.

the refrigerator, where most would be given to the family to take home. The ribs were taken over to the grill near the outdoor shade for cooking.

Carole called Valerie on her cell phone to find out when they would arrive. They were only a few miles away and soon drove up in Donovan's black pickup truck. Erica emerged to greet me with hugs since we had not seen each other for at least a year. I also greeted Oscar, her husband, and two-year-old Ethan, who now was able to run around on his own. A little while later, Valerie was grilling the pork chops, steaks, and hot dogs that she and Erica had brought from Farmington. Carole, with Ida's help, made the náneeskaadí and Erica made her recipe for salsa, while I worked on the green salad. Later Erica, Bessie (Carole's friend who was there for the weekend), and I worked on the potato salad. A little later Valerie mixed the fruit salad with whipped cream. The meal was a mélange of Navajo and

FIGURE 11.7 Carole makes náneeskaadí (Navajo tortillas) that will be grilled in a hot frying pan.
PHOTOGRAPH BY MARGARET RANDALL.

Anglo food with Hispano accents—a New Mexico tri-cultural mix. The grilled mutton ribs, 'ach'íí', and náneeskaadí represented the Navajo side and the green salad, potato salad, and whipped cream and fruit salad came from the Anglo side, along with plenty of pop and fruit punch. Erica's salsa with its jalapeños and the roasted New Mexican green chilies added some Hispano flavor.

Before we ate, Timothy offered a prayer in Navajo mentioning all who had come and thanking the Lord for keeping the family well and in a state of hózhǫ́ or blessing. Valerie also gave a speech thanking everyone for being there and mentioning that this was a joint celebration for Timothy, whose birthday was August 16, Aaron on August 18, and Randy a few days later. Carole, of course, was

FIGURE 11.8 Valerie mixes fruit and whipped cream salad in Carole's kitchen. PHOTOGRAPH BY MARGARET RANDALL.

born on that day, but Valerie was discrete in saying, "I won't tell you how old she really is." She thanked everyone for being there, including Margaret and me. Then she talked about the personal relationship she had with each of her family members and how important it was that they came together for this celebration. She mentioned that Erica did not come down from Salt Lake very often, so that it was special for her to be there, and Ethan seemed to be so smart and was talking a lot. She spoke about the love she had for her family and how she had learned something from each of those whose birthdays we were celebrating. Her uncle Timothy had given her advice, and she had always been able to go to him when she had a decision to make. Her mother had given her life itself. Randy was the first to graduate from high school, and that was important in helping her to decide to do the same. Aaron would always be her baby brother, and she would always take care of him and make sure he had the things she had never been able to have. She turned to her relationship with her sons and told a poignant story about Jacob's first day at school the past week. She took off the whole morning from work to be with him at kindergarten. But he settled in quickly to his new surroundings and soon said, "Mom, you can go now." She felt both a little abandoned by him, but also proud of his growing independence. Valerie's speech (in the same tradition as thank-you speeches given at more public ceremonies like the Navajo Enemy Way when visitors have come to help or be fed) embodied the values of k'é, family and kin relationships, and how important they were to her and those gathered for the celebration.

We lined up for the food, piled our plates high, and ate our fill. When it came time for the cake, Valerie and Carole lit the candles. A reluctant Aaron was encouraged to blow out the candles, but he got a lot of help from Haley, Timothy, and even little Ethan, while Carole and Valerie looked on. We all sang "Happy Birthday" four times.

Birthday parties like this one are a relatively new family event, not part of the Navajo cultural tradition. But, along with Thanksgiving and Christmas dinners and the occasional postgraduation meal, they now function to bring Eva's children and grandchildren back to the homes at Yellow Hills, the family *kéyah*, or land. Although parts of Eva's kin network were often away during the nineteen sixties

FIGURE 11.9 Valerie serves Oscar (Erica's husband) while Ida and Louise fill their plates in the family hooghan.

PHOTOGRAPH BY MARGARET RANDALL.

FIGURE 11.10 Valerie and Carole light the birthday candles in the hooghan after everyone has finished their meal.

PHOTOGRAPH BY MARGARET RANDALL.

FIGURE 11.11 Timothy, Haley, and Ethan blow out the birthday candles while Valerie and her son, Dylan, and brother, Aaron, look on. PHOTOGRAPH BY MARGARET RANDALL.

when Joe went to work on the railroad, Carole attended school, or Eleanor's husband commuted to his job in Gallup, Eva's children and grandchildren are now more widely dispersed in Gallup, Salt Lake, Farmington, and Albuquerque. During the weekdays, Eva and Carole are often the only ones staying at Yellow Hills, while others have more jobs and rental apartments or homes in their new locations.

Not all family get-togethers are Navajo adaptations of American celebrations. Many have important religious significance. The next weekend would involve another family gathering, this time to help Timothy who had been designated as a stick receiver for an Enemy Way ceremony. Since Valerie's graduation from the University of New Mexico, there have been three large ceremonies that have brought many of Eva's children and grandchildren together along with more distant kin and clan relatives. The first was Valerie and Donovan's wedding in October 2002, and the second was participation in an

Enemy Way by Timothy's daughter, Rolinda, during the summer 2004. In July 2006, Timothy, himself, was a patient in an Enemy Way and then had been selected as the stick receiver just a month later. In between there were smaller Native American Church meetings and Blessing Way ceremonies.

These occasions emphasize the importance of place in Navajo life, and the significance of Yellow Hills with its cluster of houses that have been the central location for this family since Eva's childhood. Yellow Hills was once one of the two places in a seasonal migrational cycle—herding at Mountain with a White Neck or Deep Valley in the summer versus cultivating the fields and using the flatlands for winter forage at Yellow Hills. In the twenty-first century it has become a gathering place rather than a homestead, one that is used to keep a more scattered kin network together. As I have explained previously, the centrality of place is also linked to the value of k'é or those positive relationships of compassion, cooperation, friendliness, unselfishness, and peacefulness. K'é relationships are primarily kin relationships, starting with those who have come up and out of the same mother's womb (*bił hajíííjéé'*). Clan relationships are also defined as k'é relations or as part of the large category of shik'éí or my relatives. Since every Navajo person has four matrilineal clans, many of those who participate in larger ceremonies like a wedding, a graduation party, or an Enemy Way are related by clan. For Anglos like myself, place and kinship are not so easily coterminous and are often shifting from one bilateral kindred to another. Family occasions such as Thanksgiving or Christmas may be held at a parent's or in-law's home or later in life at the house of a brother or sister. The connection with place shifts once a parent dies or moves to a retirement center. For the Navajo with a universe set between four sacred mountains and with families residing in local areas for more than 150 years in many cases, the extended family homestead and surrounding land become part of a family's identity, particularly a matrilineal clan segment or group of women, their children, and grandchildren.

The emphasis on k'é and place is also evident in Valerie and Donovan's wedding, which took place in the fall of 2002. Valerie in her musings in chapter 10 had wanted an Anglo-style wedding and was even considering two wedding ceremonies, one Anglo and the other Navajo. In view of the importance of place in solidifying family and even Navajo identity, it was significant that Valerie and Donovan decided to hold a traditional Navajo wedding at Carole and Eva's residence group. This contrasts to Valerie's sister, Erica, who married her Puerto Rican boyfriend in a small ceremony in Salt Lake, or Valerie's brother JR who lives with Frances and two daughters but has never had an official wedding (typical of second and third Navajo marriages of the past). Although it was not arranged, Valerie's wedding contained all the important elements that Eva's and Eleanor's weddings did six decades ago. It brought together two matrilineal kin networks who gather together in a hooghan on the woman's kéyah or land.

With the help of Valerie's uncles, a hooghan was constructed. Following an old Navajo tradition, Donovan's parents, sisters, relatives, and Donovan arrived at the homesite on horseback. The groom's family entered the hooghan and sat on the north side. Valerie, the bride, was dressed in a traditional Navajo velveteen blouse and skirt, with her hair tied in a *tsiiyéél*, and entered carrying the wedding basket with the cornmeal mush, followed by her relatives who sat on the south. The singer or medicine man presided, and the couple sat to the west, opposite the door. The hooghan was decorated with an American Flag and a tapestry containing symbols from the Peyote religion. The singer instructed the couple to wash their hands in water poured from a Pueblo wedding vase. Then Valerie fed Donovan from the basket of mush, and he fed her in turn (they took some from each of the four directions of the basket). This ceremony added some nontraditional touches. The couple exchanged rings. The medicine man blessed the marriage certificate with a prayer, and the medicine man asked for the wedding cake to be brought in and the couple again fed each other, this time with the cake rather than the mush.

The introductions of each set of relatives began and most of the significant members of each party spoke about the future of the couple. Then we all filed out of the hooghan (in a clockwise direction) and lined up for a Navajo meal, including the same sort of mix I described for the August birthdays. Afterward Valerie and

Donovan cut and served their wedding cake, provided by Uncle Beam and daughters, and opened their presents, which were household items and a pair of matching Pendleton blankets.

Metaphors of Weaving and Stirring

It is possible to see the elements in birthday parties and weddings as deriving from a different culture—Anglo or Navajo. The occasion itself may be structured as an Anglo event (a birthday or a graduation party) but with Navajo elements (mutton stew, fried bread) threaded in with Anglo ones (the birthday cake, singing "Happy Birthday"). Or the event may be structured as a Navajo one (the Kinaaldá, or a marriage ceremony) with Anglo elements (an American flag, corn grinders used instead of a mano and metate) or scenarios (exchanging wedding rings) woven into it. Some scenarios take an Anglo element (e.g., a wedding cake) and use it in a Navajo way—the couple feeding each other. Other scenarios (cutting a wedding cake, opening gifts) are behavioral events tacked onto a Navajo event, adding to its richness and complexity.

Even if we look at an event like a wedding meal there are additional layers of borrowing, amalgam, and meaning that go beyond the simple Anglo/Navajo dichotomy. At one level there is the contrast between the mutton stew, on the one hand, and the potato salad and hamburgers, on the other, or the Navajo corn mush and the American wedding cake. Ironically, however, even the mutton originally comes from the introduction of sheep into Navajo life through contact with the Spanish in the eighteenth century and corn itself was adopted through contact with Pueblo peoples before then. These can be seen as elements from different cultural traditions woven together into the same tapestry or rug, distinct yet part of a new whole.

But as we listen to Valerie talk about her own identity as a young Navajo woman, the metaphor of stirring or blending seems more appropriate—just as Valerie was stirring together the cornmeal and water for her 'alkąąd. She sees herself as molded in the image of Changing Woman through her puberty ceremony and as the educated, goal-oriented woman she has become—a sort of seamless blend of American and Navajo ways of thinking about the self. The meaning of the Navajo marriage as hazhó'ó sooké or "sitting together nicely," in beauty and peacefulness, blends together Anglo ideas about love and commitment with Navajo goals of reciprocity and mutual aid.

Valerie and Donovan have continued in their pursuit of professional careers and have evolved into a dual-worker family. Their son Jacob was born in May 2001 in Albuquerque. He seems like an American boy entranced with Spiderman and trucks. But his parents are teaching him Navajo as well as English, and he often spends weekends at Yellow Hills. In the summer of 2004, Donovan was relocated to the Shiprock Indian Health Service, and the family moved to Farmington, first to an apartment and later to a rental house. They have sold their house in Albuquerque, and have purchased a new home built to their specifications on the outskirts of Farmington. Valerie got a job as an office manager at a behavioral health center in Farmington. She began taking courses on social work at the local community college and was soon promoted to caseworker at the center.

Valerie and Donovan's son, Dylan, was born in September 2005, and Valerie returned to work just before Christmas, putting both boys in the local day care center that Jacob had attended prior to his brother's birth. Valerie is beginning to take over some of the holiday celebrations, cooking Thanksgiving dinner at her Farmington home, for example. JR and Frances, after a six-month stay in Albuquerque where they worked in fast food restaurants, returned to Sheep Springs to live in Carole's house. Carole is finding her role as a babysitter and grandmother to Haley, the five-year-old daughter of JR and Frances, a satisfying one. Haley's little sister, Hillary, was born in March 2006 and is another welcome addition to the household.

Eva is approaching eighty years of age and is having more difficulty walking, so she rarely visits her planted fields in the summer or herds her few goats, letting them roam around the homestead. Randy divorced his wife Barbara in the spring of 2005 and brought his son Randall to Sheep Springs from Salt Lake to attend school and be nearer to his paternal family. Randy and Ruda, who is often at his hooghan next door, cook and clean for Eva, tasks she no longer can

FIGURE 11.12 Carole with her grandchildren.
PHOTOGRAPH BY MARGARET RANDALL.

do for herself. She rarely weaves anymore; her last rug was one she made for me, a brown and white, hand-spun rug with my name on it. She still attends Enemy Way ceremonies and was an important participant in her granddaughter Rolinda's Blessing Way during the fall of 2005. At this small family ceremony she chanted along with the singer and his wife, staying awake all night to help protect her granddaughter from disturbing dreams. Though she may not spend hours at her loom any more, weaving is an apt metaphor for the way in which she, her daughter Carole, and Valerie have constructed their lives.

NOTES

Notes to Chapter One

1. In June 2004, Valerie and her family moved to Farmington, New Mexico, when her husband, a civil engineer with the Indian Health Service, received a transfer.
2. The Navajo word "hooghan" means "a place where there is living." In the nineteen sixties it usually referred to a *hooghan nímazí*, or round hooghan, made of pine logs placed in log-cabin style with a rounded cribbed roof made from beams and covered with dirt or tar paper and a smoke hole for a fire, or more often, the pipe of a woodstove. In Sheep Springs in the nineteen sixties many families lived in one- or two-room log cabins, often chinked with mud or with cement like Eva's. Some families still lived in hooghans, while others kept hooghans for traditional Navajo ceremonies.
3. Navajo Chapters are community organizations first started by the Bureau of Indian Affairs in 1925 when Indian Agents felt the need to have some local political organization. They became centers for resistance to the Navajo Stock Reduction Program and the BIA abandoned them (Kluckhohn 1962:158). They were revived by the Navajo Tribal Government in the nineteen fifties and have since become the local political organization, structured in accordance with American political tradition, with an elected president, vice-president, secretary, and now an office staff. Many tribal programs are administered through the 109 local Chapters.

4. The Enemy Way is a three-day ceremony to cure illness contracted because of contact with non-Navajos. It is different from a "chant" (hatáál) since it does not use a rattle to accompany songs, but rather, a drum. The patient is also called by a different term and it is possible to have two hataałii (singers) or even four. It is on the "ghost way" side rather than the "blessing way" side and particularly is supposed to dispel the influence of foreign ghosts (*'ana'í bich'į̨dii*) (Haile 1938:17). In recapitulating the ceremony first performed in mythical times, a bell-stick is taken from the main patient's camp to a group of Navajos in another area, designated the stick receivers. A young girl from the stick receiver's kin group takes care of the stick and also leads the dancing around a bonfire on each of the three nights. While a group sings accompanied by a small, water-filled drum, women and younger girls choose male partners and lead them in a slow shuffle step around the fire. Males must pay the women for the dances (usually a quarter or two). The first night takes place at the stick receiver's residence, the second at a place midway toward the patient's camp, and the third at the patient's camp itself. During the three days there are elaborate exchanges between the two groups, the patient's group first being fed and given gifts during the time they are at the stick receiver's camp, and the stick receiver's group receiving hospitality and gifts when they arrive at the patient's camp the morning of the last day and night. (See Witherspoon 1975:56–64.) After World War II, the Enemy Way ceremony was held for many returning veterans to counteract their contact with either Japanese or German dead. Because of the female-led round dance that is performed each night, the ceremony is often called a "Squaw Dance." This term may seem pejorative, but it is still commonly used on the Navajo Reservation. (See also chapter 7.)
5. I realize I have just written the tried-and-true fable of entry that anthropologists since Malinowski and Firth have used to establish "ethnographic authority," a sense that the reader should believe what we write because "we were there" (Clifford 1988). This fable has been analyzed and critiqued in a number of ways, but many of us still find it useful in beginning texts that focus on women, even as we are grappling with new, more dialogical ways to write about our relationships with women in non-Western cultures. Ruth Behar uses the trope of the first encounter in her first chapter of *Translated Woman* (1993) when she describes her initial meeting with Esperanza the street peddler and so-called bruja or witch at a cemetery on the Day of the Dead in 1983. Though not the first metaphor of the chapter (which is taken up with a story of the talking Serpent, a story to guide us into the complications of telling stories), Behar's image of the woman carrying calla lilies "like something out of one

of Diego Rivera's epic Indian women canvases" is striking. When Behar asked to take her picture, Esperanza asked, "Why?" That the exotic portrait talked back to the *gringa* anthropologist conveys the relationship Behar wants to project as the overarching relationship that produces the book. In contrast, Lila Abu-Lughod tells a story of "return" or reentry into the field to begin her book, *Writing Women's Worlds* (1993). She uses this story of returning with her father to present gifts to the Haj and his family as a way of stating how the Haj's reaction and the book itself bridges two worlds: one Western and one Bedouin. While most classic ethnographies have often included a personal narrative of encounter at the beginning of the book (and then adopted the position of the omniscient narrator above the text), I have tried to link the connections I have to the Navajo Reservation to issues that have impacted Navajo lives, and the intersection of my own family's history with that of the Navajo and with Eva, Carole, and Valerie throughout the book. Rather than applying the metaphor of bringing a story across a border or the one of bridging two worlds, I look toward creating a set of narratives that illustrate how Eva, Carole, Valerie, and I are part of one world, one political economy, yet separated by class, race, and sets of cultural meanings. We have different positionalities and bring sometimes differential and sometimes overlapping cultural notions to our interactions and conversations.

6. Most anthropologists rely on one or two (or sometimes more) informants/consultants during their field research with whom they develop close bonds and are often "adopted" or become family members. Some of these relationships are described in Casagrande's *In the Company of Man*, one of the first book-length treatments of anthropologists' relationships with consultants. Since 1960 there has been a growing literature on the anthropologist's personal connections to members of the communities they study. *Strangers to Relatives: The Adoption and Naming of Anthropologists in Native North America* (Kan 2001), a collection of articles, describes the variety of personal relationships anthropologists have forged with Native Americans in a wide range of cultures from the Northwest Coast (Tlingit, Kwakwaka'wakw) to the Midwest (the Lakota, Northern Cheyenne) to the East Coast (the Seneca). The use of names, kin terms, and informal adoption into families, lineages, or clans have been used to incorporate well-known anthropologists like Lewis Henry Morgan, Franz Boas, and William Fenton as well as recent field researchers into Native American communities.
7. The batten (a broad, smooth stick about eighteen inches to two feet long) is placed vertically in between every other thread on the upright loom and turned horizontally so that it makes a shed, then

the weaver inserts the weft. The comb is used to pound the weft down and the batten is removed so the opposite group of warp strings can be brought forward, and the batten inserted again to make a new shed.

Notes to Chapter Two

1. 'Asdząą Hashkéhí was a clan relative of Eva's grandmother (possibly a sister or parallel cousin). Since Eva's grandmother died young and her mother was raised by another clan relative, the exact genealogical links are unclear; however, among the Navajo, such "blood" linkages make no difference. A maternal ancestor is always thought of as *shimá sání*, my grandmother.
2. This story is significantly different from that recorded in Franc Newcomb's book *Hosteen Klah: Navaho Medicine Man and Sand Painter* (1964). According to Newcomb, 'Asdząą Ts'ósí, also called 'Asdząą Tsoh, worked for the wife of an army lieutenant at Fort Sumner, but left this employment in the summer of 1866 to marry Hoskie Nolyai. She was pregnant when she went with her uncle Dziłtł'ahnii Yázhí, his wife, her aunt, and her aunt's Apache husband to Fort Wingate. They were allowed to leave Fort Sumner and were accompanied by American soldiers as far as Wingate (Bear Springs near Gallup) where they camped in the piñon trees. Hosteen Klah, according to this account, was born in December 1867. In Newcomb's version, the Navajos were enumerated and given ration cards, but when no sheep arrived, they traveled to Fort Defiance. They did not receive sheep or other supplies until the summer of 1869 (Newcomb 1964:59–62).
3. In the first version of this story, Eva added the following details, "And then from there, as quickly as they could, they traveled to Washington Pass. Through the canyon where they had moved; there were houses there. There was where our late grandmother was. There they pounded rabbitbrush and herbs found on the mountain with hot rocks. Then they dressed her feet with them, they said. That is how my late mother told the story."
4. In 'Asdząą Hashkéhí's narrative of return to her homeland, a place of rootedness, a central theme is that of assistance from animals, natural elements, and kin. 'Asdząą Hashkéhí makes her way back with the help of a dog, a companion who protects her. At the river (the Rio Grande near present day Albuquerque, New Mexico), she addressed the "Collected Waters" and "Water's Child," and they receded so she was able to cross. The "Collected Waters" have been gathered from each cardinal direction and are important elements in the Rain Ceremony (Reichard 1950:609), while "Water's Child" refers

to spring water (Reichard 1950:609). In Navajo belief, plants, animals, and elements of the natural environment like water have human-like properties. They are animated, move, and, in this case, can provide assistance and help (Schwarz 1997:35–48).

5. According to Wesley Thomas, based on his interviews with Navajo elders, there are four genders: the first is the female-bodied woman, the second the male-bodied man, the third (nádleeh) the male-bodied woman, and the fourth (*dilbaa'*) the female-bodied man (Thomas 1999:9–12).
6. Newcomb in her biography spelled his name, Hosteen Klah (Newcomb 1964). I have used the more phonetically correct spelling Hastiin Tł'aaí, which means "Left-Handed." Navajo ceremonies or hatáál (sings) are given for one or more patients in order to cure illness caused by improper contact with supernaturals, animals (bears, snakes, deer), or other natural phenomena (wind, lightning); they are two-, five-, or nine-night chants performed by a specialist (a singer or hataałii) who has gone through a long apprenticeship in order to learn the songs, story, and ritual procedures that constitute a particular chant. The Night Chant (often called the Yé'ii Bicheii Dance) and the Mountaintop Way (often called the Fire Dance) in their nine-night versions, are the more elaborate of the Navajo chants, performed usually in the fall months. The Enemy Way (Squaw Dance) is performed during the summer months. Other common chants are Beauty Way, Navajo Wind Way, and Chiricahua Apache Wind Way. Blessing Way is the central ceremony used to protect and bless patients; it is performed for pregnant women, soldiers leaving for active duty, and songs from the Blessing Way are part of the house blessing ceremony and the girl's puberty ritual, the Kinaaldá.
7. Eva had visited Navajo Community College (now Diné College) several years before to try and find who had possession of Tł'aaí's jish, but she was told that the College did not have any of the items. Charlotte Frisbie lists the Wheelwright Museum of the American Indian as having in 1977: a partial Night Way bundle donated by Tł'aaí; a Wind Way bundle and an uncataloged Hail Chant bundle, both probably donated by Tł'aaí; as well as several sets of prayer sticks, the first of which were donated by Tł'aaí's relatives. She says these were donated to the NCC museum in 1977 (Frisbie 1987:243, 247). In 1994 we viewed a number of plumed wands that probably came from Tł'aaí, plus the contents of a Wind Way medicine bag that was his (including a bundle of mirage stones or hadahoniye'). We also saw several Earth bundles (which are part of the Blessing Way) and Talking Prayer Sticks, which were not associated with Tł'aaí. Under the provisions of NAGPRA (the Native American Graves Protection and Repatriation Act), all U.S. museums had to

catalog Native American sacred items and make these lists available to tribes. Thus, in 1994 the Wheelwright was in the process of listing these items for possible repatriation to the Navajo Tribe. Tł'aaí's relatives have since requested that his paraphernalia remain at the Wheelwright Museum. Only Navajo singers and family members can access them.

8. These women married two brothers and in some historical sources they are referred to by their husbands' names: Mrs. Sam Manuelito (Gladys) and Mrs. Jim Manuelito (Irene).
9. Charlotte Frisbie describes the transfer of eleven jish from the Wheelwright Museum to the NCC Cultural Center Museum on August 17, 1977. Eight of these were complete, and some certainly belonged to Hastiin Tł'aaí. These included jish from the Night Way, Enemy Way, Life Way, Blessing Way, Red Ant Way, Shooting Way, Beauty Way, and Mountaintop Way. Museum personnel may have told Eva that they did not have the jish either because the jish were on loan or because the museum's policy was that only qualified chanters could have access to sacred materials (Frisbie 1987:341–48). As of March 1986, however, only the Night Way and Enemy Way medicine bundles had been refurbished and all of the jish were still awaiting appraisal (Frisbie 1987:352).
10. The mirage stones, flint arrowheads, and other items made from long-lasting materials are called "hard goods" in Navajo.
11. The Night Way is usually performed in its nine-night version during the fall months on the Navajo Reservation. It counteracts illness caused by improper contact with supernaturals. On the ninth night, masked dancers appear representing Yé'ii, supernatural figures or gods. They are called Yé'ii Bicheii, literally "the maternal grandfathers of the gods." They dance in front of the ceremonial hooghan.
12. Sandpaintings, or *'iikááh* (also meaning "they come") are made during many Navajo chants. They contain figures of the Holy People representing incidents in the myth that goes with the chant. They are constructed on a bed of sand out of colored, ground rock (red, yellow, blue, black, and white). Once the painting is completed (usually during the afternoon), the patient sits on the painting, the singer chants a series of songs, and presses the sand against the patient's body. The Holy People enter the painting and their healing power thus is transferred into the patient.
13. Irene Ball, who had been known as Mrs. Jim Manuelito, died in the summer of 1994.
14. Eva often "salt and peppers" her Navajo sentences with English words. When she has done so, as mentioned in chapter 1, I have put these words in boldface. In this case she uses the English terms for

the Chuska Mountains and Washington Pass instead of the Navajo place names, beginning with dziłdi, "at the mountain," the usual way of referring to the mountain range in general, and Béésh Łichíi'ii Bigiizh, "copper cut," which designates the area at the top of the pass.

15. Here as elsewhere Eva uses the term "Nahasdzáán," which means not just "earth," but Mother Earth, the female contrast to Father Sky in Navajo thinking.
16. Andy died in the late nineteen nineties, and Rena died in spring 2005.
17. Rena's family hasn't lived on the mountain for at least thirty years and perhaps longer.
18. Tó Nitsaa is up on top near Aspen Lake, about three miles north. It is a flat meadow. Rena's family used to herd up there, but never had a home there. Tł'aaí's mother would have herded in this area as well.
19. Rena refers here to her matrilineal ancestors—the mothers and grandmothers, as well as those men married into the clan—the fathers and maternal grandfathers.
20. Carole asked Rena if he had his hair cut like a Pueblo man; Rena thought that might be the case.
21. We obtained copies of several pictures of Hastiin Tł'aaí from the Wheelwright Museum. Figure 2.5 shows Tł'aaí in front of his hooghan, a structure that looks like the one described by Newcomb. Figure 2.4, taken in front of a stone building that may be the Newcomb Trading Post, shows Tł'aaí with several women. In looking at the photo on October 15, 1994, Carole, Eva, and I discussed who the women might be. One is likely to be his sister, Ahdesbah. Another might be Daisy, and the other three could be Lucy, Charlotte, and Evelyn.
22. Ben is the son of the woman who was raised with Grandma Sandman and thus a clan brother.
23. For the most recent discussion of the literature on nádleeh, as well as a critique of Anglo approaches to this subject, see Wesley Thomas, *Gendering Navajo Bodies: A Personal, Political and Philosophical Treatise*, PhD dissertation, University of Washington, 1999.
24. Will Roscoe (1988) published an article pulling together much of the material on Hastiin Tł'aaí and comparing him with We'wha, calling each a berdache, but also drawing attention to their important roles as artists, ceremonial practitioners, and innovators who also had important contacts with white scholars that led to the preservation of indigenous knowledge. Today many would object to his use of the term "berdache" because it derives from Persian and Arabic terms denoting "kept boy" or "male prostitute"—two very negative labels (Jacobs, Thomas, and Long, 1997:4). The Roscoe article,

however, is a sympathetic and careful portrait using most of the important sources.

25. I think Rita Berland's mother is 'Asdzą́ą́ 'Áhidiidlį́. Rita Berland is the aunt of Eddie Foster who still lives there. According to my genealogies in 1965, lineage 176 included Rita Berland and Eddie Foster. In 1965 Rita was forty-five years old, Eddie was twenty-seven, and a younger brother Joe was seventeen. Eddie and Joe's mother was Emma B. Foster and she was married to John Foster Baadaaní. Joe Foster now lives there by himself at Where Waters Cross.

Notes to Chapter Three

1. There is no simple term for this unit in Navajo. Navajos often talk about this group by naming either the senior woman or man and indicating the children as well, for example, 'Asdzą́ą́ Ts'ósí dóó ba'áłchíní (Thin Woman and her children) (Lamphere 1977:70). Witherspoon calls it the "Subsistence Residential Unit" (1975, chs. 9, 10). I (and other anthropologists) have used the term "camp," though Navajos often object that this makes their residence sites seem temporary and impermanent, which they are not.
2. In rereading my field notes, I discovered Eva had told me shortly after I started living with her that Anita has always lived with her in-laws rather than her mother since she had no mother and father and no brothers and sisters. Anita was from the Naschitti area, ten miles south of Sheep Springs. She had been married before, and Leonard Sandman was a child from that marriage. Eva then recalled that maybe Anita had a brother—someone named Wallace Benally. Frank, the oldest son, thus lived virilocally all of his married life, while Allen Sam, the second son, lived uxorilocally, first with his wife, Francis (who lived at Bitis 'Adeetiin or Roads Passing Over with Kiyaa'áanii relatives about three miles south of Yellow Hills). She died in the mid–nineteen forties when she strained herself carrying wood. In the early nineteen fifties, Allen Sam married his second wife, Alice, and lived uxorilocally with her at Kin Dah łizhiní or Black Houses Sitting There, about five miles northwest of Yellow Hills. This was where he was living when I met him in the nineteen sixties. Allen died around 1976.
3. Later in this chapter I describe the reason Eva's parents moved to Yellow Hills in the early nineteen thirties. There the extended family increased as Eva's sister married, as Anita's son Leonard married and had children, and as Eva herself married. The breakup of this group is described in chapter 5.
4. Two Grey Hills style rugs (named after the Trading Post at Two Grey Hills where the trader helped weavers develop these characteristics)

are black-bordered rugs with intricate designs (e.g., step patterns, zigzags) using white, black, and natural tan and brown colors. Two Grey Hills rugs are among the most expensive and highly prized on the Reservation.

5. Because the numbers 666 are considered by some to be "the mark of the beast" (cited in the Book of Revelations in the Bible), the highway began to be associated with numerous accidents, death, and the curse of the Devil. In 2003, the highway was renumbered and became New Mexico State Highway 491.
6. Patients usually wear traditional Navajo clothing during ceremonies. For women this includes a velveteen shirt, a three-tiered skirt, a woven cotton belt, and jewelry. Those who lend the patient jewelry to wear have their possessions blessed during the ceremony.
7. There are two kinds of hooghans—round ones (hooghan nímazí) and ones built in the shape of a tepee ('ałch'į' 'adeez'áhí). Most hooghans are built out of pine logs, but in the Sheep Springs area in the nineteen twenties and thirties, many hooghans and square houses were built from sandstone found in the area. Eva's parents' hooghan at Dził Zéé'asgai was a round one with a foundation of stone, but the roof was hastily put together with wood and flour sacks.
8. There was a rock foundation with rocks stacked on top and there it was attached.
9. This was Hastiin Tł'ááshchí'í biye,' or Harry C.'s father. He was Dziłtł'ahnii and Rena's mother's brother. Thus he was Eva's *bidá'í* or maternal uncle. He lived on a mesa called Blue Mountain Sitting over near Rena Nelson's current house.
10. Diné Chíí's mother was married to Shoemaker, who also married Thin Woman, or the woman I call "Shoemaker's Wife" in chapter 4. These two women were sisters; sororal polygyny was common in the early twentieth century. Eva took care of Thin Woman for many years.
11. Eva reminded me that at Łizhin Deez'áhí there was just one hooghan, a house made out of rocks that Benjamin Sherman hauled.
12. Peter Begay's grandmother was named 'Asdzą́ą́ Yázhí (Little Woman).
13. As in previous chapters, boldface type indicates words that Eva spoke in English.
14. The terms "hózhǫ́" and "hóchxǫ́'í" are perhaps the two most important concepts in Navajo thought and worldview. Hózhǫ́ has been translated as beauty, harmony, blessing, balance, and pleasant conditions. It describes a state of all that is positive—the way things should be. It's opposite is hóchxǫ́'í, a state that has been described in English as one of disharmony, disorder, evil, or unpleasant conditions. The purpose of Navajo ceremonies (hatáál) is to bring a

patient who is ill due to contact with dangerous elements (those that are *báhádzid*) from a state of hóchxǫ́'í to one of hózhǫ́.

15. In one place, thirty-five hundred goats were shot and left there.
16. If Eva's narrative happened during the goat sale of 1934, Eva would have been only six years old. There was also a sale of sixteen thousand sheep and fifteen thousand goats in the fall of 1935. Other oral histories tell of the slaughter of goats and sheep on other parts of the Reservation. (See *Navajo Livestock Reduction: A National Disgrace,* 1974.)
17. Ben, who usually knew about such matters, reported that her son had been found at the Thursday night movie at the Newcomb Chapter and had been sent back to school.
18. In the mountain area, the Navajo Tribe has modernized a number of springs by building on a stone base with a rising pipe that holds a dangling hose. One can drive a pickup underneath and fill several barrels of water. We only filled a few jugs.
19. In reading over this passage, Eva laughed about Ben's trickery.
20. In rereading this passage, Eva remembered other foods they used to find in the mountains. She said she also used to eat *xosh*, the red fruit of the cactus, and another one, *xosh diltǫhii*, and also the fruit of the big yucca (*hashk'aan*). They would build a fire and roast these; "it tastes like a banana," Eva commented. Another food they would eat was *ndíshchíí'bitát'ah* (pine under the skin). "You cut back the bark of the pine tree and the juice is inside. You put a little knife in the tree and pull it out [and the liquid comes out]. You can also drink the same juice on the aspen tree. You take off the skin and put a can underneath it and it drips into the can. You can chew it and drink it." They also used to eat the gray rabbit (*gałbáí* and *gahtsoh*). They also used to mix the red sumac berries (*chiiłchin*) with white flour.
21. In another interview Eva explained more about Ben's weaving. "Ben even wove back then when he was little. He was about fourteen or fifteen years old then. He doesn't weave anymore. When we finished the rug, we would iron it. There was no electricity then. We just warmed the iron on the stove and then ironed the rug, which was then taken to the store for us."
22. Gesturing with her hands, Eva indicated that the loom was only two feet tall.

Notes to Chapter Four

1. He used to know Blessing Way (Hózhǫ́ǫjí), Knife Way or Flint Way (Béshee), and Navajo Wind Way (Niłch'ihjí). He also knew a chant having to do with insects and frogs and perhaps Deer Way (Bį́į́h).

Most Navajo ceremonies or chants focus on the healing of a patient and the transformation of their state from one of hóchxǫ́'í (danger, negativity) to hózhǫ́ (a state of harmony, blessing, or positiveness). Illness is caused by contact with dangerous elements in an inappropriate context. For example, Navajo Wind Way is performed for those who have symptoms that stem from improper contact with winds, particularly whirlwinds, snakes, or cactus. Blessing Way (Hózhǫ́ǫ́jí) is one of the most important chants and is performed to protect the patient from dangerous elements and to create a state of hózhǫ́. Many singers learn Blessing Way first and then later become an apprentice to learn other chants.

2. Helen was another daughter of Shoemaker's Wife. She grew up with Eva, met a man from Crystal whose name was Daniel Francisco, and moved over to Crystal after she married him. She eventually became a nurse at the Public Health Service Hospital in Shiprock. Another daughter, April, was married to Sam Gould (Eva's mother's brother). They had a daughter by the name of Marie Gould, who was badly burned when a campfire caught her dress on fire. She always had a limp. She went off to school, and after she graduated, she lived in Gallup and worked at a hospital and also at a Laundromat. Carole used to travel with Grandma Shoemaker to Gallup so the old woman could visit her granddaughter, Marie. The mother, April, had died in childbirth when Marie was born. Marie later moved to California. She had three children and eventually moved back to Newcomb. A fourth daughter (in addition to Elsie, Helen, and April) was Rosalyn, who married James Peter. He was a medicine man. They had four children: Pierce, Dorothy, Minnie Barney, and Johnson Peter.
3. Eva's narrative was originally recorded in Navajo. In this sentence and in other parts of this book, the boldface words indicate English, which she often uses in the midst of her Navajo sentences.
4. Eva named those who planted these fields. They were 'Atsidí Yázhí (Little Silversmith who was Mary Joe's brother), 'Asdzą́ą́ 'Ałnáos'áhí (Cross Hills Lady), Hastiin Bitis 'Adeetiin (Mr. Roads Passing Over), Ben Yazzie (Lillian Togasala's father, whose English name was Philip Sam), Harry Chee's father, Benjamin Sherman's father, John Smith, and Diné Chíí's father, along with Eva's father. Later, in revising this passage, Eva also added Lena Denetclaw's father who was called Peshlaki, Rena's father (Hastiin Sinil), and Shoemaker (Ké'ííł'íní), who was married to Grandma Sandman's sister. Again, this list outlined the important men from surrounding residence groups, plus one widow (Cross Hills Lady). These families were the crucial ones in Eva's social world and since I knew most of their sons or daughters (some deceased or in their seventies during the nineteen

nineties), Eva was communicating to me the structure of the farming community in terms of people I would recognize.

5. Tó łibáí, or gray water, is a common Navajo name for distilled liquor.
6. This indicates he performed the chants that would counteract sickness caused by improper contact with bears.
7. I asked who Hashtł'ishnii Nééz was and where he came from. Eleanor said, "He was from around here somewhere. He still has a son from over there. And then one from Mexican Springs. He also has a daughter from there, who is of the Tsi'naajinii [Black Streak Wood People] Clan. The one that was called Tł'ízí łání [Many Goats] was of the Tł'ízí łání [Many Goats] clan. He was my paternal grandfather [shinálí]."
8. Sam Manuelito was one of the brothers married to Hastiin Tł'aaí's nieces.
9. These are names of three Navajos, one woman and two men, who were probably helpers and aides to the schoolteacher or teachers. Eva is not sure where Lula came from, so these were probably Navajos who did not come from the local area, were not related to the children, but who had English skills and could help translate, given the fact that most of the children spoke no English.
10. There were not any laws against corporal punishment then.
11. That is, "our noses were pressed to the grindstone."
12. This part of the interview was conducted largely in English. Eva and I were talking up on the mountain with Carole. Then Carole went off for a while, and for the next part of the interview, Eva continued in Navajo in response to my questions in English. Since Carole was not there to translate, during some answers she spoke primarily in English with a few scattered phrases in Navajo. The English is in boldface type, and the Navajo is in regular type (as before in the text).
13. In listening to the tape recording of this section later, Eva laughed at Don pulling the eggs out of the chicken, calling him a "crazy old man" even though he was a teenage boy.
14. He was born for Tł'ááshchí'í, Eva's father's clan, and thus a cross-cousin or *bizeedí.*
15. Eva's oldest brother Allen was married to Frances, whose mother was 'Asdzą́ą́ Bitis 'Adeetiin (Roads Passing Over Woman). Frances had three sisters, Lillian Togasala, Susan, and Sadie. Emerson was a child of Frances and Allen Sam.
16. Literally, "I ate mush."
17. This means they have agreed to the marriage.

18. As Maureen Schwarz points out, "Consumption of the pinches of mush taken from each of the cardinal directions ensures that the type of knowledge associated with each particular point in the Navajo cosmology will be incorporated into the marriage," (Schwarz 1997:72).
19. As Maureen Schwarz comments, immoral acts on the part of ancestors of the Navajo "rendered certain types of blood dangerous to health and well being because the blood embodies the essence of libidinous desires and sexual activities gone awry" (2000:2). Not all blood is dangerous, however, partly because the woman herself is married or sexually active. The blood shed during a woman's first and second menstrual cycles is holy and has the power to heal, while that shed during all later periods can be very dangerous (2000:5). Contact with menstrual blood can cause rheumatism or arthritis. Schwarz's account does not mention cases where the girl or woman herself ingested menstrual blood, resulting in illness or even death.
20. In this case, kinaaldá refers to the girl herself. In Navajo the term can mean either the ceremony or the girl who is going through the ritual. See Schwarz 1997:172–229 for a complete description of the symbolism of the Kinaaldá.
21. It is unusual for a man to "mold" the kinaaldá, but apparently Diné Chíí' did this for Eva in both her ceremonies. Peter Begay's father (a relative) who also knew Blessing Way (which includes the "house songs" always performed at the beginning of any part of the Blessing Way) officiated at both ceremonies. It is common for a medicine man or singer to be called after one of the chants that he knows, hence the name "Wind Way Singer."
22. Here Eva indicates that the kinaaldá is not supposed to run too far, just a little way at first, and then a little farther each time she runs.
23. Eva ran in all four directions, not just toward the East. She had to time her running so that she completed it about the time the song ended. It was important for her to run in one direction, then come back to the hooghan, enter it, and go around the central fire in a clockwise direction (sunwise, the sacred and ritually correct direction used throughout all Navajo ceremonies). Then she returned outside through the door, which faces East, and ran in another direction. Presumably she ran to the East first, then to the South, West, and North (the ritually appropriate order).
24. Eva also said, "If you don't have a Kinaaldá, you won't have a good figure; you'll have a hunchback by the time you are fifty."
25. Eva is referring to the very important part of the cake cutting in early morning of the last day of the ceremony, when the kinaaldá takes some cake from pieces cut in each of the four directions and buries it in the ground at the very center of the pit after the last center piece

has been removed. This is an offering to Mother Earth and symbolizes the return to Mother Earth of the reproductive energy that empowers her (Schwarz 1997:222–23). Eva also mentions the buckskin hair tie that she wore throughout the ceremony, which is made from the skin of a deer that was not killed with an arrow or gun, but by hand.

26. That is, Eva was just a little girl.
27. This was clearly a story to tease Eva and there was lots of laughter and banter at the end between Eva, myself, and Eleanor.
28. Guyman was the nickname for Frank Sandman, Eva's older brother.
29. Tł'ááshchí'í Bidághaa' (Tł'ááshchí'í Clansman with a Mustache) was Eva's father's brother. He was born in Newcomb and then moved to the Crownpoint area near White Rock.

Notes to Chapter Five

1. World War II brought the Navajo into greater contact with the Anglo world. American Indians were made citizens in 1924, and they were drafted into the armed services beginning in January 1941. By the end of the war, some thirty-six hundred Navajo men had served in the military (Underhill 1956:242). So many young men and older boys left for the service or jobs that the high schools in Shiprock and Tuba City suspended commencements in 1942 for the duration of the war (Boyce 1974:99). Both men and women worked in a variety of wartime activities. More than eight hundred men were hired to convert Fort Wingate into an ordnance depot, while another fifteen hundred worked on the Bellemont depot near Flagstaff. Hundreds of Navajos became migratory farm workers scattered over the West, and others migrated to the West Coast for jobs in aviation plants, shipyards, and naval installations (Parman 1976:286–87, Bailey and Bailey 1986:200). More than eighteen thousand six hundred of the twenty-five thousand Navajo men and women over nineteen years of age during the war years either served in the military or were employed in the war effort (Bailey and Bailey 1986:200). In Eva's family, her sister Eleanor, her clan sister Rena Nelson, and others were pulled into the migratory labor force. Eva's brother Grant, who was twenty years old in 1940, joined the service, as did Ben Watchman. Harold Foster (Eva's maternal cousin or clan brother) was seventeen and in high school at Fort Wingate when he signed up to serve in the Marines and become a Code Talker. The four hundred members of these specially trained Marines used Navajo as a code to communicate on battlefields in the Pacific, the only code that was never broken by the Japanese. The idea for the Code Talkers came from Philip Johnson, a missionary's son raised on the Navajo

Reservation who spoke fluent Navajo. The first group of twenty-nine recruits supervised by Johnson devised a code in Navajo where clan names stood for different Marine Corps units, names of birds denoted airplanes, the commanding general was "war chief," and a major general was "two star" (Frank in Kawano 1990:9). Harold was a radio war chief at Iwo Jima and saw military duty at Nagasaki and Sasebo at the end of the war (Kawano 1990:45).

2. During the war, government funds were cut. Anglos employed in the Indian Service (BIA) and in schools and hospitals left the Reservation either for military duty or war-related employment. Five hospitals and eighteen day schools were closed (Bailey and Bailey 1986:200). New Deal programs like the Civilian Conservation Corps (CCC) and the Works Progress Administration (WPA) were abandoned, and the Navajo Stock Reduction Program was not as stringently enforced, due partly to the dismissal of the range riders and partly to the policies of one superintendent (Parman 1976:286–89). Just as more Navajos, like Grant, Harold, and Eleanor, were being pulled into the white world, those who remained on the Reservation were more isolated from government institutions.
3. As in previous chapters, boldface text indicates that Eva was speaking in English.
4. Carole thought that her father had stayed until shortly after her birth in 1948, probably six years after Eva was married. "My grandmother used to tell me that he stayed around until I was one or two months old because he made that cradleboard for me."
5. Carole added, "In those days they used to say, 'Oh, that man will help you within your future life and, and buy you things, and keep you well off.' Those are the things that I used to hear a lot, from my grandmother, you know. And I don't know if that's right, but they would just give you anybody else that they think is capable of marrying you."
6. Maureen Schwarz learned of similar practices from her consultants. "To control blood loss and to aid recovery from childbirth, she [a grandmother] may bind her daughter's abdomen with a layer of warm damp, cedar branches held in place by a tightly wrapped sash. . . . The binding is done as soon as possible after childbirth, in the hospital or immediately after the mother and child return home" (Schwarz 1997:136). Here Schwarz is relying on Waxman 1990:192 and her interviews with Sadie Billie, 7/10/91; A. Begay, 7/26/91; Tsosie, 8/4/92; and Knoki-Wilson, 8/10/92. Sadie Billie said her mother wrapped a sash belt around her, "To get the uterus to get back to the normal size real quick. And she said that if you don't do that then your stomach will begin to hang" (Schwarz 1997:136–37).

7. Maureen Schwarz writes, "A relative in attendance may give the child an herbal emetic at this time. Once the child has vomited up the mucus and amniotic fluids it swallowed while in the womb, a pollen blessing may be administered, which is followed by the first molding. A female relative dips her right forefinger into pollen and administers it to the child's mouth to foster its physical development and to the top of the child's head to foster its mental development. Then saying a brief prayer, she spreads pollen in front of the child in offering (Wilson 1980:20; Oscar Tso, 8/9/92). I was told this was done as a notification to the Holy People that a new 'track' on the pollen path of life is starting on the earth's surface" (Schwarz 1997:134–35).
8. My dates here come from the community census that I obtained in 1965 from the Chapter development officer. I think they are reasonably accurate for those born after 1920, since the census was based on individuals' census cards. According to these records, Margaret would have been born in 1932. Her mother's clan was Honágháahnii and her father's clan was Tódích'íi'nii.
9. Although Aaron clearly left Eva, she says she "let him go" in the sense that she did not try to persuade her parents or other relatives to put pressure on Aaron to return.
10. Dan Foster was Eva's mother's sister's son. He was the older brother of Harold, who served as a marine Code Talker, and of Donald, who was staying with Eva when her mother was away picking piñons and who pulled the egg from the chicken so they could get enough to eat (see chapter 4).
11. On another occasion, Eva said that the police did not come get her. Instead, she had to sign the paper. She maintained that she was the one who brought the complaint. "Aaron was running around with Margaret, that's why." After Eva left and went to Shiprock, then Aaron went back over to his mother's. "My mom went with me, I just told the judge I didn't want him any more. Ever since he went around with that woman" (Field notes, 1965).
12. Between 1944 and 1946, the annual per capita income fell from $199.60 to $80, about the same as it had been in 1940; however, inflation had cut into the buying power of these dollars. Bailey and Bailey estimate that Navajo income in 1946 was 40 percent of what it had been in 1936; between 1944 and 1946, buying power had dropped by almost two-thirds (Bailey and Bailey 1986:220). Missionaries, the American Legion, and the Daughters of the American Revolution began to bring the story of Navajo deprivation to national attention. *Time Magazine* published a story on November 3, 1947, describing the Navajo as facing starvation, " . . . from 25,000 to 30,000 Navajos

are lingering in the state between malnutrition and starvation. The whole Tribe's diet averaged only 1,200 calories and many have nothing to eat but bread and coffee" (Boyce 1974:221). The federal government began to provide relief funds (though only $5.00 per person per month), and private charities sent food and clothing. A shipment arrived from the Denver Relief Committee, organized in my home city. January 1949 was particularly difficult since a blizzard dropped thirty-five inches of snow on the Western Reservation, causing many newborn lambs to die, flocks to starve without hay or other food, and schoolchildren in isolated communities like Navajo Mountain to be stranded as trading post supplies ran out (Boyce 1974:238–39). I vaguely remember a huge snowstorm in Denver when I was a child, since we shoveled the snow from the driveway at the side of the house and the resulting piles were much taller than I was. What I do not remember was whether our Presbyterian church was involved in the relief effort. Government relief payment rose to $39 a family by 1949, but it was clear that a longer-term solution was necessary. In 1948 Secretary of the Interior Julius Krug presented the "Krug Report" to Congress, which made a series of recommendations. This was the basis for the Navajo-Hopi Long Range Rehabilitation Act, passed by Congress in 1950 (Bailey and Bailey 1986:232). It provided $90 million over a ten-year period for range improvement, irrigation projects, the building of roads, and most importantly, $4.7 million for hospitals and $25 million for schools.

13. By 1994, I had forgotten all of the details she described and was surprised to find them in my field notes.
14. My field notes also indicate that "His Pinedale wife already had a son and two daughters. He had one daughter with the Pinedale lady. The Smith Lake wife was [his] 1st [wife]." The sister of Timothy and Randa who died in the spring of 1996 was the daughter of the Pinedale wife, born after he came back from the service. Joe probably did not come back over to Sheep Springs to live with his mother until 1947 or 48" (Field notes, November 30, 1965).
15. The Enemy Way, 'Anaa'jí, often referred to as a "Squaw Dance" when Navajos are speaking in English, is a three-day ceremony that is conducted during the summer months. The ceremony cures illnesses due to contact with non-Navajos or "enemies." Enemy Way ceremonies were often held for World War II veterans on their return home from the service because of their contact with the enemy dead.
16. My field notes indicate that they went to Delta, Colorado, to pick sugar beets. Carole told me during a 1994 interview that Joe was an alcoholic at that time, and "I don't know if I was taken with them or stayed with my grandma." When Eva and Joe returned they stayed in the same hooghan where Mary Sandman lived in the cluster that

included Frank Sandman's and Leonard's home, made up of two log cabins side by side, i.e., with one adjoining wall.

17. Levy and Kunitz indicate that tó łibáí may have been made as early as 1910 (reported by the Franciscan Fathers at St. Michael's) and as late as 1954 (as reported by Adams) (1974:66). They suggest that bootlegging was practiced by wealthy men who often paid a relative or retainer to buy liquor and bring it back to the residence group. Then other men were given liquor in return for services and a "party" would take place later at night in the hooghan (Levy and Kunitz 1974:77). This seems like a slightly different pattern than the one described by Eva and Eleanor. Here a group of economically average Navajo men waited for the bootlegger and probably shared in the payment as well as in the wine, a more egalitarian arrangement than described by Levy and Kunitz. It also seemed more occasional and not done to excess, i.e., not associated with passing out or with accidents like the one that killed Frank Sandman in 1960.
18. A more recent study of drinking patterns by Levy and Kunitz included both female and male interviewees (McCloskey 2000) and confirms that Navajo women have been drinking for decades, often to the detriment of their families.
19. By this time, Mary Sandman, her married children, and their families had begun to spend summers on Shoemaker's Wife's summer land. This arrangement had been worked out by Eva's father since he was a clan relative of Grandma Shoemaker. The area was very near a spring and included a large cornfield as well as a nearby grazing area. It was not nearly as far from the summer Chapter House and the main dirt road up on the mountain; however, the sheep herd was probably taken over the same trail Mary had used to get to Ben Bimá's place, a few miles to the east and at a slightly lower elevation along the mountain "bench" area.
20. Paul died as a young man in the early nineteen eighties. He left behind two children by his first wife and three children by his second wife.
21. My grade school friend Elaine Smith Dunlap has a slightly different theory of what was important during our grade school years. She feels that each child emerged from their family and began to see how their experiences were different than those of other children. Social relationships, friendships, and the peer group became important sites for communicating values, rather than the classroom itself. How one got along with others and was integrated within small clusters of friends was more important, at this stage, than the actual content of school books.

22. The Mormon Placement Program, described by Carole in detail below, is one where young Navajo girls and boys were placed in Mormon homes in towns throughout Utah during their school years, returning to the Reservation during the summer months.
23. Mabel and Bernice were the daughters of Aaron (Carole's father) and Margaret (his second wife). Mabel was two years younger than Carole, and Bernice was four years younger.
24. Carole laughed as she remembered this.
25. In other words, the person who led the Blessing Way songs during the all-night ceremony in the hooghan.
26. During the nineteen sixties, when more girls were away at boarding schools or on the Mormon Placement Program and hence were not with their families when they reached menarche, families began having only one rather than two ceremonies (as prescribed from mythological times when Changing Woman had two ceremonies). Some girls were away from home and did not tell their mothers about their first menstruation and hence did not have a Kinaaldá at all. Others had a ceremony during the summer months although they had reached menarche during the school term when away from their families. Thus, in this period, although the number of Kinaaldá may have even increased because of the growing population, more and more girls and their families did not participate. The increasing number of converts to Evangelical Christian sects may have also been a factor, since these churches prohibited participation in traditional Navajo ceremonies.
27. At the time, the Mormon missionaries used the Sheep Springs Chapter House both for youth activities and for church services. They lived in a small trailer next to the trading post, run by a Mormon, Evan Lewis. The Mormon church was being planned when I was living in Sheep Springs in 1965–66, and was probably completed in the late nineteen sixties.
28. Ella Ann Tsosie was the daughter of Grant, Eva's brother; Mabel and Ethel were the daughters of Eleanor, Eva's sister; Walter was the son of Frank Sandman; and Johnnie and Paul were Eleanor's oldest sons.
29. This group includes most of the cousins and classificatory sisters and brothers of school age in the residence group where Carole lived. There were four households: (1) her mother, Eva, Joe, and her grandmother; (2) Frank Sandman, Eva's oldest brother, his wife, Anita, and their children; (3) Anita's son, Leonard Sandman, his wife, and their children; and (4) Eleanor, Eva's older sister, her husband Tom Yazzie, and their children.
30. In earlier times Navajos buried their dead by either removing the body from a hooghan, taking it northward, and placing it in a rock

shelter or shallow grave; or they collapsed the hooghan down around the dead person, making the old house a grave. By the early nineteen sixties, most Navajos were turning over the preparation of the body and burial to funeral homes since dead bodies were so very dangerous and a source of illness and misfortune. Several communities, including Sheep Springs, had constructed small community graveyards.

31. The male hooghan is an older form of Navajo housing made of logs standing lengthwise and built in the shape of a teepee ('ałch'į' 'adeez'áhí) with a square entranceway built out from the east side. The female hooghan or hooghan nímazí is round and built from cribbed logs laid horizontally, usually with six to eight sides. The dirt roof placed over a cribbed log ceiling gives the top a rounded appearance.

Notes to Chapter Six

1. In the summer of 1965 I was accompanied by Terry Reynolds who was a graduate student in anthropology, first at Stanford and later at the University of British Columbia (UBC). We borrowed the winter house of a Sheep Springs family who was living in their summer cabin on the mountain, and the daughter in the family became our interpreter. Later, Terry got to know Eva, Carole, and members of other Sheep Springs families through me. Carole spent time with Terry in California where Terry was teaching after the death of her baby (see chapter 7). Terry completed her own dissertation research in the Sheep Springs area and received her PhD from UBC.
2. In fact, Vogt says very little about drinking in his monograph. He does indicate that for the first time, Indians were able to drink with Anglos and not be considered breaking the law, since bartenders near bases in the Midwest and East had probably never heard of Indian prohibition (Vogt 1951:97). However, he does not mention where his subjects learned to drink, what army drinking patterns were, and how these may have impacted Navajo veterans.
3. (As in previous chapters, the quotes from Eva are translated from Navajo; the words she spoke in English are in boldface type.) Pauline Chee, Frank and Anita's oldest daughter, was born in 1937, so Eva was probably talking about the War years or slightly afterward, but before Joe entered Eva's life, which would have been the mid–nineteen fifties. I tend to agree with Carole's assessment, that the War did provide a context for learning to drink. Certainly, even if Grant, Leonard, Joe, Andy, and Tom had been drinkers before the War, binge drinking during the war (even if it were with American soldiers and did not entail passing a bottle around and passing

out) was not the same as cocktail hour drinking in private homes, which was the middle-class, Anglo pattern for the period. Wartime experience may have provided the background for solidifying a Navajo male drinking group among in-married males as well as two brothers in the kin group. Andy, Joe, and Tom were in-laws, while Leonard was Anita's son by an earlier marriage and thus an in-law as well. Only Grant and Frank Sandman were brothers and clan members, though Frank/Gaaman had not served in the war. He was too old to have been drafted and had also been injured in the house fire during the nineteen thirties.

4. Eva and Carole felt that at the time there were no laws against liquor. National prohibition lasted from 1919 to 1933. Indians were always prohibited liquor, on and off reservations. Indian prohibition was repealed in 1953, though the possession and sale of liquor on the Reservation continued to remain illegal, even up to the present period. Thus there has always been a surreptitious aspect to Navajo drinking. To put a sign up calling attention to bootlegging was clearly something that Tom and Eleanor were worried about.
5. Carole and Eva later told me that Shoemaker's Wife and Eva had hitchhiked to Gallup to visit Grandma Shoemaker's daughter, Mary. On the way back, they caught a ride with someone else and then took a detour to Fort Defiance, then through Crystal, and back over Washington Pass. It was somewhere on the mountain pass that the car accident occurred.
6. Kunitz and Levy's study of drinking patterns on the Western Navajo Reservation during the nineteen sixties indicates that many Navajo women were abstainers (about 25 percent of their sample of forty-five women), while, of those who did drink, about half, including many who lived in Reservation extended-family groups, started drinking at home with their families. The other half, like Eva, were induced to drink by their husbands, a pattern more prevalent in an agency town like Tuba City (Kunitz and Levy 1994:117–22). Kunitz and Levy also found that most women in extended-family residence groups and agency towns had stopped drinking at the time of a second interview twenty-five years later, while more women in the border towns continued to drink. Overall, however, between 77 percent and 96 percent of women in these three contexts had stopped drinking later in their lives. The Native American Church was important in helping a number of the men in this study to stop drinking; the role of NAC and other religious experiences for women is not explored, perhaps because the sample of women was so small. It is clear that Eva's experience was not atypical for women of her generation.
7. Joe's behavior was appropriate etiquette around a stranger. Navajos often seem reticent or shy to "pushy" Anglos. In describing similar

Apache behavior, Keith Basso explains that Apaches, especially when dealing with a stranger and children coming home from boarding school, will wait silently before beginning a conversation until each party becomes comfortable with the other. Apaches (and Navajos as well) do not rush to fill up silences (Basso 1970:217–18, 219–21).

8. At that time, most Navajos slept in their daytime clothes and then changed the next day or when it was important to be wearing a clean set of clothes. I followed Navajo custom, thus making it easy to share sleeping space with Navajo families, allowing all of us to retain our modesty, which is important in Navajo culture. It was also appropriate that I avoid any appearance of being close to a Navajo man of my age or older, since, for example, if a couple is seen together alone in a pickup truck, it is assumed that they have an intimate sexual relationship. As a single woman, I was careful to follow Navajo women's suggestions as to how I should behave around men.
9. These are all dangerous animals or beings. Improper contact with them brings illness, thus shouting them at someone is threatening and also profanes something that has sacred and potentially harmful powers.
10. During this ceremony, the singer, with the aid of several men, prepares a large sandpainting made from ground rock (in the colors of black, blue, red, yellow, and white) on the floor of the ceremonial hooghan. The painting depicts Diyin Dine'é (Holy People) from a specific event in the creation myth that describes the origin of the ceremony. After the painting is completed, the singer chants songs from the ceremony while the patient sits on the painting. The Diyin Dine'é come to infuse the painting with their power and the singer presses the sand on the patient's body, helping to cure the patient.
11. During 1965–66, Evan Lewis, the trader, approached the Chapter for permission to build a Mormon church on reservation land about three hundred yards behind the trading post. The church was built during the nineteen seventies. By the eighties, it was the center of Mormon activity in Sheep Springs. On January 16, 1966, Evan made a presentation to the Sunday afternoon Chapter meeting. "Evan explained that they had had a meeting in June where people voted for the establishment of a Mormon chapel, across the road from the Chapter House. Then there were complaints about it being close to the windmill where people needed to water their stock. So a site south of the trading post was decided on and more than one hundred people signed a petition in favor; however, they wanted to find out how many people were still in favor. There were comments from several people, and finally a vote was taken, eighty-seven for and one or two against." In my experience in the nineteen sixties,

Chapters rarely voted on issues until a consensus was reached. If there was a real division of opinion, nothing was done. This accords with my analysis of the importance of consensus (as opposed to hierarchical) decision making in Navajo life (see *To Run After Them*, pages 38–41).

12. In their most recent book (2000) based on a study in Tuba City and Shiprock, Kunitz and Levy indicate that Navajo drinking patterns are shifting in younger generations. Navajo young men are drinking with their peers and not with older relatives, and many are influenced by off-reservation drinking contexts in the army or in college or off-reservation work contexts. More young men are drinking in bars during weekends and there is more effort to "maintain control" rather than binge drink. Navajo women in this study were more likely to drink (i.e., fewer were lifelong abstainers) but there were still high numbers who had ceased drinking (about 50 percent in all contexts studied). Nevertheless, Navajo women drink less then Navajo men (fewer than 10 percent of Navajo men are abstainers). Those women profiled by McCloskey (2000) who became alcohol-dependent have a history of dysfunctional family experiences. Risk factors include a mother's drinking, childhood physical and sexual abuse, absence of supportive family relationships, and a husband's drinking, among others. This level of social dysfunction has not been found in Eva's immediate family since Eva's conversion experiences in the early nineteen sixties. McCloskey argues that higher education levels, family support, and steady employment can mitigate these negative factors and help women stop drinking or prevent alcohol from becoming a factor in their lives (2000:148). This is certainly true for Carole and Valerie, where their strong sense of family, their religious values, the importance of kin support in their lives, and their histories of employment and education have protected them from alcohol dependency.
13. Walter's father is Frank Sandman, Eva's older brother.
14. Eva used "Nihookáá' Dine'é," the more formal term for the Navajo People.

Notes to Chapter Seven

1. Carole came back to Sheep Springs fairly regularly that winter. I was asked to take her back to school the next Sunday, February 27, and my notes indicate she was visiting her mother the following weekend (March 4–6).
2. On the first night, the "stick receiver's" group receives the rattle stick, feeds the patient's group, and hosts an all-night singing (led by the patient's group who carry the drum and drumstick and who

stand near a large bonfire that burns all night). Dancing takes place during the evening. A young female relative on the stick receiver's side cares for the rattle stick and chooses a partner for each dance. Other young girls and women follow suit; the boys and men must pay the girls for the dances (hence the Anglo name Squaw Dance). Early in the morning, the stick receiver's group distributes cloth, candy, pop, and other gifts to the patient's group. Then the stick receiver's group moves to a place halfway toward the patient's camp and stays there for the night. The singing and slow shuffle-step dancing are repeated. On the morning of the third day, the stick receiver's group (usually young men riding horses) makes a mock attack on the patient's camp. The stick receiver's group sets up camp nearby and are fed by the patient's group. Then they are given gifts of cloth, candy, pop, and cracker jacks, followed by a full meal of mutton stew, fried bread, and coffee. Later that day, there is a "blackening ceremony," which is culminated by an attack on a scalp that represents the "alien" or "enemy." Following this is another night of singing and dancing (Witherspoon 1975:56–64). (See also chapter 1.)

3. His parents were Joe and Stella Ben. Joe died in 1993; he had a heart attack and did not survive. Stella died around August 1, 1996; she had diabetes and then had to have kidney dialysis. She died in Farmington at the San Juan hospital—she was going through dialysis and her heart got weaker and she just died. Wallace has four sisters: Ella, Mary, and Rose, and a younger one, Della, and a number of brothers, perhaps five. Carole was working during the funeral and stopped by the Catholic church in Shiprock and the family was cleaning up after the guests had gone home. She talked with Della Ben and said she was sorry she could not go to her mom's funeral, and she told her how important Wallace's parents had been to her.
4. Carole told me that Tina was about three and a half months old when she died on Carole's birthday, August 26. This would mean that Tina was born around May 10. School usually ends during the last week of May and graduation is often on Memorial Day weekend.
5. Lena Denetclaw lived about a hundred yards to the west of Eva's house. Carole often asked Lena for rides, since her mother did not drive. Although Carole could have driven, it is possible that she was too distraught to do so.
6. Terry Reynolds had done fieldwork with me in Sheep Springs during the summers of 1965 and 1966, and she was teaching at California State University at Northridge during the school years.
7. George died in August 2001 in a motorcycle accident on the Navajo Reservation. Valerie, Carole, and Eva attended the funeral and

reception in Shiprock and had a chance to meet George's other children and his father's relatives.

8. Roslyn Johnson is the daughter of Frank Sandman, Eva's older brother who died in the fire. She is Carole's cross-cousin (bizeedí), but one of the women who is very close to Carole and who is often called upon for rides, help at ceremonies, and babysitting. She has also been present at the birth of several of Carole's children.
9. It is very typical to refer to someone (in this case, MacArthur) not by his or her real name but by their relationship to someone else, Jay's father or Harry Chee's sister. Using a given name as a term of reference is considered impolite and too direct. Also, Navajos often use nicknames instead of given names and these may change throughout a person's lifetime. MacArthur Junior is referred to as JR, and then—an even shorter name—Jay.
10. In August 1973, I started living with Peter Evans in a collective household in Providence, Rhode Island, when I was teaching at Brown University. I did not receive tenure in May 1974, when Peter was in Brazil for the calendar year of 1974. In May 1975, I interviewed for and accepted an Associate Professorship at the University of New Mexico. I put off starting the position until January 1976, since I wanted to accept a Ford Foundation Fellowship at the Bunting Institute at Radcliffe College in Cambridge, Massachusetts. I taught at UNM during the spring and fall semesters in 1976, and spent the calendar year in Rhode Island in 1977, working on a research project there. I returned to UNM for three more semesters (spring and fall 1978 and spring 1979), spending the summers in Rhode Island, then took a trip to Brazil during the summer of 1979. I resigned my UNM position in the fall of 1979 and returned to Brown. My son, Peter Bret, was born in the spring of 1980. Peter, Peter Bret, and I spent summers in New Mexico, and I returned again in the calendar year of 1982 to conduct a research project. Thus between 1975 and 1985, I was in New Mexico frequently and made trips from Albuquerque to Sheep Springs often, especially during the summer months and also around the Christmas or Thanksgiving holidays.
11. The man's English name was Elton Thompson.
12. Elton, like MacArthur, was from Mexican Springs. Eva thought the two men were related. MacArthur is 'Áshįįhí (Salt Clan) and Táchii'nii yáshchíín. MacArthur's mother remarried when he, his brother Sam, and his sister Helena were little children. Her sister raised them. His mother now lives in Crystal. One of his aunt's daughters lives in Mexican Springs and was an important friend of Carole's during the years she was married to MacArthur.

13. Like Carole, Lee Joe and Helen had taken advantage of the possibility of new housing and moved from their traditional residence group into one of the new houses in the "suburb" behind the trading post. Their house was just two doors away from Carole's.
14. The green truck that Carole had been driving belonged to MacArthur.
15. The Relocation Program in the nineteen fifties provided financial incentives and some minimal training to relocate Navajo men and their families to urban areas. It was part of the general policy of the fifties that led to the termination of a number of Native American reservations and programs, to assimilate Native Americans to American life. Rather than promote the creation of jobs on reservations (a policy adopted in the sixties), relocation was based on the notion that Indians should move to urban areas, take wage jobs, and not continue to be "wards of the state." Most studies indicate that relocated Native Americans had severe problems adjusting to urban areas where they lacked support, kin, and tribal networks and often found themselves living in skid row areas with low-paying and often temporary jobs. Unemployment and high levels of alcohol abuse were typical.
16. Bessie was married to Larry Keedah, Carole's father's brother's son, who came from Sheep Springs. Larry and Carole were both "born for" the Kiyaa'áanii clan and thus called each other brother and sister. Again, a kinship tie created the connection between Bessie and Carole. So even friendships, like that expressed in English as "my best girl friend," are really founded on kin ties.
17. MacArthur developed diabetes shortly after leaving Carole and eventually became blind.
18. Nora married into the Watchman family, the family I first lived with when I came to Sheep Springs in the summer of 1965.

Notes to Chapter Eight

1. This woman was the daughter of MacArthur's mother's sister, the person who raised him. In Navajo she is his sister, though in English she would be called a "cousin." Navajos often use the term "cousin/sister" to indicate those who are members of the same clan, and hence sisters, in Navajo, but who would be referred to as cousins in English.
2. Linda was the youngest daughter of Leonard and Louise Sandman. They all lived in a five-bedroom house in the new housing area for a while. Previously, they had lived across the road from Carole and Eva near Yellow Hills. Leonard's mother was Anita Sandman who had been married to Eva's brother, Gaaman or Frank Sandman,

who died in the hooghan fire. Leonard had married Louise, who was Joe Price's sister. Many of the Sandman daughters went on the Mormon Placement Program and spent a number of years in Utah.

3. Rena Nelson is Eva's clan sister (see chapter 3). It was her grandmother who raised Eva's mother. Rena and her husband Andy Nelson lived about a quarter-mile east of Eva's house at Yellow Hills in a residence group composed of Rena and Andy, Rena's sister, Mary Parkett, and her married children. Rena had two older children by another marriage; David is the oldest son of both Andy and Rena and is Carole's age. When David and his wife moved to a house in the new housing area, Rena, like Eva, was a frequent visitor in her child's new house and often a co-resident.
4. Ditto is the nickname for Elena, Randa's oldest daughter. Randa is Eva's second oldest son. Ditto is the same age as JR and about five years younger than Valerie. Of all the cousins (children of Eva's sons) and cousin/sisters (children of Eva's sister Eleanor) Ditto is the closest in age to Valerie.
5. Marilyn Morris is the daughter of Daisy Morris and her first husband. Daisy and Paul lived across the road from Carole and Eva in the large, Benjamin Sherman extended-family residence group. Marilyn is from the Bit'ahnii clan (the same clan as Joe Price and Helen Joe). She worked at the store with Carole, and they were good friends.
6. Central Avenue is the section of historic Route 66 that passes through Albuquerque. It stretches from the west side of town through the downtown area, passes the University of New Mexico, and goes east toward the Sandia Mountains. Between the university and state fairgrounds are a number of motels that in the late nineteen seventies were still attracting a middle-class clientele. The Sheep Springs trip would have been in 1978–79 when I was teaching at the university.
7. Elsie Gould is the daughter of Haskie and Rebecca Charley. She is Kiyaa'áanii (Carole's father's clan) and so she is Carole's cross-cousin. They live a half-mile north of Eva's home just off the highway.
8. These are all areas where there are scattered homesteads; Tocito and Little Water are fairly near Newcomb where the school is located, while Burnham is far to the east off dirt roads and near a new strip mine.
9. By the mid–nineteen sixties, after the second circle of corn husks was laid across the poured batter, families often covered the cake with a layer of wax paper or wet paper sacks. Then a shallow layer of dirt was added before the fire was put on top. The layer of paper sacks,

in addition to the layer of dirt, kept the fire from burning the top of the cake.

10. "Binálí," or paternal grandparent, often called "-nálí" when speaking English.

Notes to Chapter Nine

1. During the Clinton administration, Richardson served as U.S. representative to the United Nations and as secretary of energy. He was elected governor of New Mexico in 2002 and re-elected in 2006.
2. I attended one graduation reception for two of Anita Sandman's grandsons—Roselyn's son, Henry, and Glen's son, Michael. I also received an invitation for a reception at a motel in Window Rock given by a Sheep Springs family residing in Fort Defiance. Families who have more resources and are in Reservation towns or border towns may be able to give more elaborate receptions.
3. These same elements—mutton stew; fried bread; American-style salads with Jell-O, carrot and raisins, or whipped cream and fruit; punch or soda pop; as well as cookies or candy—are always part of meals served for baby showers or funerals. Cakes are not appropriate at funerals, but are often part of baby showers—or especially birthdays—if there is an extended-family celebration of a birthday, which may not be very usual in some families. Thanksgiving feasts that include members of an extended family usually substitute turkey and store-bought pies for mutton stew, and always include additional Anglo foods like salads, potato chips, fruit punch, and soda pop.
4. When our son Peter Bret graduated from Albuquerque High School in 1998, several of his friends had receptions at their homes the afternoon of the Saturday graduation or the next day. These usually featured a buffet spread (sometimes including southwestern dishes like homemade enchiladas), a graduation cake, and ice cream. We had a small brunch on Sunday for our community, my mother and sister who were visiting for graduation, several of Peter Bret's teachers, and a few of his friends. Valerie and her boyfriend Duane, who were living with us, also attended. My impression is that some Albuquerque High School students bow to family wishes in terms of attending these celebrations, but would prefer to be off with their friends, even though friends do attend each other's receptions.

Notes to Chapter Ten

1. Kneel down bread is like a tamale. It consists of fresh, green corn that has been removed from the cob and pounded into a kind of

mush. Then it is packed into corn husks, much like a tamale, and the little packets are baked in a hole in the ground for several hours. Families usually make kneel down bread in the summer and early fall during the corn harvest, and some families often sell it by the roadside, especially in the Shiprock/Fruitland area where families have large plots of irrigated land.

2. The College Enrichment Program at the University of New Mexico is a summer program for incoming students to give them an orientation to college, help them register for the appropriate classes, and provide them with some study skills.
3. Lucille Stillwell was Director of American Indian Student Services when Valerie was in college. During her sophomore year, and when Duane was a freshman, I put them both in touch with Lucille. She was able to recommend that Valerie take one or two short courses offered by the library staff that emphasized study skills and computer skills. She also helped them find courses in which they could do well, and she encouraged them to take courses about Native American cultures. Valerie took two semesters of Navajo language as well.
4. CAPS, or the Center for Academic Program Support, is the academic counseling center at UNM, which offers drop-in help for math and English classes as well as tutoring for other courses. As an instructor, I find it very difficult to get my students to go over to CAPS and get help with studying to improve their grades.
5. Academics was the title of the course that helped students learn how to take notes, write an outline for an essay, and put together a research paper.
6. Alan was one of my graduate student advisees in the Department of Anthropology.
7. Valerie meant they were interested in the personal side of her life.

REFERENCES

Aberle, David F.

1961 The Navaho. *In* Matrilineal Kinship. David Schneider and Kathleen Gough, eds. Berkeley: University of California Press.

1966 The Peyote Religion. Chicago: University of Chicago Press.

1967 The Navaho Singer's 'Fee': Payment or Prestation? *In* Studies in Southwestern Ethnolinguistics. Meaning and History in the languages of the American Southwest. Dell H. Hymes and William E. Bittle, eds. Pp. 15–32. Studies in General Anthropology 3. The Hague: Mouton and Company.

1991 The Peyote Religion Among the Navajo. Second Edition. Norman: University of Oklahoma Press.

Abu-Lughod, Lila

1993 Writing Women's Worlds: Bedouin Stories. Berkeley: University of California Press.

Bailey, Garrick and Roberta Glenn Bailey

1986 A History of the Navajos: The Reservation Years. Santa Fe: SAR Press.

Basso, Keith H.

1970 "To Give Up on Words": Silence in Western Apache Culture. Southwestern Journal of Anthropology 26(3):213–30 (Autumn).

1996 Wisdom Sits in Places: Landscape and Language Among the Western Apache. Albuquerque: University of New Mexico Press.

Beck, Nanibaa

2006 David Aberle: A Trusted Friend and Gracious Anthropologist To The Diné People. Paper presented at the Annual Meeting of the Society for Applied Anthropology, Vancouver, Canada, March 30.

Behar, Ruth

1993 Translated Woman: Crossing the Border with Esperanza's Story. Boston: Beacon Press.

Benedek, Emily

1995 Beyond the Four Corners of the World. New York: Alfred A. Knopf.

Boyce, George

1974 When Navajos Had Too Many Sheep. San Francisco: The Indian Historian Press.

Brown, Dee

1971 Bury My Heart at Wounded Knee. New York: Holt, Rinehart and Winston.

Casagrande, Joseph B., ed.

1960 In the Company of Man: Twenty Portraits by Anthropologists. New York: Harper and Brothers.

Clifford, James

1988 On Ethnographic Authority. *In* The Predicament of Culture. Pp. 21–54. Cambridge: Harvard University Press.

Faris, James C.

1990 The Nightway: A History and a History of Documentation of a Navajo Ceremonial. Albuquerque: University of New Mexico Press.

Frisbie, Charlotte J.

1967 Kinaaldá: A Study of the Navaho Girl's Puberty Ceremony. Middletown, CT: Wesleyan University Press.

1987 Navajo Medicine Bundles or Jish: Acquisition, Transmission, and Disposition in the Past and Present. Albuquerque: University of New Mexico Press.

Iverson, Peter and Monty Roessel

2002 Diné: A History of the Navajos. Albuquerque: University of New Mexico Press.

Jacobs, Sue-Ellen, Wesley Thomas and Sabine Long, eds.

1997 Two-Spirit People: Native American Gender Identity, Sexuality, and Spirituality. Urbana: University of Illinois Press.

Kan, Sergei

2001 Strangers to Relatives: The Adoption and Naming of Anthropologists in Native North America. Lincoln and London: University of Nebraska Press.

Kawano, Kenji

1990 Warriors: Navajo Code Talkers. Flagstaff: Northland Publishing Company.

Keith, Anne

1964 The Navajo Girls' Puberty Ceremony: Function and Meaning for the Adolescent. El Palacio 71(1):27–36. Santa Fe: Museum of New Mexico.

Kluckhohn, Clyde

1966 The Ramah Navaho In Smithsonian Institution Anthropological Papers 79. Bureau of American Ethnology, Bulletin 196. Washington, DC: U.S. Government Printing Office.

Kluckhohn, Clyde and Dorothea Leighton

1962 The Navaho. Rev. edition. Garden City, New York: Doubleday Anchor Books.

Kunitz, Stephen J. and Jerrold E. Levy

1994 Drinking Careers: A Twenty-Five-Year Study of Three Navajo Populations. Tucson: University of Arizona Press.

Lamphere, Louise

1977 To Run After Them: The Social and Cultural Bases of Cooperation in a Navajo Community. Tucson: University of Arizona Press.

1990 Historical and Regional Variability in Navajo Women's Roles. Journal of Anthropological Research 45(4):431–456, Navajo Ethnology (Winter 1989). Albuquerque: University of New Mexico, Department of Anthropology.

Levy, Jerrold E. and Stephen J. Kunitz

1974 Indian Drinking: Navajo Practices and Anglo-American Theories. New York: John Wiley and Sons.

Locke, Raymond Friday

1976 The Book of the Navajo. Los Angeles: Mankind Publishers.

McCloskey, Joanne

2000 Risk and Protective Factors Affecting Navajo Women's Drinking Behaviors. *In* Drinking, Conduct Disorder, and Social Change: Navajo Experiences. Jerrold E. Levy and Steven J. Kunitz, eds. Oxford: Oxford University Press.

McGreavey, Susan

1993 Daughters of Affluence: Wealth, Collecting, and Southwestern Institutions. *In* Hidden Scholars: Women Anthropologists and the Native American Southwest. Nancy Parezo, ed. Albuquerque: University of New Mexico Press.

Miller, Darlis A.

2007 Matilda Coxe Stevenson: Pioneering Anthropologist. Norman: University of Oklahoma Press.

Navajo Community College Press

1973 Navajo Stories of the Long Walk Period. Prepared under the supervision of Ruth Roessel. Tsaile, AZ: Navajo Community College Press.

1974 Navajo Livestock Reduction: A National Disgrace. Compiled by Ruth Roessel and Broderick H. Johnson. Chinle, AZ: Navajo Community College Press.

Newcomb, Franc

1964 Hosteen Klah. Norman: University of Oklahoma Press.

1966 Navajo Neighbors. Norman: University of Oklahoma Press.

Parman, Donald L.

1976 The Navajos and the New Deal. New Haven: Yale University Press.

Parsons, Elsie Clews

1921 Hopi Mothers and Children. Man 21:98–104 (July).

Reichard, Gladys

1950 Navaho Religion: A Study of Symbolism. New York: Pantheon Books.

Roscoe, Will

1988 We'wha and Klah: The American Indian Berdache as Artist and Priest. American Indian Quarterly 7(2) (Spring).

Schwarz, Maureen Trudelle

1997 Molded in the Image of Changing Woman: Navajo Views on the Human Body and Personhood. Tucson: University of Arizona Press.

2001 Allusions to Ancestral Impropriety: Arthritis and Rheumatism in the Contemporary Navajo World. American Ethnologist 28(3):650–78.

Terrell, John Upton

1970 The Navajos: The Past and Present of a Great People. New York: Harper and Row.

Thomas, Wesley K.

1999 Gendering Navajo Bodies: A Personal, Political and Philosophical Treatise. PhD dissertation, University of Washington.

Thompson, Hildegard

1975 The Navajos' Long Walk for Education: A History of Navajo Education. Tsaile, AZ: Navajo Community College Press.

Underhill, Ruth

1956 The Navajos. Norman: University of Oklahoma Press.

Vogt, Evon Z.

1949 Navajo Veterans: A Study of Changing Values. Reports of the Rimrock Project Values Series, no. 1. Papers of the Peabody Museum of American Archaeology and Ethnology, Harvard University 41(1). Cambridge, MA.: Peabody Museum.

Waxman, Alan

1990 Navajo Childbirth in Transition. Medical Anthropology 12:187–206.

Werner, Oswald and Kenneth Begishe

1968 Styles of Learning: the Evidence from Navajo. Unpublished MS.

Wilson, Ursula

1980 Traditional Child-Bearing Practices among Indians. *In* Life Cycle of the American Indian Family. Pp. 13–26. Janice Kekahbah and Rosemary Wood, eds. Norman, OK: American Indian and Alaska Native Nurses Association Publishing Company.

Witherspoon, Gary

1975 Navajo Kinship and Marriage. Chicago: University of Chicago Press.

1977 Language and Art in the Navajo Universe. Ann Arbor: University of Michigan Press.

Young, Robert

1961 The Navajo Yearbook, 1951–1961: A Decade of Progress. No. 8. Window Rock, AZ.: Navajo Agency.

Zolbrod, Paul G.

1984 Diné bahane': The Navajo Creation Story. Albuquerque: University of New Mexico Press.

NAVAJO PRONUNCIATION KEY*

1. There are four basic vowels in Navajo:
   a as in *art*
   e as in *met*
   i as in *sit*
   o as in *note*
2. Vowels may be short or long, length being indicated by a doubling of the letter. The quality of the vowel is not affected by length except that long "i" is pronounced as in *seen* or *machine.*
3. Vowels may also be nasalized. The nasalized pronunciation is indicated by a hook underneath the affected vowel, as in *Mą́'ii.*
4. A tone marker over a vowel, as in *Tó* or *dine'é* indicates a rise in pitch. Long and short vowels alike can be high tone or low.
5. Navajo has the following diphthongs that require special mention:
   ai as in *kite*
   ei as in *day*
   oi as in *buoy*
6. While many Navajo consonants are unfamiliar, they can be reasonably well approximated by a casual reader. There are two characters in the Navajo alphabet, however, which do not appear in the standard English alphabet. They include the glottal stop ('), as in *Mą́'ii* or *dine'é,* and the voiceless glide (ł), as in *Níłch'i.* The former is pronounced like the break between the two elements of the familiar English expression, "oh, oh." The latter is pronounced by unvoicing the "l" familiar to speakers of English. Or it can be roughly approximated by pronouncing it as if it were "sh" in a word like *push* or *shoot.*

   The Navajo consonant *tł',* as in *Tł'aai,* is similar to the English "cl," as in *closet,* but pronounced as *tł* with a puff of air. (The tip of the tongue touches the alveolar ridge and there is a lateral relase.)

* This is a simplified guide adapted from Zolbrod (1984:xi) for readers who wish to approximate the Navajo terms used here. For a more detailed guide, see Goosen; Young and Morgan 1943; or Young and Morgan 1980.

INDEX